JRWalla

DIFFUSION PROCESSES AND FERTILITY TRANSITION

SELECTED PERSPECTIVES

Committee on Population

John B. Casterline, Editor

Division of Behavioral and Social Sciences and Education

National Research Council

D1509573

NATIONAL AC

Washingt   D.C.

NATIONAL ACADEMY PRESS • 2101 Constitution Avenue, N.W. • Washington, D.C. 20418

NOTICE: The project that is the subject of this report was approved by the Governing Board of the National Research Council, whose members are drawn from the councils of the National Academy of Sciences, the National Academy of Engineering, and the Institute of Medicine. The members of the committee responsible for the report were chosen for their special competences and with regard for appropriate balance.

This study was supported by the Andrew W. Mellon Foundation, the William and Flora Hewlett Foundation, and the United States Agency for International Development's Office of Population, under award no. CCP-A-0095-00024-02. Any opinions, findings, conclusions, or recommendations expressed in this publication are those of the author(s) and do not necessarily reflect the views of the organizations or agencies that provided support for the project.

Library of Congress Cataloging-in-Publication Data

Diffusion processes and fertility transition : selected perspectives /
Committee on Population ; John B. Casterline, editor ; Division of
Behavioral and Social Sciences and Education, National Research Council.
    p. cm.
Includes bibliographical references and index.
  ISBN 0-309-07610-2 (pbk.)
  1. Communication in birth control—Developing countries—Congresses.
  2. Fertility, Human—Developing countries—Congresses. I. Casterline,
John. II. National Research Council (U.S.). Committee on Population.
III. National Research Council (U.S.). Division of Behavioral and Social
Sciences and Education.
  HQ766.5.D44 D54 2001
  304.6′32′091724—dc21
                            2001004922

[*Availability from program office as desired.*]

Additional copies of this report are available from National Academy Press, 2101 Constitution Avenue, N.W., Lockbox 285, Washington, D.C. 20055; (800) 624-6242 or (202) 334-3313 (in the Washington metropolitan area); Internet, http://www.nap.edu

Printed in the United States of America
Copyright 2001 by the National Academy of Sciences. All rights reserved.

Suggested citation: National Research Council. (2001). *Diffusion Processes and Fertility Transition: Selected Perspectives.* Committee on Population. John B. Casterline, Ed. Division of Behavioral and Social Sciences and Education. Washington, DC: National Academy Press.

THE NATIONAL ACADEMIES

National Academy of Sciences
National Academy of Engineering
Institute of Medicine
National Research Council

The **National Academy of Sciences** is a private, nonprofit, self-perpetuating society of distinguished scholars engaged in scientific and engineering research, dedicated to the furtherance of science and technology and to their use for the general welfare. Upon the authority of the charter granted to it by the Congress in 1863, the Academy has a mandate that requires it to advise the federal government on scientific and technical matters. Dr. Bruce M. Alberts is president of the National Academy of Sciences.

The **National Academy of Engineering** was established in 1964, under the charter of the National Academy of Sciences, as a parallel organization of outstanding engineers. It is autonomous in its administration and in the selection of its members, sharing with the National Academy of Sciences the responsibility for advising the federal government. The National Academy of Engineering also sponsors engineering programs aimed at meeting national needs, encourages education and research, and recognizes the superior achievements of engineers. Dr. Wm. A. Wulf is president of the National Academy of Engineering.

The **Institute of Medicine** was established in 1970 by the National Academy of Sciences to secure the services of eminent members of appropriate professions in the examination of policy matters pertaining to the health of the public. The Institute acts under the responsibility given to the National Academy of Sciences by its congressional charter to be an adviser to the federal government and, upon its own initiative, to identify issues of medical care, research, and education. Dr. Kenneth I. Shine is president of the Institute of Medicine.

The **National Research Council** was organized by the National Academy of Sciences in 1916 to associate the broad community of science and technology with the Academy's purposes of furthering knowledge and advising the federal government. Functioning in accordance with general policies determined by the Academy, the Council has become the principal operating agency of both the National Academy of Sciences and the National Academy of Engineering in providing services to the government, the public, and the scientific and engineering communities. The Council is administered jointly by both Academies and the Institute of Medicine. Dr. Bruce M. Alberts and Dr. Wm. A. Wulf are chairman and vice chairman, respectively, of the National Research Council.

iii

COMMITTEE ON POPULATION

JANE MENKEN *(Chair)*, Institute of Behavioral Sciences, University of Colorado, Boulder

ELLEN BRENNAN-GALVIN, Population Division, United Nations, New York

JANET CURRIE, Department of Economics, University of California, Los Angeles

JOHN N. HOBCRAFT, Population Investigation Committee, London School of Economics

F. THOMAS JUSTER, Institute for Social Research, University of Michigan, Ann Arbor

CHARLES B. KEELY, Department of Demography, Georgetown University

DAVID I. KERTZER, Department of Anthropology, Brown University

DAVID A. LAM, Population Studies Center, University of Michigan, Ann Arbor

CYNTHIA LLOYD, The Population Council, New York

W. HENRY MOSLEY, Department of Population and Family Health Sciences, Johns Hopkins University

ALBERTO PALLONI, Center for Demography and Ecology, University of Wisconsin, Madison

JAMES W. VAUPEL, Max Planck Institute for Demographic Research, Rostok, Germany

KENNETH W. WACHTER, Department of Demography, University of California, Berkeley

LINDA J. WAITE, Population Research Center, University of Chicago

BARNEY COHEN, *Director*

Preface

The past fifty or so years have witnessed phenomenal changes in the fertility behavior of couples in most developing countries—a dramatic shift away from an environment in which large families were the norm and few couples practiced any form of contraception to a situation today in which smaller families are the norm and most couples know and use some form of contraception. Before 1960, substantial improvements in life expectancy were achieved but fertility declines were rare. Indeed there is some evidence to suggest that levels of childbearing rose in many countries, developed as well as developing, in the fifteen years following World War II.

Since 1960, total fertility rates (TFRs) have fallen in virtually every major geographic region of the world, transcending political, social, cultural, economic, ethnic, and religious boundaries. For example, in 1970, women in South Asia could be expected to bear 6 children over their reproductive lives. Today, the figure is down to 4.2 children per woman. In Latin America and the Caribbean, fertility fell by more than 2 children per woman over the same period: from a TFR of 5.2 in 1970 down to 3.1 in 1991. Only in parts of Sub-Saharan Africa has fertility remained consistently high.

What factors are responsible for the sharp decline in fertility? Despite extensive debate and controversy over the past twenty years, the factors responsible for fertility decline are still not fully understood. Demographers have struggled to explain differences in the timing and speed of fertility transitions between countries and the contribution of prior mortality decline, socioeconomic change, organized family planning programs, and the diffusion of various norms and ideals related to childbearing to these differences.

In 1995, the National Research Council's (NRC) Committee on Population initiated a research program to review what was known at that time about the determinants of fertility transition in developing countries and to identify policy-oriented lessons that might lead to policies aimed at lowering fertility. As part of that program, the committee organized a workshop called "Social Processes Underlying Fertility Change in Developing Countries" to learn more about the roles of diffusion processes, ideational change, social networks, and mass communications in changing behavior and values, especially as related to childbearing. There has been increased interest over the past few years within the demographic community concerning the role of diffusion processes in the fertility transition. A new body of empirical research is currently emerging from studies of social networks in Asia (Thailand, Taiwan, Korea), Latin America (Costa Rica), and Sub-Saharan Africa (Kenya, Malawi, Ghana). Given the potential significance of social interactions to the design of effective family planning programs in high-fertility settings, efforts to synthesize this emerging body of literature are clearly important.

The papers in this volume were first presented at the Committee on Population Workshop on Social Processes Underlying Fertility Change in Developing Countries, which was held January 29 and 30, 1998, in Washington, D.C. The workshop was supported by the Andrew W. Mellon Foundation, the William and Flora Hewlett Foundation, and the United States Agency for International Development's Office of Population.

The Committee on Population is grateful to the many individuals who made substantive and productive contributions to the project. Most important, we are indebted to the authors of the papers for their willingness to participate and to contribute their special knowledge. The committee is also grateful to past and present members John Bongaarts, John Casterline, Mark Montgomery, and Alberto Palloni, who served on a subcommittee (chaired by John Casterline) that assumed responsibility for organizing this workshop. In addition, the committee thanks Steven Sinding, who attended one of the planning meetings and provided valuable advice. The committee would also like to acknowledge the role of the NRC staff who managed the workshop: Barney Cohen, project director; LaTanya Johnson and Brian Tobachnick, project assistants; and Laura Penny, contract editor.

The papers have been reviewed by individuals chosen for their diverse perspectives and technical expertise, in accordance with procedures approved by the NRC's Report Review Committee. The purpose of this independent review is to provide candid and critical comments to assist the authors and the NRC in making the published report as sound as possible and to ensure that the report meets institutional standards for objectivity, evidence, and responsiveness to the purpose of the activity. The committee thanks the following individuals for their participation in the review of the papers in this report: Charles Hirschman, University of Washington; Ronald Rindfuss, University of North Carolina, Chapel Hill; and Thomas W. Valente, University of Southern California. Although these individuals provided constructive comments and suggestions, responsibility for the final content of this volume rests solely with the authoring committee and the NRC.

Jane Menken, *Chair*
Committee on Population

Contents

DIFFUSION PROCESSES
AND
FERTILITY TRANSITION

1

Diffusion Processes and Fertility Transition: Introduction

JOHN B. CASTERLINE

By the early decades of the twentieth century, it was apparent that a historic change had occurred in childbearing patterns in Western societies. Whereas in the past women had borne an average of five or more children by the end of their reproductive years, under the newly emerging fertility regime, the norm was roughly two children per woman (Livi-Bacci, 1999). The decline had occurred in the space of a generation or two, and was in no sense a silent revolution. Instead, this was a development noted by social scientists and laymen alike, and widely regarded as a fundamental departure from childbearing patterns in the past (Szreter, 1993). Among social scientists, the decline in fertility was generally viewed as but one element in a larger transformation in the family and its functions, with far-reaching implications for Western societies (Davis, 1945). The fertility decline in the West, largely completed prior to World War II, has been followed in the second half of the twentieth century by comparable fertility declines in Asia, Latin America, and, most recently, Africa (United Nations, 2000). By any criteria, the fertility decline of the late nineteenth and twentieth centuries must be ranked as among the more profound social changes of this era. Accordingly, it has begged for explanation, and social scientists have applied themselves to this task from the 1930s to the present.

Not surprisingly, the earliest efforts to explain the decline in fertility linked it with the other social and economic changes that were themselves

John B. Casterline is senior research associate at The Population Council, New York.

a major preoccupation of social scientists, particularly the massive economic transformation labeled "industrialization," and the concomitant shift in settlement patterns toward greater concentration of populations in towns and large urban centers. Industrialization and urbanization, it was argued, resulted in a substantial increase in the costs of rearing children and a decrease in the benefits children conferred on older generations (Thompson, 1929; Davis, 1945; Notestein, 1945, 1953). By mid-century, arguments along these lines held sway as the dominant explanation for fertility decline in the West. Some scholars also emphasized the importance of mortality decline as a precondition (Davis, 1963), and in the emerging field of social history there was an interest in the causal contribution of changing notions about family life (Aries, 1962, 1980; Caldwell, 1982) and declining adherence to long-dominant religious and ethical systems (akin to the secularization argument rearticulated by Lesthaeghe and collaborators in the 1980s [Lesthaeghe, 1983; Lesthaeghe and Surkyn, 1988]).

By the time rigorous quantitative research was initiated on the European fertility decline and the emerging declines in Asia and Latin America, the presumption was that variables such as modes of production, urbanization, and levels of schooling, themselves indicators of basic economic and social structural changes that had taken place in these societies, would largely account for the decline in fertility. Hence it came as some surprise when researchers associated with the European Fertility Project at Princeton discovered that the empirical associations between the standard battery of economic and social indicators and fertility decline in fact were rather modest in strength (van de Walle and Knodel, 1967; Knodel and van de Walle, 1979; Watkins, 1986). In hindsight, this may have been a mistaken conclusion, drawn from aggregate-level studies that were incapable of detecting the many linkages at the household level between social and economic change and demographic change (see, e.g., Kertzer and Hogan, 1989). In any case, confronted with these findings from the Princeton project, scholars turned to other explanations to augment, or even to supplant, the dominant theoretical framework in which the primary causal forces underlying fertility decline were mortality decline and the paradigmatic economic and social changes that occurred in Europe in the nineteenth and early twentieth centuries.

One set of alternative explanations that came to the fore has usually been collected under the label "diffusion." As we shall note below, the arguments classified as "diffusion theories" vary somewhat in their emphasis, and particularly in what they regard as the unique causal contribution of diffusion theory. What unites them is an overarching model of social change in which attitudes and behaviors become more prevalent in a population through their spread from some individuals to others, through informal face-to-face social interaction or at a distance through the mass media (Rogers, 1962; Brown, 1981; Valente and Rogers, 1995). Diffusion theory usually stresses the innovative nature of the attitudes or behaviors that spread—the common phrase is "innovation diffusion"— but for most scholars this is not an essential feature of this theoretical perspective. For example, Retherford and Palmore (1983), in one of the more extended reviews of the contribution of diffusion theory to research on fertility, distinguish "discontinuous" from "continuous" innovations, the former being entirely novel introductions into a population and the latter involving modification of something already present in the population (and thus not an innovation in the strictest sense of the term). Instead, what sets diffusion explanations apart from the mainstream theories that were formulated in the early and middle decades of the twentieth century is the assertion that fertility decline is not simply an adaptive response to changes in demographic, economic, and social structures; rather, it reflects the spread of certain key attitudes (e.g., about the costs and benefits of children) and behaviors (e.g., birth control technologies). For most scholars who have argued the case for diffusion theory, the crucial point is that the spread of attitudes and behaviors is not bound tightly to societal structural changes, rather, it has an independent dynamic of its own, and hence can account for a unique portion of the variation in the timing and pace of change (Bongaarts and Watkins, 1996). Some scholars have gone so far as to propose that diffusion theory can substitute for theories that feature economic and social structural changes (Cleland and Wilson, 1987; Watkins, 1991). The more common stance is that the two sets of explanations are complementary, not competing, with diffusion theory adding further independent factors to an enlarged theory of fertility decline (Retherford, 1985; Montgomery and Casterline, 1996). These are Cleland's (this volume) "pure" and "blended" diffusion models, respectively.

Early efforts to apply diffusion theory to fertility change were not submitted as challenges to the dominant social scientific theories of demographic transition; rather, they were directed to the more practical and programmatic goal of accelerating the adoption of contraception (Bogue, 1967; Palmore, 1967; Rogers, 1973). Although not recognized at the time, in hindsight the first articulation of a diffusionist argument that ran counter to, or added a significantly new element to, the demographic transition theory developed by Davis, Notestein, and others, was Coale's address to the International Union for the Scientific Study of Population (IUSSP) General Conference in Liège (Coale, 1973). In this influential paper, Coale proposes that sustained marital fertility decline has three preconditions, one of which can be viewed as primarily a function of societal structural changes (birth control must be perceived as advantageous) and the other two of which can be viewed as somewhat independent of changes in social and economic structures (birth control must be "within the calculus of conscious choice" and couples must have at their disposal the means of avoiding births). In the decade following this paper, scholars increasingly came to perceive that the latter two preconditions could change through diffusion processes, that is, the spread through a population of attitudes and behaviors (Knodel and van de Walle, 1979; Retherford and Palmore, 1983). As Lesthaeghe (this volume) reminds us, a great virtue of Coale's framework is that it acknowledges the causal contribution of both the diffusion of innovative attitudes and behaviors and changes in economic and social structures (the latter affecting parental calculations about the costs and benefits of children). In Coale's framework neither set of explanatory factors is neglected, in contrast to much of the literature of the past two decades that has touted the contribution of one set at the expense of the other. Lesthaeghe cogently argues that much needless dispute would disappear if the field returned to Coale's full framework of three preconditions—each one necessary—for fertility decline.

While scholars struggled with the intellectual challenge of isolating the causes of the fertility declines that occurred in Europe in the past and that were under way in developing countries in the present, public policy concerns about rapid population growth in developing countries provided an entirely separate motivation for examining the explanatory power of diffusion theories. If the main obstacle to fertility decline in developing countries was not that couples did not perceive birth control to be in their interests (the argument of Davis's [1967]) famous dismissal of the potential returns from investments in family planning programs), but rather that birth control was regarded as either unacceptable or infeasible, then programs that attempted to inform couples about birth control, legitimize its practice, and make services and supplies more conveniently available and affordable would have the potential to accelerate the decline in fertility. Beginning in the 1960s, there was an enormous financial investment in "purposive diffusion" of birth control (Retherford and Palmore, 1983) through government and private family planning programs. Whether these programs were having a net impact on the timing and pace of fertility decline, and how substantial that impact was in relation to the financial cost of these programs, were research questions of utmost importance beginning in the 1970s and continuing into the 1990s (Bongaarts et al., 1990). Because these questions have been addressed in numerous other articles and volumes, they are not singled out for separate attention in this volume. However, it is worth noting that one very important issue, not considered at any length in this volume, is the extent to which social diffusion might condition the impact of formal programs, either amplifying or dampening their impact (Montgomery and Casterline, 1998).

Once the concept of innovation diffusion gained general currency in the field around 1980 (through, for example, widely read articles by Knodel [1977] and Knodel and van de Walle [1979]), the term "diffusion" appeared with increasing frequency in the literature on demographic change. Initially this reflected the frustration described above with the apparently poor performance of explanatory theories that ignore diffusion dynamics (Cleland and Wilson, 1987; Watkins, 1990; Bongaarts and Watkins, 1996; Kirk, 1996). Increasingly in the 1990s, the concept has been employed in fresh empirical studies that have yielded direct evidence supportive of one or more variants of diffusion theory (Montgomery and Casterline, 1993; Rosero-Bixby and Casterline, 1993; Entwisle et al., 1996; Kohler, 1997; Rutenberg and Watkins, 1997; Munshi and Myaux, 1998; Kohler, 2000). Diffusion explanations have been applied not only to fertility decline but also to mortality change (Montgomery, 2000), and to the experiences of both historical and contemporary populations.

The main objective of the January 1998 workshop organized by the National Research Council (NRC) Committee on Population, from which the papers contained in this volume are drawn, was to assess the potential contribution to our understanding of fertility decline of explanations that invoke the concept of diffusion. The twofold question motivating this workshop was, "How might diffusion dynamics affect the timing and pace of fertility change, and how might the magnitude of those effects be ascertained through rigorous empirical research?" This question reflected the committee's unease with the existing research literature. The committee noted several tendencies in the literature that undermined the contribution of innovation diffusion theory. The first was the tendency to construct arguments that relied heavily, or exclusively, on innovation diffusion theory or, worse, only portions of innovation diffusion theory (as described below). The committee felt the need for a more balanced treatment of diffusion in fertility theory and research, a treatment that allowed full play to the potentially powerful implications of the concept of innovation diffusion while not losing sight of the other determinants that together make up a comprehensive theory of fertility change. A second weakness in the literature was the common failure to employ the concept of diffusion in a manner that would permit rigorous assessment of causal contribution. That is, although it may be descriptively accurate to say that fertility decline "diffuses," in the sense of reaching societies and subgroups at different times, the same descriptive generalization applies to virtually all social change. Surely if diffusion theory is to make a significant contribution to demography, it must be informative about the determination of the timing and pace of demographic change. It was with these concerns in mind and with the aim of contributing to a more balanced and insightful treatment of diffusion effects on reproductive change that the committee organized the Workshop on Social Processes Underlying Fertility Change in Developing Countries.

This introductory chapter begins with a synopsis of the treatment of diffusion in the fertility literature, highlighting the inadequacies in this literature alluded to above. From this emerges a theoretical stance, labeled here "the social effects model," that combines the causal effects of innovation diffusion and other determinants (such as demographic and socioeconomic factors). Variants of this model are the primary focus of the papers in this volume, although other diffusionist perspectives are also represented here. Key features of the social effects model are reviewed, with reference to the papers in this volume. The Introduction concludes with a discussion of theoretical developments and empirical investigations that promise to advance our understanding of the contribution of innovation diffusion to reproductive change.

KEY ELEMENTS IN DIFFUSION THEORY

The influential pieces in the literature on fertility decline that invoke the term "diffusion" are, with few exceptions, subscribing to the same theoretical propositions. The crux of innovation diffusion theory is an argument that has two closely linked, yet distinguishable, key elements that correspond to the two terms in the phrase "innovation diffusion": fertility decline is the consequence of the increased prevalence of attitudes and behaviors that were previously very rare or absent in the population (i.e., they are *innovative*), and their increased prevalence is the consequence of the spread of these attitudes and behaviors from some segments in the population to others (i.e., a *diffusion* process). Although it is natural to join these two elements together—and, indeed, absent the other, the explanatory contribution of each element is severely weakened—a frustrating aspect of much of the pertinent research literature is the extent to which one element has been stressed to the neglect of the other. The consequence has been a diversity in theoretical emphasis that, because it has often gone unnoticed, has led to some confusion. We identify three distinct emphases in the research literature on fertility change that have been heavily influenced by innovation diffusion theory and concepts.

In some portions of the literature, the emphasis is on the *innovation* component of "innovation diffusion." This has yielded two distinct bodies of work:

- One body of work stresses the innovativeness of the exercise of deliberate fertility control. Modern fertility control as the diffusion of a *behavioral innovation* (use of certain types of birth control techniques and technology, heretofore unknown or rare) is the main theme of this literature.

- A second body of work that focuses on the innovation half of the "innovation diffusion" concept stresses the spread of novel ideas. These are the so-called *ideational theories* of fertility transition. The basic argument is that declines in fertility occur because of the growing strength of certain knowledge, attitudes, and values.

One might characterize these two literatures as concerned with the question "What diffuses?"

Another set of papers, by focusing on the phenomenon of "diffusion," draws somewhat different conclusions about the explanatory contribution of innovation diffusion theory:

- This third body of work focuses on the *social dynamics* of the spread of innovative information and behaviors, such as birth control practices. The fundamental premise motivating this literature is that changes in the attitudes and behaviors of some individuals can influence the likelihood that other individuals will change their attitudes and/or behaviors. This describes a social dynamic that in the aggregate over time results in a diffusion process, that is, the spread of attitudes and behaviors through the population. In theory, this dynamic can alter both the timing and the pace of fertility decline, and hence is properly classified as a causal factor.

One might characterize this body of work as preoccupied with the question "How does diffusion occur?"

By no means are these various literatures in contradiction with each other, nor are they even exclusive of each other. There is, in fact, considerable overlap among the three. One can view the differences as primarily, although not entirely, a matter of different weightings of the two key elements of innovation diffusion theory. However, this tendency to slight one or the other key element has seriously limited the contributions of innovation diffusion theory to the explanation of fertility change. This is apparent if each literature is subjected to a critical review.

Behavioral Innovation

This body of work stresses the *innovativeness* of the exercise of deliberate fertility control. Fertility decline is the consequence of the spread of innovative birth control techniques and technologies. The spread can be spontaneous or directed.

This is the issue that Carlsson (1966) isolates in his seminal piece on fertility decline in nineteenth-century Sweden. At the time of Carlsson's article, it should be noted, there was already a relatively well-developed literature on the diffusion of new technologies, particularly agricultural technologies (Ryan and Gross, 1943; Beal and Bohlen, 1955; Griliches, 1957). Carlsson sets two arguments in opposition: fertility decline as an adjustment to changed social and economic circumstances that employed already known and accepted behaviors, against fertility decline as the consequence of the widespread adoption of birth control techniques that were for the most part unknown or unacceptable to previous generations. Carlsson concludes that the Swedish evidence on balance refutes the second argument.

The most articulate and sustained effort to defend the behavioral innovation argument came from scholars involved in the Princeton European Fertility Project. A cardinal principle in this project was that in pretransition populations, family limitation was an alien concept, and effective techniques to avoid pregnancy were largely unknown. This is implicit in Coale's (1973) three preconditions for marital fertility decline, one of which is that means of birth control must be known and available. This is the "able" condition in Lesthaeghe's contribution to this volume. That birth control was innovative behavior in historical European (and selected non-European) populations has been argued persuasively by Knodel and van de Walle, both separately (Knodel, 1977; van de Walle, 1992) and jointly (Knodel and van de Walle, 1979). Watkins (1986) has adhered to this interpretation of the historical European evidence. However, most of the evidence that birth control was a behavioral innovation is indirect.

During the past decade, further efforts have been made to uncover more direct evidence. Limited empirical materials from the European past can be brought to bear on this question; however, the gradual accumulation of evidence from literary and other sources raises doubts about the validity of the Princeton position in its simplest and purest versions (Szreter, 1993; Santow, 1995). More direct evidence can be gathered for contemporary non-European populations. In these populations, some researchers see clear evidence in pretransition societies of widespread awareness and acceptance of fertility regulation techniques, if not for limiting family size, then certainly for the purpose of spacing births (Bledsoe et al., 1994; Mason, 1997). By no means is there consensus on this issue, however. Cleland (this volume), updating an earlier review (Cleland and Wilson, 1987), concisely summarizes evidence for maintaining his position that pretransition populations are not familiar with birth control techniques, especially for the purpose of limiting the number of births, and therefore their widespread adoption during fertility transition should be regarded as truly innovative behavior.

Much dispute remains, therefore, on the relatively straightforward questions of whether the increasing prevalence of contraception as fertility transition progresses represents the spread through the population of innovative techniques and technologies and whether this spread is the critical catalyst to transition. For our purposes, an equally important question is: What might the answer to this question contribute to our understanding of the underlying determinants of fertility transition? If the answer is affirmative—that practice of birth control is the adoption of innovative behavior—how much has our understanding of the causes of fertility decline been advanced? The gain is far less than the intensity of the debate would imply, in our view, because this literature tends to neglect the related question of how the innovative birth control techniques and technologies reach individuals. The latter is a question about the diffusion process, and must be addressed if the argument is to provide any explanatory leverage. That certain behaviors were once alien and then become commonplace is itself a limited causal insight, more a description of social change than a theory for why and how the change came about.

The arguments of most of the scholars named here are not as crude as the previous paragraphs might suggest. The proposition that birth control is innovative behavior typically is coupled with a recognition that child-bearing motivations change over the course of transition, and that the reasons why these motivations change is itself a question that must be addressed. Cleland (this volume) proposes that mortality decline is the key factor motivating fertility decline in contemporary developing countries; and Lesthaeghe (this volume) emphasizes that for fertility to decline, all three of Coale's preconditions must be present, including the perception that restricting fertility is advantageous (the "ready" condition).

In short, whether or not the increased prevalence of birth control during the course of fertility transition constitutes behavioral innovation is undeniably a significant question. Were it to be answered in the negative, this would be a serious blow to innovation diffusion theory's contribution to causal models of fertility transition. Yet by itself this question is insufficient, as becomes clear when we ask what an affirmative answer would contribute to theories of reproductive change. An emphasis on behavioral innovation must be complemented by theory and research on diffusion processes, that is, those processes through which behavioral innovations spread through a population. This is the emphasis of the second body of work reviewed below.

Ideational Change

A second body of work is closely related to the first because in both literatures the heart of the argument is the nature of the innovation rather

than how the diffusion comes about. While the first body of work emphasizes *behavioral innovation*, the second emphasizes the spread of *innovative
ideas*. Since Cleland and Wilson's (1987) influential piece, it has been
common to speak of *ideational theories* of fertility transition. The basic
argument is that fertility declines because of the presence of certain knowledge, attitudes, and values that either were not present previously or that
grow significantly in strength. Although the innovative character of the
ideas figures into the argument—and ultimately makes this argument
difficult to distinguish from the behavioral innovation argument just discussed—this literature sets itself apart by its determination to contrast
ideas from material conditions as possible causes of fertility change. Note
that material conditions can include technological innovations, such as
methods of contraception. Among the ideas identified in this literature
are the notion of family limitation, knowledge/attitudes/values about
modern contraception, and ideas about family behavior (the roles of
women and children).

Falling under this label are major contributions to the literature on
fertility transition that differ significantly among themselves in the substance of their arguments. Caldwell's theoretical pieces on fertility transition written in the late 1970s and collected in his 1982 book (Caldwell,
1982) attribute considerable causal power to the spread of Western ideas
about family life, through schools and through the mass media. But the
foundation of his theory is an argument that changes in modes of production—material conditions—alter the costs and benefits of children, and in
this respect his theory is much larger than the ideational change argument (and, indeed, is on the whole compatible with the conventional
demographic transition theory formulated several decades earlier). Similarly, Freedman (1979) suggests that new consumer aspirations, diffused
through international networks of communication and transportation,
constitute one of the powerful motivations to reduce family size. In doing
so he adds content and specificity to a theory that at its core emphasizes
the determining power of changes in social and economic conditions.
Perhaps the most sophisticated contribution that might be classified in
this body of work is Lesthaeghe's research on fertility change in Europe
(Lesthaeghe, 1983; Lesthaeghe and Surkyn, 1988). Lesthaeghe argues that
secularization and the emergence of an emphasis on individual autonomy
and self-actualization together explain important features of fertility
trends and differentials in Europe in the twentieth century. But like
Caldwell, Lesthaeghe also attributes considerable causal power to changing economic structures.

In contrast, Cleland and Wilson (1987) explicitly reject the notion that
fertility decline can be explained by changes in structural conditions. Instead, they argue, the relatively autonomous spread of information and

values about fertility regulation has been the primary stimulant of contemporary fertility transitions. Cleland repeats, and updates, this crucial point in his contribution to this volume. After reviewing the accumulated empirical evidence up to the present, he maintains the position articulated in his widely cited piece with Wilson, namely that "the case that the *idea* of marital fertility regulation was a true innovation both in Europe and elsewhere remains robust despite widespread skepticism" [our italics].

There are many disturbing aspects of the baldest statements of the ideational change argument. Several of these have already been identified by Mason (1992) and Burch (1996). For one thing, the favoring in ideational explanations of ideas about contraception is arbitrary and unnecessary. There is every reason to give equal or greater weight to ideas that influence the demand for children, namely, ideas about the costs and benefits of children, the roles of women and children, and so forth. The more fundamental problem with this literature, however, is its implicit behavioral model. It is common in this literature to perceive ideas and material conditions as alternative, even competing, causes of fertility change, a definition of the terms of the debate that demands that ideas can be separated from material conditions. Most social science theory does not accommodate such a relationship between ideas and material conditions: Palloni (this volume) makes this point by drawing on mainstream sociological theory, and Carter (this volume) recounts the rejection by anthropology early in the twentieth century of the notion of autonomous cultural diffusion, supplanted by functionalist theory that emphasized the capacity of societies to invent their own idiosyncratic solutions to common human problems. Most social scientists recognize that ideas are grounded in social and economic institutions (see review in Hechter, 1993). This insight is valid at any level of aggregation, from the individual to the society. From this perspective, the disjuncture between material conditions and ideas found in some of the pieces in this body of work is a fiction. This key point is underscored by empirical work carried out in developing countries during the past two decades, some of it inspired by the ideational argument, that plainly reveals that the ideas that bear on fertility and family planning decisions more often than not are ideas about material conditions—changing labor and commodity markets, new economic opportunities, and so forth (Casterline, 1999b). An opposition between material conditions and ideas simply does not fit such empirical evidence, and this should come as no surprise: cultural systems cannot be detached from social and economic systems to the degree that some of this literature presumes.

A rejection of the causal contribution of changes in material conditions does not necessarily follow from an emphasis on ideational change.

As already argued, innovation diffusion theory can augment, rather than displace, theories that focus exclusively on the causal effects of changing societal structures. Most social science theory accords some limited autonomy to ideas. Exercising this limited autonomy, certain innovative ideas may have led fertility transition, indeed acted as the key catalyst to fertility transition. At issue, then, is whether it is plausible that ideas led the way, and what those ideas might be. On these points, too, there are some reasons for skepticism about the validity of the ideational change argument.

Ironically, social scientists have as often been impressed with the resistance of cultural systems to change as with their capacity to stimulate change. "Cultural lag" is a venerable, if simplistic, concept in sociological research on development and social change (Ogburn, 1922). Some demographers point to the rapidity of the decline of fertility in many societies as evidence of the causal contribution of changing ideas, the assumption being that ideas (values, norms) are generally capable of more rapid change than social and economic structures (Bongaarts and Watkins, 1996). This assumption is sensible, and yet there is a substantial amount of social science research on societal change that reveals that norms and values are slow to change because they are so deeply wedded to individual and group identities (Geertz, 1973). In the case of fertility, the more common case may be that fertility reduction is an effort to maintain existing norms and values in the face of changing material conditions (Casterline, 1999a). That is, family limitation is a new strategy for achieving long-standing goals (Montgomery and Chung, 1999). Santow and Bracher (1999) beautifully describe how this generalization applies to the decline of fertility among southern Europeans in Australia. And some analyses of the East Asian fertility transitions—the most complete to date of the non-European transitions—conclude that they were motivated above all by a desire to achieve socioeconomic goals that were grounded in established familial norms and values (Greenhalgh, 1988).

In short, on its own the ideational change argument is unsatisfactory on several counts. A divorce of ideas from structural conditions is artificial; in fact, it may often be ideas about material circumstances that are most influential in reproductive decision making. By specifying an opposition between ideas and material circumstances, the ideational change argument impedes the development of a satisfactory theory of fertility change. It follows that the ideational change argument must be embedded in a larger theory that encompasses a more complete set of causal factors. A second point is that, as with the behavioral innovation argument reviewed above, the ideational change argument should be accompanied by theory and empirical research on how ideas become more prevalent—diffuse—in a population. That certain ideas come to the fore and stimulate changes in reproductive behavior is more a description of change than an explanation. Propositions about how ideational change comes about (its timing, its pace) can be derived from the diffusion portion of "innovation diffusion" theory, as discussed below. It is not surprising that many of the prominent pieces in the ideational change literature propose that the ideas establish and strengthen themselves in a society through a diffusion process (e.g., Cleland and Wilson, 1987). What is lacking in this body of work is a formal and rigorous development of diffusion processes as a causal force. Like the literature reviewed above that emphasizes behavioral innovation, the main deficiency of the ideational change literature is that the governing theory and the empirical research are incomplete.

Social Dynamics

A third body of work that draws on innovation diffusion theory is more concerned with the diffusion process, that is, with the question "How does diffusion occur?" The focus of this literature is the *social dynamics* of the spread of innovative information and behaviors. By social dynamics, we mean the interdependencies among individuals in their behavioral decisions, in this case with respect to reproductive behavior. The key premise underlying this body of work can be concisely stated as follows (see Palloni, this volume): "Changes in the knowledge and behaviors of some individuals affect the likelihood that other individuals will change their knowledge and/or behaviors." Concretely, one might posit that if one woman in a community begins using a modern contraceptive, for example, this in itself changes the likelihood that other women in the community will adopt contraception, net of other characteristics of the women and the community. To borrow language from epidemiology, a social contagion process occurs.

Like the two literatures just reviewed, the social dynamics literature tends to concern itself with information and behaviors that are innovative. The explanatory contribution of this argument is not limited, however, to ideas and actions that are novel. Social dynamics can help account for increased prevalence of already existing knowledge (e.g., the advantages of small families) or behaviors (e.g., coitus interruptus), provided that other conditions have changed. Moreover, an emphasis on knowledge and values is characteristic of this literature, but without the tendency found in the ideational change literature to set ideas and material conditions against each other. One can view the social dynamics argument, therefore, as subsuming key elements of both the behavioral innovation and ideational change arguments.

What distinguishes the social dynamics literature is its attention to the diffusion process itself. This process can be viewed as an emergent outcome of the accumulated decisions of many individuals. The argument is that the very dynamics of this process can influence individuals to make decisions that differ from the decisions they would make in isolation from this process. For example, individuals who are predisposed to use a modern contraceptive might not do so because so few of their peers use contraception or because of the struggles with side effects that they have observed among their friends. Or, in contrast, individuals who have been reluctant to use a modern contraceptive might feel secure in beginning use once they observe that many of their friends use one and seem to derive benefit from use. Elsewhere, we have proposed that two mechanisms provide the behavioral foundation for social dynamics (Montgomery and Casterline, 1996; see also Palloni, this volume): *social learning*, the process through which individuals gain knowledge from others (through informal or formal social interaction, and including the mass media); and *social influence*, the process through which some individuals exert control over others, by virtue of their power or authority. Social learning and social influence are both types of what we shall term *social effects*, a key concept in this essay. Social learning and social influence are perhaps the most powerful and pervasive types of social effects that bear on fertility, but other types of social effects also can be identified (see next section).

Although there are early contributions to this literature by Bogue (1967), Palmore (1967), Freedman and Takeshita (1969), Rogers (1973), Crook (1977), and Rogers and Kincaid (1981), it is during the past decade that research on social dynamics and reproductive behavior has intensified. Several teams of researchers have submitted both conceptual and empirical pieces: Casterline, Montgomery, and collaborators (Rosero-Bixby and Casterline, 1993; Montgomery and Casterline, 1993; Lee and Casterline, 1996; Montgomery and Casterline, 1996); Watkins and collaborators (Watkins, 1990; Bongaarts and Watkins, 1996; Buhler et al., 2000; Kohler et al., 2001); and Entwisle and collaborators (Entwisle et al., 1996; Godley, 2001). Burch (1996) and Kohler (1997) are other strong contributors to this literature. This work has drawn inspiration from a rapidly expanding literature in sociology (especially the social network literature: Marsden and Friedkin, 1993; Valente, 1995; Hedström and Swedberg, 1998) and in economics (especially the literature on social learning and the literature on neighborhood effects: Case and Katz, 1991; Bikhchandandi et al., 1992; Ellison and Fudenberg, 1993; Shiller, 1995; McFadden and Train, 1996; see also Arrow, 1994). These literatures describe models similar in structure that assume essentially the same underlying behavioral mechanisms. Related literatures in epidemiology, geography, and communication are reviewed in Valente (1995).

For the purposes of the current overview of innovation diffusion theory and fertility transition, the crucial point is that the social dynamics argument adds distinct, and plausible, elements to causal models of fertility change, what we have termed social effects. Social effects can accelerate or retard the process of fertility change, a point that is developed further in this introduction and in the papers collected in this volume. Explaining fertility change is a matter of accounting for the timing and pace of change, and social dynamics can affect either one. More debatable is whether the social dynamics argument has anything to say about why fertility transition occurs at all. This can be restated as a question of the contribution of social effects to the determination of "equilibrium" levels of fertility. Durlauf and Walker (this volume) use economic theory to describe several types of social effects, with an emphasis on fertility change but with some commentary on theoretically plausible effects on equilibrium levels as well. Similarly, research in social psychology indicates that social influence can modify behaviors even under conditions of relative stability in the surrounding social, economic, and cultural structures (Cialdini and Trost, 1998). Whether this occurs to any meaningful extent with respect to fertility is an issue that requires more theoretical and empirical investigation. For now, assessing the causal impact of social effects on the timing and pace of fertility change is sufficient challenge and is the primary focus of the papers in this volume.

It is natural to imagine that social effects operate through informal social interaction—that is, through social networks—and hence it is hardly surprising that much of the recent empirical work on social effects on reproductive behavior has included the collection of extensive data on social networks. In adopting social network models, fertility researchers can draw on the theory, concepts, and tools of a rich subfield of sociology (Degenne and Forse, 1999) that have been applied to the problem of innovation diffusion from the 1950s (Coleman et al., 1957; Coleman et al., 1966) to the present (Valente, 1995). However, personal social networks are but one means through which social effects might operate, and it would be a mistake to limit social effects to this channel. In particular, it is clear that the mass media are another channel through which one set of individuals can affect another. Individuals become aware of what other persons are thinking and doing by reading newspapers and magazines, listening to radio, and watching television. Although exposure through social networks and through the mass media are clearly fundamentally different modes of contact with other persons, both can be channels for social effects as defined above, and both fit within the general social effects model to be described in the next section.

An important question is what relationship exists between social effects that operate through personal networks and social effects that operate through the mass media. To begin with, it is plausible that each set of effects conditions the nature and magnitude of the other. In this vein, in their review of mass media effects on reproductive behavior, Hornik and McAnany (this volume) suggest that exposure to other persons through social networks can amplify or dampen the effects of mass media exposure, both by affecting the receptivity of individuals to mass media messages, and, once individuals are inclined to adopt an innovative idea or behavior acquired through mass media exposure, by encouraging or discouraging them from acting on their desires. Alternatively, the two channels may substitute for each other as sources of information or influence (Valente and Saba, 1998). Yet another possibility is that mass media exposure leads to a modification of the patterns and/or content of interpersonal communication (Valente et al., 1996). Because of these various possible relationships between social effects via personal networks and via the mass media, social network analysis alone cannot provide a complete assessment of the contribution of innovation diffusion theory. It is with this in mind that this collection of papers includes the Hornik and McAnany review of the research literature on the mass media and fertility.

The literature that has concerned itself with social dynamics—how diffusion occurs—yields testable hypotheses about the timing and pace of fertility change (see next section of this essay; also Palloni, this volume). Despite this considerable strength, the social dynamics argument falls short of providing anything like a sufficient foundation for a theory of fertility change, for the simple reason that it provides little guidance as to why individuals might be prepared to change their reproductive behavior and which innovations will have appeal. Hence, although the social dynamics argument is attractive on formal grounds because it lends itself naturally to the articulation of causal propositions, the argument must be said to lack essential content. As we have stressed throughout this section, satisfactory explanatory theory must join innovation and diffusion, the former providing content and the latter describing process, and it must recognize the causal contribution of societal structural changes.

From this review of the three distinct thematic emphases in the literature on innovation diffusion and fertility change—behavioral innovation, ideational change, and social dynamics—two principal conclusions emerge. First, each emphasis on its own is incomplete and, in particular, is unable to support full-fledged theory about the causes of fertility transition, that is, why onset is early or late and why pace is slow or rapid. Second, the literature that emphasizes social dynamics—that is, diffusion processes, how diffusion occurs—has been the latest to develop and would seem to offer particular advantages when it comes to the formulation of explanatory models. For this reason, the present collection of papers is weighted toward this latter emphasis—how diffusion occurs—although the question of what diffuses is discussed at some length by several contributors (Cleland, Lesthaeghe).

THE SOCIAL EFFECTS MODEL

The formulation and empirical investigation of the social effects model is guided by the premise that *changes in the knowledge and behaviors of some individuals affect the likelihood that other individuals will change their knowledge and/or behaviors.* This describes a social contagion process or, following Erbring and Young (1979), an "endogenous feedback" process. The usual hypothesis is that social effects operate in addition to (or "on top of") other determinants of changes in fertility behavior (Palloni, this volume).

The premise stated above rings true; it possesses "face validity." But we should press ourselves and ask why such social dynamics might occur. In the previous section, social learning and social influence were identified as specific mechanisms through which social effects might operate, in this instance to affect the timing and pace of fertility change. It may be helpful to make this less abstract by describing those circumstances under which it is highly plausible that these sorts of mechanisms might be in play (Montgomery and Casterline, 1993):

(1) When individuals are uninformed about behavioral choices they might make, for example, information about available contraceptive technologies. Those individuals who learn about, or who adopt, certain contraceptive methods can serve as sources of information for others. Or advertisements in the mass media might bring new contraceptive technologies to the attention of individuals. In these circumstances, the social effects consist of *information flow.*

(2) When individuals are uncertain about the benefits and costs of certain fertility decisions they might make. Risk aversion can be an impediment to the adoption of innovative behaviors that would appear to offer net benefit to the individual. The experiences of some individuals offer concrete demonstration to others of the possible benefits and costs of making the same reproductive choices. In these circumstances, the social effects can be termed *demonstration effects.*

(3) When social norms prohibit certain reproductive behaviors, for example the use of induced abortion to limit family size. If group norms are determined, in part, by the behavior of group members, then individual decisions to adopt innovative behavior can modify the group norms that others later confront when contemplating adoption of innovative behaviors (Bicchieri et al., 1997). (This effect is potentially very pow-

erful if the violation of group norms by merely a minority of the group is sufficient to undermine those norms and render innovative behaviors acceptable.) In these circumstances, the social effects consist of *change in normative context*.

An emphasis on the circumstances in which social effects are likely to be powerful is an important feature of our argument. The expectation is that effects of substantial magnitude are only likely to operate in rather special circumstances, namely where lack of information, risk aversion, or norms are obstacles to the adoption of behavior that is otherwise desirable from the standpoint of individual (or couple) cost-benefit calculus. There is a danger of either underestimating or exaggerating the magnitude of social effects. On the one hand, conventional models that either omit or do not feature social effects may miss entirely their tremendous potential to powerfully accelerate or decelerate changes in attitudes and behaviors, as is clearly evident in formal simulations (Rosero-Bixby and Casterline, 1993; Burch, 1996; Hedström, 1998; and other literature reviewed in Durlauf and Walker, this volume). On the other hand, the temptation to exaggerate the magnitude of social effects takes two forms: first, failure to recognize that these effects in their full strength are probably limited historically and to certain social contexts; and, second, failure to recognize that social effects are but one set of factors in a larger model of the determinants of fertility.

As should be clear from the critique above of the ideational change argument, by no means are social effects restricted to knowledge about contraception. Included within *demonstration effects* are effects on the perceived costs and benefits of children: through interaction with others, couples may modify their perceptions of the net value of an additional child. Similarly, although it is not clear from the definition above, included within *information flow* is the spread of new algorithms for weighing the many separate costs and benefits of children. As Mason (1992) points out, calculation of the net value of children is a complex task, and hence couples almost certainly rely on simplified calculation procedures that are part of the cultural toolkit. Revision and reinterpretation of these procedures is an ever-present possibility, following discussions with other persons or observations of their experiences (the latter being an example of *demonstration effects*), or as a result of mass media exposure that alters what Hornik and McAnany (this volume) term the "frame" that guides individuals when making decisions.

It is essential to be clear about the contribution of social effects to *causal models* of fertility change, a concern of several papers in this volume (particularly Palloni). A simple algebraic representation will assist in structuring this discussion:

$$Y_{i,t} = X_{i,t} \beta + \alpha \sum Y_{j,t-1} W_j + \varepsilon_{i,t} \tag{1}$$

where:

Y   is an indicator of fertility behavior
X   are sets of conventional determinants of fertility
W   are weights for the salience of the jth person for the ith person
i   denotes the ith person or couple
j   denotes the jth person or couple
t   denotes time period

and

β, α, ε are parameters

This is a model for fertility *dynamics*, hence the explicit subscripting by time. Imagine Y_i to be innovative fertility behavior, namely termination of childbearing after two live births. This behavior is affected by the conventional determinants X and, in addition, by exposure to the fertility behavior of others Y_j. A more elaborate formulation might include on the right-hand side, in addition to the fertility behavior of others (Y_j), their reproductive knowledge and attitudes, and perhaps also other behaviors and attitudes that might plausibly affect fertility decision making (e.g., other persons' views about how much schooling children should obtain). Parameter α, which in the simple expression of equation (1) is a single parameter that summarizes the cumulative effects of the behaviors of all persons j (as weighted by W_j), represents an overall social effect, that is, the combined effects of the behaviors of other persons j on the fertility behavior of person i. This social effect is assumed to operate with some lag. This equation is a concise representation of more elaborate models of the same form developed in Palloni (this volume) and, among recent contributions to the literature, Marsden and Friedkin (1993), Strang and Tuma (1993), Valente (1995), Friedkin (1998), and Van den Bulte and Lilien (in press).

Nothing in the formulation of equation (1) requires that persons j from which the social effect α originates be confined to the personal social network of person i. The only requirement is that person i be aware of the behaviors of persons j and not indifferent to those behaviors (i.e., persons j are salient social actors for person i). This formulation allows for social effects operating indirectly and at a distance, including through the mass media.

A fundamental feature of equation (1) is that it encompasses both social effects and the effects of the conventional determinants X. In this specification, the two types of effects are combined additively. This is consistent with the argument presented earlier in this Introduction and by other scholars (Mason, 1992; Burch, 1996; and, in this volume, Palloni, Carter, and Lesthaeghe) that there is no theoretical basis for setting structural and innovation diffusion explanations in opposition to each other. Equation (1) can be viewed as one algebraic articulation of Cleland's (this volume) "blended model."

Further features of equation (1) deserve some attention because they point to issues that are examined by one or more papers in this volume. A first point is that the equation does not require that social effects result in more rapid fertility change. For the social effects to accelerate fertility decline, two restrictions must be placed on α. First, it must be positive in sign (i.e., the weighted social effect across all j must be positive). Second, and a corollary of the first, those individuals who have changed their behavior (the innovators) must be more salient to individual i, that is, they must have larger W_j than other individuals X. The first restriction rules out negative feedback effects, such as rumors about detrimental health side effects of contraception. But negative feedback effects are by no means uncommon, especially with respect to innovative behaviors and technologies about which little is known, such as modern contraceptive technologies (Lesthaeghe, this volume; Casterline and Sinding, 2000). The second restriction means simply that innovative fertility behaviors must have more appeal than customary fertility behaviors. It is plausible that this is often the case on the eve of fertility transition, if the social and economic calculus has changed in such a manner as to make additional children less valuable to parents (e.g., because of substantial mortality decline). Or the calculus may not have changed, but technologies heretofore unavailable happen to satisfy long-standing desires. Such may be the case, for example, with respect to the adoption of modern medical technologies and methods of personal hygiene that lead to improvements in child survival. Hence a more complex but realistic specification than equation (1) would make the social effect α conditional on the outcome of individual cost-benefit calculus: an individual i will be especially alert for behaviors of other individuals j that are in his or her interest. Note that this line of reasoning gives clear primacy to cultural, social, and economic explanations for fertility change. These account for the fact that individuals are prepared to adopt innovative behaviors.

Without these two restrictions, the social effects model, rather than offering an explanation for the rapidity of many fertility declines, instead provides good reason to expect fertility to be resistant to change. Indeed, perhaps it was the relative absence of retarding social effects that explains the rapid declines in countries such as Thailand and Colombia (Knodel et al., 1984, at times imply as much for the case of Thailand), and the dominance of certain social effects that explains the slow pace of decline in other settings such as Pakistan (Sathar and Casterline, 1998). In this vein,

Potter (1999) argues that various sorts of social effects have contributed to the maintenance of contraceptive practices in Brazil and Mexico that have proven to be highly disadvantageous to the health of women and undesirable on other grounds as well.

A related issue is how to account for the decisions of the earliest adopters of innovative behavior. As Pollak and Watkins (1993) point out, a pure social effects model cannot account for the behavior of the vanguard group (termed "trendsetters" by Pollak and Watkins), and this is a weakness of any theory that places heavy weight on social effects. This problem is addressed in equation (1) through the $X_{i,t}$ β term—the effects of conventional determinants, what Durlauf and Walker (this volume) refer to as "exogenous forcing variables," and presumably the stimulus for the earliest adopters. This alone does not resolve the problem, however, because if this model is to enjoy any advantage over models that exclude the social effects term ($\alpha \Sigma Y_{j,t-1} W_j$) the vanguard group must exert more influence than others in the population. Given these two problems, it is not surprising that social effects models perform much more effectively as ex post explanations than as predictive theories; ex ante it is, in practice, difficult to know which persons will assume the role of trendsetters and why these persons, and not others, will exert disproportionate influence on the behavior of others (Kreager, 1993; Pollak and Watkins, 1993). This is but one aspect of a larger theoretical problem raised by Carter (this volume) and elaborated on by Carley (this volume): individuals are not passive recipients of relatively limited amounts of discrete information about the attitudes and practices of other persons; rather, they must sift regularly among large volumes of information coming from persons both nearby and distant (e.g., through the mass media), much of it contradictory. Typically the outcome of this process will be a reliance on some pieces of information and not others (i.e., selective social learning), and, perhaps of more profound importance, a transformation of the information received, so that it fits better with past experience and/or with existing beliefs. How to explain the relative salience of the voluminous bits of social information to which individuals are exposed is among the most challenging problems confronting researchers who wish to employ the social effects model. For this reason, the joining of cognitive psychology and social network research, as in Carley (this volume), may be critical to the formulation of successful social effects models.

This discussion draws attention to one further issue about the social effects model, namely the role of perceptions. Although the social effects term on the right-hand side of equation (1) contains the behaviors of persons j, ordinarily it is not those behaviors themselves that matter but rather person i's perceptions of those behaviors. As Durlauf and Walker (this volume) note, it is the expectation of the choices of others in the populations that bears on the decision of any particular person (see also Valente et al., 1997; Montgomery and Chung, 1999). This again makes the case for an integration of models for cognition and social interaction, for which Carley's review (this volume) provides much helpful guidance.

IMPROVING RESEARCH ON SOCIAL EFFECTS

Although several of the seminal contributions to the literature on innovation diffusion and fertility change were published a decade or more ago, systematic rigorous research on this topic—both theoretical and empirical research—is still in its infancy, with much of this work very recent. This is especially the case when it comes to research guided by the social effects model. The work to date can be faulted for its simplicity, and yet this is a common feature of a research literature in the early stage of development. In addition to reviewing existing research, the authors of the chapters in this volume identify ways in which research on social effects might be improved. The needed improvements are both conceptual and practical. We consider four ways in which research on this topic might be advanced. The first three are conceptual, with each one having direct implications for the design of empirical research: consideration of a broader set of types of social effects, better specification of the structure of social relations, and more explicit attention to the dynamics of social systems. The fourth concerns data collection requirements.

Types of Social Effects

As noted above, the mechanism for social effects that has received the most attention to date is *social learning*, that is, that individuals obtain information from others (about the likelihood of children dying, about the costs and benefits of children, about contraceptive technology, etc.) that informs their reproductive decisions. It is plausible that social learning can exert a powerful effect on reproductive decision making, but other types of social effects also deserve consideration. Already mentioned above was *social influence*, that is, that some individuals have the power to constrain the decisions of others (due to authority, deference, cumulative obligations, etc.). It is natural to group these two types of social effects together, because in structure they closely resemble each other, as reflected in expressions such as equation (1).

In contrast, the type of social effect that sociologists term *social comparison* (Carley, this volume; Palloni, this volume) can take an altogether different form. Theories of social comparison have a very long heritage in sociology (Festinger, 1954; Merton, 1968). The fundamental notion is that an individual assesses his or her needs and well-being through comparison of his or her circumstances to those of others. The conclusions drawn from this comparison are a function of the relative status of the individuals, and this is what gives social comparison theory its power and complexity. Individuals are assumed to respond differently to a recognition that higher status individuals have certain attitudes or behaviors than to a recognition of the same attitudes and behaviors among lower status individuals. One particular form of social comparison is social competition, and another is social emulation (Hedström, 1998; Palloni, this volume). Although social emulation generates effects that are nicely represented by equation (1) and similar expressions, social competition effects would appear to require a different specification, in which the degree of dissimilarity between the individual and his or her peers enters explicitly into the modeling. To date there has been little effort to examine how social comparison and its subtypes (including emulation and competition) might affect reproductive decisions.

Another type of social effect that can be subsumed under social influences but is distinct enough to be noted separately is *social coercion* (Molm, 1997). In all societies, individuals make some decisions under orders from others. The orders may be issued in personal relationships or, at the other extreme, in codified rules that are enforced through institutionalized power. This applies to reproductive decisions, if not fertility outcomes then the direct determinants of fertility: marriages can be arranged, and contraception and induced abortion can be prohibited. In northern Ghana, for example, senior men are granted decision making authority over many aspects of young women's lives, and in effect operate as gatekeepers for the diffusion of innovative reproductive behaviors (Adongo et al., 1997).

Much of the literature on social effects on reproduction presumes relatively passive social exposure. This can simplify the modeling of social effects, particularly if one is prepared to assume that social exposure is exogenous to reproductive decision making. It is clear, however, that in many instances this assumption is untenable: individuals make choices about with whom they interact and to what they are exposed (Carley, this volume). Indeed, at the extreme individuals actively seek information that might assist them in making decisions, about reproduction and other types of outcomes (Pescondido, 1992; Boulay, 2000). Whether information that has actively been sought can be assigned a causal role is a matter of dispute, and raises basic philosophical questions about the nature of causality in the social sciences (Pearl, 2000): Can factors that are deliberately employed by individuals to achieve desired ends be regarded as "causal" in any sense? What is the causal standing of mediating variables? However one answers these basic questions, the possibility (indeed, virtual certainty) of active information seeking certainly complicates the assessment of social effects on reproduction and, more concretely, demands that equation (1) be augmented with an equation for the determination of social exposure (i.e., social effects $\alpha \sum Y_{j,t-1} W_j$ as an outcome).

An entirely different set of social effects can be grouped under the concept of *social capital*. Social capital refers to the access to resources, of all kinds, provided by social relations. It can be viewed as a property of individuals and higher aggregations, such as local communities. Since James Coleman developed this concept and coined the term in the late 1980s (Coleman, 1988), social capital has been the subject of a burgeoning body of research, initially in sociology (Putnam, 1995; Portes, 1998) and more recently in economics (Knack and Keefer, 1997). The concept has become extremely influential in the development literature, with an accumulating body of empirical studies indicating that individuals and communities possessing certain types of social capital fare better in terms of standard development outcomes (Woolcock, 1998; Narayan and Pritchett, 1999). For the purposes of modeling reproductive change, the value of the concept is threefold. First, it adds to the explanatory models for various determinants of fertility, such as schooling, income, and health status. In this respect social capital is only an indirect determinant of fertility, and thus does not enter directly into models of fertility such as equation (1). Second, social capital may bear directly on the perceived costs and benefits of children. Augmenting one's social capital can be a motivation for having, or not having, children. This argument is developed in Astone et al. (1999) and tested empirically with survey data from the United States in Schoen et al. (1997). (Although use of the term social capital is recent, this particular argument has a longer history in the fertility literature. For example, it figures prominently in Caldwell, 1982.) As Palloni (this volume) points out, social structure itself is transformed by changes in fertility, and individuals may recognize this and take this into account when making decisions about reproduction. Third, and more germane to social effects as defined here, social capital as a property of individuals and communities—to whom individuals are connected, the resources they can obtain through those relationships, their trust in those relationships—can affect the scope and magnitude of social effects on fertility. In terms of equation (1) and the social effects term $\alpha \sum Y_{j,t-1} W_j$, the concept of social capital encompasses both the composition of the j other persons and the structure of the W_j, that is, the salience attached to the knowledge and actions of those other persons. In this respect, although the concept of social capital would not appear to bear on the basic structure of the social effects model, it may well lead to significant improvements in the application of this model in empirical research, informing decisions about the content of data collection instruments and the specification of equations at the analysis stage (Lin, 1999).

Structure of Social Relations

There has been a tendency in the fertility literature to view social effects as the outcome of informal social interaction in local personal social networks. These networks are often treated as unstructured, homogeneous, and static. As Carter (this volume) and Carley (this volume) stress, this can simplify social relations to such an extent as to lead to serious bias in the assessment of the nature and magnitude of social effects. To rectify this shortcoming, theory and empirical research must be improved in a number of respects.

First, there must be more precise measurement of patterns of informal and formal social interaction. This can be viewed as a question of how to determine the composition of persons j and the structure of weighting matrix W_j. Heterogeneous mixing will be the norm in virtually all settings, with important implications for the expected magnitude of social effects (Akerlof, 1997) and for the design of data collection exercises. The literature on social networks—conceptualization and measurement—is now well developed and provides more than adequate instruction (Strang, 1991; Wasserman and Faust, 1994; Degenne and Forse, 1999). As Carley proposes (this volume), the modeling of social network effects needs to be more attentive to complexity in network "nodes" (types of actors) and network "ties" (types of linkages and the exchanges that occur through them). An excellent example of the lack of development of the fertility literature in this respect is its neglect of the "structural equivalence" argument of Burt (1987, 1992). According to this argument, rather than being swayed by the overall prevalence of certain attitudes and behaviors in their social network, individuals are more affected by the attitudes and behaviors of those persons j with whom they share a "structurally equivalent" network position. This argument has clear implications for the construction of the matrix W_j. In the fertility literature, apparently only Valente (1995) has tested Burt's influential hypothesis in empirical analysis.

Second, patterns of social relations are not static but rather undergo continual evolution and transformation, and this must be taken into account in any effort to assess the nature and magnitude of social effects. Theory and methods for considering social network evolution are under active development (Carley, 1999, this volume). Almost certainly this implies longitudinal observation in empirical research.

Third, research on social effects on fertility must allow for both localized and long-distance effects. The mass media (Hornik and McAnany, this volume) are the most dominant means for social effects over a distance, but indirect social relationships can take other forms as well, as described in the burgeoning literature on "globalization" (Calhoun, 1992; Kearney, 1995). A particular type of model that deserves more attention in the fertility literature is the two-step model of Katz and Lazarsfeld (1955), in which innovative ideas and behaviors are transmitted relatively long-distance to elites (perhaps via the mass media), who in turn affect other individuals in their local communities. Watkins and Hodgson (1998) describe such a process with respect to the diffusion of fertility control in Kenya: Kenyan elites were exposed to innovative reproductive behaviors in other countries—inadvertently through their schooling and professional activity and deliberately through the recruitment efforts of international agencies—and then subsequently undertook local activities that eventually modified the attitudes and behaviors of other segments of the Kenyan population. There is a risk, however, of placing too much emphasis on social effects that transcend and penetrate small-scale groups; the continuing importance of local communities should not be overlooked (Cox, 1997; Watts, 1999).

Social Systems

Social effects can be represented in simplified form in equations such as equation (1). However, because these effects operate over time and consist of interdependencies among community members, an assessment of the full impact of social effects on social change can only be obtained through the construction and estimation of social systems that contain the implied feedbacks. As yet, research on fertility change has hardly begun to entertain such system models, although a few scholars have made initial efforts in this direction (Durlauf and Walker, this volume; Kohler, 2000). (See also Gregersen and Sailer, 1993; Hallinan, 1997.)

Feedbacks are a fundamental feature of these system models. It is also likely that the models will need to allow for social effects that are nonlinear in form: thresholds, ceilings, and marked variation in the magnitude of the effects as the prevalence of attitudes or behaviors evolves (Durlauf and Walker, this volume; Hornik and McAnany, this volume; Palloni, this volume). This is a common proposition in the sociological literature; see, for example, the influential pieces by Granovetter and Soong (1983, 1986). (See also literature reviewed in Valente, 1995.) An intriguing concept is "tipping point"—that once an attitude or behavior achieves a certain prevalence in a community, adoption by others in the community becomes much easier and occurs rapidly. This notion has recently caught the imagination of a popular audience through Gladwell (2000).

The data requirements for the construction and estimation of social system models are daunting. Surely for the foreseeable future the models will be highly simplified and will obtain parameters by assumption rather than empirical measurement. Nevertheless, interest in such models is growing in demography (see, e.g., Blanchet, 1998), and it is reasonable to expect substantial progress over the next few years. Among other dividends, this effort, if accompanied by continued disciplined empirical work, should improve our capacity to assess the nature and magnitude of social effects on reproductive behavior.

The Need for Empirical Data

In light of the several-decades heritage of interest in applying innovation diffusion theory to the study of fertility transition, it is somewhat puzzling that the literature contains so few rigorous empirical studies. The most influential conceptual pieces were published more than a decade ago, and several of them more than two decades ago (Coale, 1973; Knodel and van de Walle, 1979; Watkins, 1986; Cleland and Wilson, 1987). As of the early 1990s, nearly all the empirical research that attempted explicitly to test hypotheses derived from innovation diffusion theory had been carried out either by Donald Bogue and his students or by Everett Rogers and his students (see reviews in Retherford and Palmore, 1983 and Valente, 1995). It is by any measure a rather small body of empirical work, especially in the context of an explosion of empirical research on fertility and fertility transition during the 1970s and 1980s. How can this neglect of social diffusion processes be explained?

Certainly unavailability of the necessary empirical data accounts in part for the paucity of research. The major survey programs—the World Fertility Survey and the Demographic and Health Survey—have collected very little of the information required for estimation of any variant on the social effects model. This in turn can be interpreted as an implicit rejection, or at least lack of interest, in innovation diffusion theories (Cleland and Wilson, 1987). There is surely some truth to this, but in our view the obstacles are as much practical as ideological. The data requirements are demanding and, more importantly, entail somewhat different data collection designs than have been standard in the field. The key features of data collection that would permit the estimation of the social effects model are:

- Measurement of social exposure, including some of the following: informal social interaction with kin, friends, neighbors, and workmates; formal social interaction with program agents (health and family planning workers, school teachers); and mass media exposure.

- Measurement of individuals' perceptions of the attitudes and behaviors of other persons.
- Prospective data collection, so that social exposure and perceptions at earlier times can be related to later attitudinal and behavioral transitions.

Longitudinal designs, achieved through prospective data collection, are especially critical for obtaining valid estimates of *causal* effects, such as those specified in equation (1) (Palloni, this volume).

In principle, social effects should be considered at all levels and via all mechanisms: personal social networks, local social organizations, influential elites, the mass media, and program personnel (health workers, school teachers, and so forth). In practice, simplification is unavoidable: no one data collection exercise can afford to obtain data that permits estimation of social effects at all these levels. In any case, if the social effects model is specified in full generality, it admits too many possibilities and lacks sufficient structure for these effects to be precisely and confidently identified (Montgomery and Casterline, 1998). Researchers have no recourse but to engage in some simplification, primarily through deletion, in their investigation of social effects. This requires an informed and in-depth understanding of the structure of social relations in the society where the investigation is occurring, as proposed by Carter (this volume). A good rule of thumb is that researchers' protocols for sampling social networks (informal, formal, and long-distance) should to the extent possible mimic the sampling habits of the actors under investigation (Palloni, this volume).

All this seems a daunting undertaking. And yet data collection carried out in the 1970s (as reviewed in Retherford and Palmore, 1983, and Valente, 1995) and during the past decade (Kincaid et al., 1996; Valente et al., 1997; Entwisle and Godley, 1998; Boulay, 2000; Casterline et al., 2000; Kohler et al., 2001) demonstrates that it is feasible to design projects that conform to the principles just enunciated. Despite the recent progress, it remains the case that the more imposing barrier to research on innovation diffusion and reproductive behavior is not the underdevelopment of theory but rather the lack of data that will support rigorous empirical testing of theory already in place. A number of the papers in this volume nicely demonstrate that a rich collection of concepts and theories are awaiting empirical investigation (Cleland, Palloni, Carter, Carley).

THE PAPERS IN THIS VOLUME

Despite an interest in innovation diffusion theory among demographers that extends back at least to the 1960s, and the publication more than a decade ago of widely read pieces that argued vigorously that research on the determinants of fertility change should give far more attention to diffusion dynamics (Knodel and van de Walle, 1979; Watkins, 1986; Cleland and Wilson, 1987), research on the contribution of diffusion remains undeveloped. One reason for this, just noted, is the scarcity of data that will support the estimation of the models implied by innovation diffusion theory, including the basic model we have termed the "social effects model." A more fundamental explanation for this state of the field, however, is that many of the efforts to date have employed incomplete or imbalanced conceptualizations of diffusion effects.

The aim of this collection of papers is to fill in some of the existing gaps and achieve a better balance than has characterized the literature to date. A deliberate effort has been made to represent the various social science disciplines that have given systematic attention to diffusion processes (either recently or in the past)—sociology (Palloni), anthropology (Carter), social and cognitive psychology (Carley), and communication sciences (Hornik and McAnany). (Economics is the major oversight; an economic analysis was presented at the 1998 workshop [Durlauf and Walker, this volume].)

As indicated above, the existing literature on fertility transition that was influenced by innovation diffusion theory tends to focus either on innovation—What are the innovative attitudes or behaviors that diffuse?—or on diffusion—By what process do attitudes and behaviors spread through the population? The latter has been given far less attention than the former, and hence this is the emphasis of the majority of the papers in this volume. Palloni reviews the evolution of theory and models of diffusion in sociology, and then presents and critiques a more complicated version of the social effects model of this introduction. Carley provides a concise yet comprehensive overview of research findings from social and cognitive psychology that speak to the general question of how individuals learn from, or are influenced by, other persons. All models implicitly, if not explicitly, make assumptions about the nature of interpersonal learning and influence. For social effects models of fertility change to become more powerful and precise, they must be informed by the behavioral research that Carley summarizes. Hornik and McAnany tackle the important problem of social effects through the mass media (with particular reference to effects on reproductive behavior). It is clear that in the contemporary world, this is an important channel for innovation diffusion, and that to ignore this channel is to run the risk of obtaining a biased impression of the impact of diffusion dynamics on reproductive decision making.

In the three other papers in this volume, far more attention is given to the issue of the content of diffusion processes—What are the innovative attitudes and behaviors that diffuse, and to what extent does this explain fertility change? Cleland reviews the fertility literature of the past four decades, for both historical Europe and the contemporary developing countries. From this he concludes that the diffusion of knowledge, acceptance, and technologies of birth control provides a parsimonious and compelling explanation for the onset of fertility decline in historical Europe and, while not as decisive for declines outside Europe in the second half of the twentieth century, it nevertheless stands as one of the primary underlying causal forces. Lesthaeghe revisits Coale's (1973) three preconditions of sustained marital fertility decline, which as noted earlier was an early theoretical statement that can be viewed as (implicitly) arguing for a central causal role for innovation diffusion. Lesthaeghe argues, illustrating his point through analysis of recent Demographic and Health Surveys data, that in positing a causal role for innovation diffusion one need not deny the central causal contributions of changes in the demand for children, itself a response to societal structural changes (demographic, social, economic). Finally, Carter observes that anthropology early in the twentieth century accorded substantial causal power to cultural diffusion, only to conclude that this was an inadequate explanation for much of the meaningful variation among societies. Carter's chapter serves as a caution against excessive enthusiasm for innovation diffusion theory. As noted earlier, the research literature on fertility transition contains examples of such excess enthusiasm. One of the conclusions that it is hoped the reader will take away from this collection of papers is that innovation diffusion is but one component in a more elaborate causal process that also involves factors such as mortality decline and economic transformation, and that the most revealing models will take due account of all these causal forces.

REFERENCES

Adongo, P.B., J.F. Phillips, B. Kajihara, C. Fayorsey, C. Debpuur, and F. N. Binka
  1997   Cultural factors constraining the introduction of family planning among the Kassena-Nankana of Northern Ghana. *Social Science and Medicine* 45(12):1789–1804.
Akerlof, G.A.
  1997   Social distance and social decisions. *Econometrica* 65(5):1005–1027.
Aries, P.
  1962   *Centuries of Childhood: A Social History of Family Life*. New York: Knopf.

1980 Two successive motivations for the declining birth rate in the West. *Population and Development Review* 6(4):645–650.

Arrow, K.
1994 Methodological individualism and social knowledge. *American Economic Review* 84(2):1–9.

Astone, N.M., C.A. Nathanson, R. Shoen, and Y.J. Kim
1999 Family demography, social theory, and investment in social capital. *Population and Development Review* 25(1):1–32.

Beal, G.M., and J.M. Bohlen
1955 *How Farm People Accept New Ideas.* Cooperative Extension Service Report 15. Ames, IA: Cooperative Extension Service.

Bicchieri, C., R. Jeffrey, and B. Skyrms
1997 *The Dynamics of Norms.* Cambridge, Eng.: Cambridge University Press.

Bikhchandandi, S., D. Hirshleifer, and I. Welch
1992 A theory of fads, fashion, custom and cultural change as information cascades. *Journal of Political Economy* 100(5):992–1026.

Blanchet, D.
1998 Nonlinear demographic models and chaotic demo-dynamics. *Population: An English Selection* (Special Issue):139–150.

Bledsoe, C., A.G. Hill, U. D'Alessandro, and P. Langerock
1994 Constructing natural fertility: The use of Western contraceptive technologies in rural Gambia. *Population and Development Review* 20(1):81–114.

Bogue, D.J., ed.
1967 *Sociological Contributions to Family Planning Research.* Chicago: Community and Family Study Center, University of Chicago.

Bongaarts, J., W.P. Mauldin, and J.F. Phillips
1990 The demographic impact of family planning programs. *Studies in Family Planning* 21(6):299–310.

Bongaarts, J., and S.C. Watkins
1996 Social interactions and contemporary fertility transitions. *Population and Development Review* 22(4):639–682.

Boulay, M.
2000 The Influence of Information-Seeking Strategies on Social Network Composition and Contraceptive Adoption Among Women in Rural Nepal. Unpublished paper presented at the annual meeting of the Population Association of America, March 23–25, 2000, Los Angeles.

Brown, L.A.
1981 *Innovation Diffusion: A New Perspective.* New York: Methuen.

Buhler, C., H.-P. Kohler, and S.C. Watkins
2000 Who Influences Contraceptive Use in S. Nyanza District, Kenya?: Evidence from a Social Network Study. Unpublished paper presented at the annual meeting of the Population Association of America, March 23–25, 2000, Los Angeles.

Burch, T.K.
1996 Icons, straw men, and precision: Reflections on demographic theories of fertility decline. *Sociological Quarterly* 37(1):59–81.

Burt, R.S.
1987 Social contagion and innovation: Cohesion versus structural equivalence. *American Journal of Sociology* 92(6):1287–1335.
1992 *Structural Holes: The Social Structure of Competition.* Cambridge, MA: Harvard University Press.

Caldwell, J.C.
   1982   *Theory of Fertility Decline.* London: Academic Press.
Calhoun, C.
   1992   The infrastructure of modernity: Indirect social relationships, information tech-
           nology, and social integration. Pp. 205–236 in *Social Change and Modernity,* H.
           Haferkamp and N. Smelser, eds. Berkeley: University of California Press.
Carley, K.M.
   1999   On the evolution of social and organizational networks. *Research in the Sociology of
           Organizations* 16:3–30.
Carlsson, G.
   1966   The decline of fertility: Innovation or adjustment process. *Population Studies* 20(2):
           149–174.
Case, A., and L. Katz
   1991   *The Company You Keep: The Effects of Family and Neighborhood on Disadvantaged
           Youths.* National Bureau of Economic Research Working Paper No. W3705. Cam-
           bridge: NBER.
Casterline, J.B.
   1999a   Conclusions. Pp. 357–369 in *Dynamics of Values in Fertility Change,* R. Leete, ed.
           Oxford: Oxford University Press.
   1999b   *The Onset and Pace of Fertility Transition: National Patterns in the Second Half of the
           Twentieth Century.* Policy Research Division Working Paper No. 128. New York:
           Population Council.
Casterline, J., M. Montgomery, S. Green, P. Hewett, D. Agyeman, W. Adih, and P. Aglobitse
   2000   Contraceptive Use in Southern Ghana: The Role of Social Networks. Unpublished
           paper presented at the annual meeting of the Population Association of America,
           March 23–25, 2000, Los Angeles.
Casterline, J.B., and S.W. Sinding
   2000   Unmet need for family planning in developing countries and implications for
           population policy. *Population and Development Review* 26(4):691–723.
Cialdini, R.B., and M.R. Trost
   1998   Social influence: Social norms, conformity, compliance. Pp. 151–192 in *The Hand-
           book of Social Psychology, Volume II,* D.T. Gilbert, S.T. Fiske, and G. Lindzey, eds.
           New York: McGraw-Hill.
Cleland, J., and C.R. Wilson
   1987   Demand theories of the fertility transition: An iconoclastic view. *Population Stud-
           ies* 41(1):5–30.
Coale, A.J.
   1973   The demographic transition reconsidered. Pp. 53–72 in *International Population
           Conference, Liège, 1973, Volume I.* Liège, Belgium: International Union for the Sci-
           entific Study of Population.
Coleman, J.
   1988   Social capital in the creation of human capital. *American Journal of Sociology* 94:S95–
           S120.
Coleman, J., E. Katz, and H. Menzel
   1966   *Medical Innovation: A Diffusion Study.* New York: Bobbs Merrill.
Coleman, J., H. Menzel, and E. Katz
   1957   The diffusion of an innovation among physicians. *Sociometry* 20:253–270.
Cox, K.R., ed.
   1997   *Spaces of Globalization: Reasserting the Power of the Local.* New York: Guilford
           Press.

Crook, N.
1977   On social norms and fertility decline. *Journal of Development Studies* 14(4):198–210.
Davis, K.
1945   The world demographic transition. *Annals of the American Academy of Political and Social Science* 237:1–11.
1963   The theory of change and response in modern demographic history. *Population Index* 29(4):345–366.
1967   Population policy: Will current programs succeed? *Science* 158:730–739.
Degenne, A., and M. Forse
1999   *Introducing Social Networks*. London: Sage Publications.
Ellison, G., and D. Fudenberg
1993   Rules of thumb for social learning. *Journal of Political Economy* 101(4):612–643.
Entwisle, B., and J. Godley
1998   Village Networks and Patterns of Contraceptive Choice. Unpublished paper presented at National Academy of Sciences Workshop on Social Processes Underlying Fertility Change in Developing Countries, January 29-30, 1998, Washington, D.C.
Entwisle, B., R.R. Rindfuss, D.K. Guilkey, A. Chamratrithirong, S.P. Curran, and Y. Sawangdee
1996   Community and contraceptive choice in rural Thailand: A case study of Nang Rong. *Demography* 33(1):1–11.
Erbring, L., and A.A. Young
1979   Individuals and social structure: Contextual effects as endogenous feedback. *Sociological Methods and Research* 7(4):396–430.
Festinger, L.
1954   A theory of social comparison processes. *Human Relations* 7:114–140.
Freedman, R.
1979   Theories of fertility decline: A reappraisal. *Social Forces* 58(1):1–17.
Freedman, R., and Y. Takeshita
1969   *Family Planning in Taiwan: An Experiment in Social Change*. Princeton: Princeton University Press.
Friedkin, N.E.
1998   *A Structural Theory of Social Influence*. Cambridge, Eng.: Cambridge University Press.
Geertz, C.
1973   *An Interpretation of Culture*. New York: Basic Books.
Gladwell, M.
2000   *The Tipping Point: How Little Things Can Make a Big Difference*. Boston: Little, Brown.
Godley, J.
2001   Kinship networks and contraceptive choice in Nang Rong, Thailand. *International Family Planning Perspectives* 27(1):4–10.
Granovetter, M., and R. Soong
1983   Threshold models of diffusion and collective behavior. *Journal of Mathematical Sociology* 9:165–179.
1986   Threshold models of interpersonal effects in consumer demand. *Journal of Economic Behavior and Organization* 7:83–99.
Greenhalgh, S.
1988   Fertility as mobility: Sinic transitions. *Population and Development Review* 14(4):629–674.

Gregersen, H., and L. Sailer
  1993   Chaos theory and its implications for social science research. *Human Relations* 46(7):777–802.
Griliches, Z.
  1957   Hybrid corn: An exploration in the economics of technical change. *Econometrica* 25:501–522.
Hallinan, M.T.
  1997   The sociological study of social change. *American Sociological Review* 62(1):1–11.
Hechter, M.
  1993   Values research in the social and behavioral sciences. Pp. 1–30 in *The Origin of Values*, M. Hechter, L. Nadel, and R.E. Michod, eds. New York: Aldine de Gruyter.
Hedström, P.
  1998   Rational imitation. Pp. 306–327 in *Social Mechanisms: An Analytical Approach to Social Theory*, P. Hedström and R. Swedberg, eds. Cambridge, Eng.: Cambridge University Press.
Hedström, P., and R. Swedberg
  1998   Social mechanisms: An introductory essay. Pp. 1–31 in *Social Mechanisms: An Analytical Approach to Social Theory*, P. Hedström and R. Swedberg, eds. Cambridge, Eng.: Cambridge University Press.
Katz, E., and P. Lazarsfeld
  1955   *Personal Influence: The Part Played by People in the Flow of Mass Communications.* New York: Free Press.
Kearney, M.
  1995   The local and the global: The anthropology of globalization and transnationalism. *Annual Review of Anthropology* 24:547–565.
Kertzer, D.I., and D.P. Hogan
  1989   *Family, Political Economy, and Demographic Change.* Madison: University of Wisconsin Press.
Kincaid, D.L., S. Pathak, and S.N. Mitra
  1996   Communication Networks and Contraceptive Behavior in Bangladesh. Unpublished paper presented at the annual meeting of the Population Association of America, May 9–11, 1996, New Orleans.
Kirk, D.
  1996   Demographic transition theory. *Population Studies* 50(3):361–387.
Knack, S., and P. Keefer
  1997   Does social capital have an economic payoff? A cross-country investigation. *Quarterly Journal of Economics* 112:1251–1288.
Knodel, J.
  1977   Family limitation and the fertility transition: Evidence from the age patterns of fertility in Europe and Asia. *Population Studies* 31(2):219–249.
Knodel, J., N. Havanon, and A. Pramualratana
  1984   Fertility transition in Thailand: A qualitative analysis. *Population and Development Review* 10(2):297–328.
Knodel, J., and E. van de Walle
  1979   Lessons from the past: Policy implications of historical fertility studies. *Population and Development Review* 5(2):217–245.
Kohler, H.-P.
  1997   Learning in social networks and contraceptive choice. *Demography* 34(3):369–383.
  2000   Social interactions and fluctuations in birth rates. *Population Studies* 54(2):223–237.
Kohler, H.-P., J.R. Bereman and S.C. Watkins
  2001   The density of social networks and fertility decisions: Evidence from South Nyanza District, Kenya. *Demography* 38(1):43–58.

Kreager, P.
  1993   Anthropological demography and the limits of diffusionism. Pp. 313–326 in *International Population Conference, Montreal 1993,* Volume IV. Liège, Belgium: Ordina.
Lee, R.D., and J.B. Casterline
  1996   Introduction. Pp. 1–15 in *Fertility in the United States: New Patterns, New Theories,* J.B. Casterline, R.D. Lee, and K.A. Foote, eds. Supplement to *Population and Development Review* 22. New York: Population Council.
Lesthaeghe, R.
  1983   A century of demographic and cultural change in Western Europe: An exploration of underlying dimensions. *Population and Development Review* 9(3):411–435.
Lesthaeghe, R., and J. Surkyn
  1988   Cultural dynamics and economic theories of fertility change. *Population and Development Review* 14(1):1–45.
Lin, N.
  1999   Building a network theory of social capital. *Connections* 22(1):28–51.
Livi-Bacci, M.
  1999   *The Population of Europe: A History.* Malden, MA: Blackwell Publishers.
Marsden, P.V., and N. E. Friedkin
  1993   Network studies of social influence. *Sociological Methods and Research* 22(1):127–151.
Mason, K.O.
  1992   Culture and the fertility transition: Thoughts on theories of fertility decline. *Genus* 48(3-4):1–14.
  1997   Explaining fertility transitions. *Demography* 34(4):443–454.
McFadden, D.L., and K.E. Train
  1996   Consumers' evaluation of new products: Learning from self and others. *Journal of Political Economy* 104(4):683–703.
Merton, R.K.
  1968   *Social Theory and Social Structure.* New York: Free Press.
Molm, L.D.
  1997   *Coercive Power in Social Exchange.* Cambridge, Eng.: Cambridge University Press.
Montgomery, M.R.
  2000   Perceiving mortality decline. *Population amd Development Review* 26(4):795-819.
Montgomery, M.R., and J.B. Casterline
  1993   The diffusion of fertility control in Taiwan: Evidence from pooled cross-section, time-series models. *Population Studies* 47(3):457–479.
  1996   Social learning, social influence, and new models of fertility. *Population and Development Review* (Supplement) 22:151–175.
  1998   *Social Networks and the Diffusion of Fertility Control.* Policy Research Division Working Paper No. 119. New York: Population Council.
Montgomery, M.R., and W.S. Chung
  1999   Social networks and the diffusion of fertility control in Korea. Pp. 179–209 in *Dynamics of Values in Fertility Change,* R. Leete, ed. Oxford: Oxford University Press.
Munshi, K., and J. Myaux
  1998   Social Effects in the Demographic Transition: Evidence from Matlab, Bangladesh. Unpublished paper, Department of Economics, Boston University.
Narayan, D., and L. Pritchett
  1999   Cents and sociability: Household income and social capital in rural Tanzania. *Economic Development and Cultural Change* 47(4):871–898.

Notestein, F.W.
  1945   Population—the long view. Pp. 36–57 in *Food for the World*, T.W. Shultz, ed. Chicago: University of Chicago Press.
  1953   Economic problems of population change. In *Proceedings of the Eighth International Conference of Agricultural Economists*. London: Oxford University Press.
Ogburn, W.F.
  1922   *Social Change*. New York: B.W. Huebsch, Inc.
Palmore, J.A.
  1967   The Chicago snowball: A study of the flow of influence and diffusion of family planning information. In *Sociological Contributions to Family Planning Research*, D.J. Bogue, ed. Chicago: Community and Family Study Center, University of Chicago.
Pearl, J.
  2000   *Causality: Models, Reasoning, Inference*. Cambridge, Eng.: Cambridge University Press.
Pescondido, B.A.
  1992   Beyond rational choice: The social dynamics of how people seek help. *American Journal of Sociology* 97:1096–1138.
Pollak, R.A., and S.C. Watkins
  1993   Cultural and economic approaches to fertility: Proper marriage or *mesalliance*? *Population and Development Review* 19(3):467–496.
Portes, A.
  1998   Social capital: Its origins and applications in modern sociology. *Annual Review of Sociology* 22:1–24.
Potter, J.
  1999   The persistence of outmoded contraceptive regimes: The cases of Mexico and Brazil. *Population and Development Review* 25(4):703–740.
Putnam, R.D.
  1995   Bowling alone: America's declining social capital. *Journal of Democracy* 6:65–78.
Retherford, R.
  1985   A theory of marital fertility transition. *Population Studies* 39(2):249–268.
Retherford, R., and J. Palmore
  1983   Diffusion processes affecting fertility regulation. Pp. 295–339 in *Determinants of Fertility in Developing Countries, Volume 2*, R.A. Bulatao and R.D. Lee, eds. New York: Academic Press.
Rogers, E.M.
  1962   *Diffusion of Innovations*. New York: Free Press.
  1973   *Communication Strategies for Family Planning*. New York: Free Press.
Rogers, E.M., and D.L. Kincaid
  1981   *Communication Networks: Toward A New Paradigm for Research*. New York: Free Press.
Rosero-Bixby, L., and J. B. Casterline
  1993   Modelling diffusion effects in fertility transition. *Population Studies* 47(1):147–167.
Rutenberg, N., and S.C. Watkins
  1997   The buzz outside the clinics: Conversations and contraception in Nyanza Province, Kenya. *Studies in Family Planning* 28(4):290–307.
Ryan, R., and N. Gross
  1943   The diffusion of hybrid seed corn in two Iowa communities. *Rural Sociology* 8(1):15–24.
Santow, G.
  1995   *Coitus interruptus* and the control of natural fertility. *Population Studies* 49(1):5–18.

Santow, G., and M.D. Bracher
  1999   Traditional families and fertility decline: Lessons from Australia's Southern Europeans. Pp. 51–77 in *Dynamics of Values in Fertility Change*, R. Leete, ed. Oxford: Oxford University Press.
Sathar, Z., and J.B. Casterline
  1998   The onset of fertility transition in Pakistan. *Population and Development Review* 24(4):773–796.
Schoen, R., Y.J. Kim, C.A. Nathanson, J. Fields, and N.M. Astone
  1997   Why do Americans want children? *Population and Development Review* 23(2):333–358.
Shiller, R.
  1995   Conversation, information and herd behavior. *American Economic Review* 85(2): 181–185.
Strang, D.
  1991   Adding social structure to diffusion models: An event history framework. *Sociological Methods and Research* 19(3):324–353.
Strang, D., and N. Tuma
  1993   Spatial and temporal heterogeneity in diffusion. *American Journal of Sociology* 99(3):614–639.
Szreter, S.
  1993   The idea of demographic transition and the study of fertility change: A critical intellectual history. *Population and Development Review* 19(4):659–701.
Thompson, W.S.
  1929   Population. *American Journal of Sociology* 34(6):959–975.
United Nations
  2000   *World Population Prospects, the 1998 Revision: Volume III, Analytical Report.* New York: United Nations.
Valente, T.W.
  1995   *Network Models of the Diffusion of Innovations.* Cresskill, NJ: Hampton Press.
Valente, T.W., P.R. Poppe, and A.P. Merritt
  1996   Mass-media-generated interpersonal communication as sources of information about family planning. *Journal of Health Communication* 1:247–265.
Valente, T.W., and E.M. Rogers
  1995   The origins and development of the diffusion of innovations paradigm as an example of scientific growth. *Science Communications* 16(3):242–273.
Valente, T.W., and W.P. Saba
  1998   Mass media and interpersonal influence in a reproductive health communication campaign in Bolivia. *Communication Research* 25(1):96–124.
Valente, T.W., S.C. Watkins, M.N. Jato, A. van der Straten, and L.-P.M. Tsitsol
  1997   Social network associations with contraceptive use among Cameroonian women in voluntary associations. *Social Science and Medicine* 45(5):677–687.
Van den Bulte, C., and G.L. Lilien
  in   Medical innovation revisited: Social contagion versus marketing effort. *American*
  press   *Journal of Sociology.*
van de Walle, E.
  1992   Fertility transition, conscious choice and numeracy. *Demography* 29(4):487–502.
van de Walle, E., and J. Knodel
  1967   Demographic transition and fertility decline: The European case. Pp. 47–55 in *Contributed Papers Sydney Conference*, International Union for the Scientific Study of Population. Canberra, Australia: Australian National University Press.

Wasserman, S., and K. Faust
    1994   *Social Network Analysis: Methods and Applications.* Cambridge, Eng.: Cambridge University Press.
Watkins, S.C.
    1986   Conclusions. Pp. 420–449 in *The Decline of Fertility in Europe,* A.J. Coale and S.C. Watkins, eds. Princeton: Princeton University Press.
    1990   From local to national communities: The transformation of demographic regimes in Western Europe, 1870–1960. *Population and Development Review* 16(2):241–272.
    1991   More Lessons from the Past: Women's Informal Networks and Fertility Decline. Unpublished paper presented at the International Union for the Scientific Study of Population (IUSSP) seminar on The Onset of Fertility Decline in Sub-Saharan Africa, Harare, November 19–22, 1991, Zimbabwe.
Watkins, S.C., and D. Hodgson
    1998   From Mercantilists to Neo-Malthusians: The International Population Movement and the Transformation of Population Ideology in Kenya. Unpublished paper presented at National Academy of Sciences Workshop on Social Processes Underlying Fertility Change in Developing Countries, January 29–30, 1998, Washington, D.C.
Watts, D.J.
    1999   *Small Worlds: The Dynamics of Networks Between Order and Randomness.* Princeton: Princeton University Press.
Woolcock, M.
    1998   Social capital and economic development: Towards a theoretical synthesis and policy framework. *Theory and Society* 27:151–208.

2

Potatoes and Pills: An Overview of Innovation-Diffusion Contributions to Explanations of Fertility Decline

JOHN CLELAND

Forks, potatoes, and contraception may not appear at first glance to have much in common but, at different times, all have been innovations that have encountered considerable resistance before becoming accepted as humdrum elements of everyday life. The first mention of a fork as an instrument for carrying food to the mouth describes its use by the wife of the Venetian Doge in the eleventh century (Visser, 1993). The incident aroused the wrath of St. Peter Damian, the cardinal bishop of Ostia, who criticized the whole procedure in a passage entitled "Of the Venetian Doge's wife, whose body, after her excessive delicacy, entirely rotted away" (Visser, 1993:189). In Northern Italy, it took a further 200 years before forks were commonly used for eating. As usual, England lagged well behind Italy in culinary matters. It was not until the early seventeenth century that Thomas Coryate introduced the fork, following a visit to Italy (Clair, 1965). Once again the instrument was condemned from the pulpit and repudiated by society. One irate preacher declared that "to touch meat with a fork was impiously to declare that God's creatures were not worthy of being touched by human hands" (Clair, 1965:181).

The initial reaction to the potato in Europe following its introduction at the end of the sixteenth century was similar to that evoked by the fork (Salaman, 1949). Opposition was widespread, partly because of its strange

John Cleland is professor and head of research unit in the Centre for Population Studies at the London School of Hygiene and Tropical Medicine. The author would like to extend appreciation to Ian Timaeus and Brent Wolff who made constructive suggestions for improvement of a first draft of this paper.

shape and subterranean character. At different times and places, the potato was accused of causing leprosy, scrofula, fever, tuberculosis, and rickets. In 1774 Frederick the Great set out to attack these superstitious beliefs. He sent a wagonload of potatoes to Kolberg to relieve a severe food shortage. After rejection of his gift by the indignant citizens, he dispatched a Swabian gendarme who convinced them that the potato was edible in the most convincing way possible: by eating one (Pyke, 1968). To overcome similar resistance in France, the government adopted a less colorful strategy. It invited the Medical Faculty of Paris to undertake an inquiry into the merits and demerits of the potato and disseminated the favorable verdict.

The example of the fork serves to remind us that even a seemingly innocent and trivial innovation may encounter resistance before more widespread (though, in this case, not universal) acceptance and incorporation into everyday life. The case of the potato is perhaps potentially more relevant to contraception because food, sex, and procreation are central concerns of all human societies. Because of this centrality, radically new products or ideas concerning these three topics are likely to arouse particularly strong reactions that often necessitate the intervention of governments or other elites.

How useful is it to pursue analogies between the spread of forks, potatoes, and contraception? To what extent can an innovation-diffusion framework help to explain marital fertility declines? These are among the key questions that will be addressed in this paper. Before doing so, however, it may be helpful to present a brief historical sketch of the role of diffusion frameworks in fertility theories.

The spread of new products or ideas between societies is such an important feature of human history that it has always formed part of broader theories of social and cultural change. Both archeology and social anthropology have been influenced heavily by diffusionism. Quantitative investigation of the diffusion of innovations also has a relatively long ancestry. It originates in the 1920s in the efforts of the U.S. Department of Agriculture to assist small farmers by encouraging them to adopt new products, such as hybrid seeds, fertilizers, and herbicides. Many of the concepts and assumptions of this early work left a profound imprint on subsequent research. These include the assumption that the new product or practice offered an indisputable benefit; an emphasis on the process of communication and a neglect of possible structural determinants of uptake of the innovation; a focus on the individual as decision maker; a concern with the roles of change agents (in this case, agricultural extension workers); investigation of the characteristics of opinion leaders, early innovators, and late innovators; and an emphasis on applied research rather than on theory building.

During the 1950s and 1960s, innovation-diffusion research blossomed, with scant regard for disciplinary boundaries. In a major synthesis at the end of this era, Rogers and Shoemaker (1971) identified 1,500 studies drawn from agriculture, anthropology, sociology, geography, communications, marketing, and other substantive areas. Not surprisingly, the burgeoning family planning movement participated fully in this enthusiasm. In terms of program design, the early medical clinic-based model gave way to a more diffusionist approach, with an emphasis on communications, incentives, and fieldworkers (i.e., change agents). Major family planning communication groups were created at Johns Hopkins University and the East-West Center.

The effect on research into family planning was also considerable. Bogue (1965) defined the field as "the systematic study of the phenomenon of family planning among populations, of the processes by which the practice of family planning diffuses throughout a community or nation and of the forces that retard or facilitate such diffusion and adoption." Some of the best empirical studies of the role of interpersonal communication in the spread of contraceptive practice date from this era. Palmore (1967) used a diffusion framework to study the discussion of family planning following a mailing of booklets to individuals in low-income, inner-city areas of Chicago. In the famous Taichung experiment, one research question was phrased as follows: "Can direct communication to systematically spaced subgroups of a population indirectly affect a much larger population by diffusion from the initial foci of direct contact?" (Freedman and Takeshita, 1969:110). The answer was emphatically positive. In India, Marshall (1971) compared communication networks for family planning with those for a new wheat variety, while Blaikie (1975) assessed the strengths and limitations of spatial diffusion theory for understanding contraceptive adoption in Northeast Bihar.

A diffusionist approach to family planning research was buoyed by numerous Knowledge, Attitudes, and Practice (KAP) surveys that indicated a widespread need for and interest in family planning; by the success of early family planning programs in Taiwan, the Republic of Korea, and Singapore; and perhaps by the illusory success of Ayub Khan's 1965–1969 program in Pakistan. Subsequently the mood changed as it became clear that adoption of contraception and declines in marital fertility would not sweep across the larger countries of Asia and Africa as fast as they had done in Taiwan, for example. Doubts were expressed about the effectiveness of family planning programs (e.g., Davis, 1969), and the validity of the results of KAP surveys was questioned (Hauser, 1967). Even Rogers (1983: 71) had to admit that "contraceptives are one of the most difficult types of innovations to diffuse." Economic theories of fertility transition, that stressed shifts in the costs and benefits of children, assumed an increasing dominance. And within the favored individual utility maximization model, there was little space for innovation-diffusion ideas. The academic climate of the time is well illustrated by the mammoth National Academy of Sciences volumes on fertility determinants in developing countries. They end with an agenda for future research. Forty topics are described, but only one reflects an interest in diffusion (Bulatao and Lee, 1983).

In the mid-1980s, the tide of demographic events and research evidence turned again, and there was a renaissance of interest in diffusion frameworks. By that time, it was clear that fertility declines, largely fueled by increases in birth control, were occurring in most of Asia and Latin America. Within a few more years, indisputable evidence of fertility change in some of the poorest countries in the world (e.g., Bangladesh and Nepal) had accumulated and there were growing signs of the onset of fertility transition in Africa. Both the pace and geographical spread of fertility decline appeared, at least superficially, to be more consistent with an innovation-diffusion style of explanation than one based on structural changes leading to reduced demand for children.

The publication of the results of two major research programs greatly strengthened the diffusionist case. The Princeton European Project analyzed aggregate demographic data for the provinces of Europe during the period of the fertility transition (Coale and Watkins, 1986). The analysis of age-specific marital fertility rates suggested that the practice of family limitation, or parity-specific birth control, was largely absent prior to 1880, with the important exception of France. Between 1880 and 1930, the practice spread with remarkable speed throughout most of Western Europe. The timing of the onset of decline was only weakly related to provincial levels of socioeconomic modernization but unmistakably linked to language, a feature most vividly demonstrated by the difference between Flemish- and French-speaking villages in Belgium (Lesthaeghe, 1977). The demographic laggards tended to be communities that were both spatially and linguistically isolated: the Celts in the United Kingdom, the Lapps in Sweden and Finland, and the Frieslanders in the Netherlands (Watkins, 1991). Moreover, there was little evidence that the decline of marital fertility in Europe was propelled by any transformation in the value of children (Knodel and van de Walle, 1986).

This Princeton orthodoxy is not without its critics. In an analysis of the Balkans, Hammel (1995) comes to the conclusion that ethnicity is only a proxy for political factors that in turn determine economic motives for childbearing. Kertzer and Hogan (1989) give a plausible economic interpretation to the persistence of high fertility among sharecroppers compared to the other economic strata in Italy. Yet the big picture has not been seriously challenged and the Princeton European Project remains the single most powerful rebuttal of demand theories of decline and provides the most convincing, albeit indirect, evidence to support an innova-tion-diffusion style of explanation.

The second major research program to reach completion in the mid-1980s was the World Fertility Survey. The raw data, cross-sectional inter-view surveys of women were very different from those available to the Princeton Project. Nevertheless, there were striking parallels in some of the findings. Once again, there was evidence of a rapid spread of birth control practices from urban to rural strata and evidence that language or other cultural factors (denoted, for example, by religious affiliation) influ-enced the onset and speed of decline (Cleland, 1985). With the clear ex-ception of Sub-Saharan Africa, differences in the level of contraceptive practice or marital fertility at national or subnational levels appeared to reflect variations in the propensity to act on family size preferences rather than variations in the nature of preferences themselves (Lightbourne, 1985). And once again, evidence of the impact of economic factors on reproduction was largely absent. For example, women's labor force par-ticipation was not a predictor of fertility in most countries (United Na-tions, 1985) nor did the shift from familial to nonfamilial modes of pro-duction have the expected effect on family size (Rodriguez and Cleland, 1981). This evidence, together with that from historical Europe, consti-tuted a major attack on the dominant economic paradigm of the previous decade and a boost to diffusion frameworks (Cleland and Wilson, 1987).

Since the 1980s, empirical work that bears directly on innovation-diffusion explanations of fertility decline has taken two very different pathways. Watkins and collaborators have investigated the content and nature of interpersonal discussions about family size and family planning in the United States and in Kenya, thereby beginning to remedy a glaring gap in the research evidence (Watkins and Danzi, 1995; Watkins et al., 1997; Rutenberg and Watkins, 1997), and Valente and collaborators have applied network theory (a rapidly growing field) to family planning in Cameroon (Valente et al., 1997). Meanwhile, Casterline, Montgomery, and Rosero-Bixby have modeled fertility trends in Taiwan and Costa Rica to test expectations derived from the diffusion framework (Montgomery and Casterline, 1993; Rosero-Bixby and Casterline, 1993, 1994). These con-tributions will be discussed later.

SPECIFICATION OF THE INNOVATION-DIFFUSION FRAMEWORK AND ITS APPLICABILITY TO FERTILITY TRANSITION THEORY

Thus far in the paper, no specification of the innovation-diffusion framework has been given. It is appropriate now to remedy this defect. The third edition of *Diffusion of Innovations* serves as an appropriate basis for the account that follows (Rogers, 1983). According to Rogers (1983:10), diffusion has four main elements. It is "the process by which (1) an innovation (2) is communicated through certain channels (3) over time (4) among members of a social system."

The characteristics of the innovation (new product, procedure, idea, or some combination of these) partly determine its rate of adoption. These include its perceived relative advantage, compatibility with norms and values, complexity, trialability, and observability. The last two features have potentially interesting implications for family planning diffusion. Reversible methods can be subjected to trial but not sterilization, for example. Observability is likely to differ between supply methods and other methods, such as withdrawal, with possible consequences for the speed of diffusion. In contrast the concepts of relative advantage and compatibility relate to familiar themes in fertility theorizing and have nothing distinctive to offer. Relative advantage simply echoes child-utility theories while compatibility corresponds to cultural theories of fertility change.

The innovation-diffusion approach is thus at its weakest in helping to understand why some innovations spread and others do not. As the vast majority of new ideas or products fail to gain acceptance, this is a damaging weakness and helps to explain why the concept of diffusion remains at the margins of mainstream theories of change.

The framework offers potentially more useful concepts to examine the process of communication. It draws heavily on sociological theories of learning, influence, and networks. Although the role of mass media and specially trained "change agents" is recognized, the importance of interpersonal communication is stressed as the most powerful channel of influence. In contrast to theories that model behavior as the outcome of isolated individual decision making or of internalized norms and values, the major concern of network theory is the ties that link people, both strong ties between close friends and weak ties with mere acquaintances (Granovetter, 1973). Such interpersonal contacts act not only as conduits for information flow but as powerful constraints on behavior. To put it at its most simple, the behavior of individuals is heavily influenced by the behavior or perceived behavior of others with whom they interact.

These concepts lend themselves readily to the study of innovations. Because innovations, almost by definition, carry an element of uncertainty, risk, and perhaps even fear, uptake is initially slow. The incidence of adoption then accelerates because of the social influence of peer groups on individuals. This self-reinforcing process is also fueled by reductions in risk and uncertainty as the innovative item becomes more common and familiar. Rogers (1983:234) call this the "diffusion effect." The term preferred in later work by Casterline and others is "endogenous feedback." In terms of Easterlin's framework, the spread of contraception reduces the psychic and social "costs" of fertility regulation (Easterlin, 1975). The incidence of adoption then falls as saturation is approached, giving an S-shaped cumulative adoption distribution over time. Early adopters tend to be of high social status and education, partly because of exposure to a wider range of communication networks. The speed of diffusion thus depends to some extent on interpersonal links between these individuals and others: hence the importance of heterophilous contacts (Rogers' term) or weak ties (Granovetter's term). The potential applicability of this model to contraception is obvious.

From this brief description, both blended and pure versions of inno-vation-diffusion explanations of marital fertility decline may be derived. Blended versions are essentially a fusion of classical demand theories and elements of the diffusion model. The fundamental cause of fertility de-cline is reduced demand for children (and/or increased supply through improved child survival) that stems from modernization in its various forms. Once the structural conditions are right, fertility decline is inevi-table but its timing may be lagged. The onset of decline can be advanced by skillful government deployment of mass media and change agents or delayed by inappropriate official efforts to promote contraception. Diffu-sion processes subsequently condition the speed and mechanisms of change. Couples do not make reproductive decisions in isolation from one another. Although the idea of birth control within marriage may or may not be new, the modern array of methods certainly is. The spread of knowledge and use of these methods accords with the diffusion model described above. Early adopters tend to be more cosmopolitan, urban, and educated, but adoption, and reduced fertility, spreads to other sec-tors, largely through interpersonal communication networks. Formal ex-positions of such a blended theory may be found in Retherford (1985) and Kohler (1997).

Under the blended theory, the engine of demographic change is the structural transformation of societies, and diffusion is the lubricant. A pure version of innovation-diffusion explanations of fertility decline ac-cords a much more central explanatory role to marital birth control as an innovation. It is an exogenous theory of change whereas the blended version is essentially an endogenous theory. Not only are modern meth-ods of contraception recent inventions, but the very idea of deliberate pregnancy regulation within marriage has been absent in most societies for most of human history. This absence of pregnancy regulation for so much of human history remains a puzzle because, as our knowledge of historical demography increases, it is becoming clear that all societies have developed ways of suppressing average fertility and family size to remarkably low levels. Total fertility rates of between four and six births appear to have been the norm (Wilson and Airey, 1999). A latent demand for pregnancy regulation exists in all societies. The "invention" of contraception offers huge advantages over previous ways of mitigating the perennial human problem of controlling numbers: celibacy; methods of abortion that were dangerous, partially effective, or both; infanticide; child abandonment; fostering; or adoption (Mason, 1997). The "invention" is largely a moral one in historical Europe: forms of behavior previously considered repugnant and fit only for illicit relationships became respectable. In the developing world, the invention was both moral and technological. Like the wheel, once invented, its global spread is inevitable and unstoppable. The nexus between sexual intercourse and conception, once broken, cannot be restored. But like the potato, both the idea of marital birth control and its material manifestations encounter resistance of a largely cultural or religious nature that condition the timing and speed of adoption. New Frederick the Greats arise at international and national levels, and cohorts of Swabian gendarmes in the modern uniform of grey suits, are dispatched from New York and Washington, D.C., to convince suspicious or fearful communities of the merits of the new idea and its products. Partly because of the effectiveness of their efforts but also because of the proliferation of communication networks, universal diffusion of contraception is achieved more quickly than the diffusion of the potato in Europe: 150 years if Europe is included and a mere 50 or so years for other major regions.

The spread of contraception has no logical, inevitable link to the level of fertility but, like other radical innovations, it has profound implications. By releasing women from the burden of frequent childbearing, it paves the way for a revolution in gender relations. More importantly for fertility theory, it allows couples to reassess the number of children they want, and this reassessment inevitably leads to a downward revision. New means make possible new motives and new attitudes toward children. This drop in the desired number of births is undoubtedly influenced by improvements in child survival that accompany or precede the spread of birth control. Whether or not this reassessment leads inexorably to replacement-level fertility or below remains to be seen, but the indications, thus far, are that it will.

These sketches of blended and pure versions of innovation-diffusion explanations of course do not imply that stark choices have to be made between rejection of both or endorsement of one. There are many possible variations on the central themes. However, the distinction is worth making for the following reason. As I shall argue below, the evidence that contraceptive practice spreads by interpersonal communication and that the reproductive habits of couples are influenced by the behavior of those around them is overwhelmingly strong and indeed blindingly obvious to anyone with first-hand experience in family planning in developing countries. Only a bigot or a theoretician who never strays from the comforts of algebraic models could attempt to explain what has happened to human fertility without invoking elements of the diffusion framework. Interest should focus therefore on the pure version of the innovation-diffusion framework, which is more controversial, more problematic, and by no means blindingly obvious.

The pure version of innovation-diffusion explanations rests on key assumptions and leads to a large number of empirical expectations, some of which can be addressed by evidence. Many are also relevant to the blended version. These are listed below.

- Fertility regulation within marriage is an innovation.
- The idea of fertility regulation within marriage and many of the methods to achieve this initially evoke feelings of uncertainty, ambivalence, and fear.
- The evidence concerning the timing of fertility transitions across societies is more consistent with expectations derived from the innovation-diffusion framework than with those derived from economic theories.
- Once a certain threshold of cumulative adoption is reached, contraception spreads rapidly throughout socially and linguistically homogeneous systems, regardless of the position of groups within the economic structure.
- Contraception, and related topics, are the subject of interpersonal communication.
- The decision of individuals to adopt contraception and the methods they choose are influenced by their perceptions of behavior of others within their communication networks.
- Declines in desired family size accompany or follow the diffusion of contraception rather than precede it.
- Contraception supercedes earlier methods of managing family size and composition.

THE EVIDENCE

Is Fertility Regulation an Innovation?

In view of universal understanding of the causal link between sexual intercourse and pregnancy, it may seem fanciful to claim that deliberate control of conception within marriage can be an innovation. Indeed it has often been claimed that coitus interruptus, nonvaginal intercourse, and prolonged abstinence are always available when the motive arises. But as Pollack and Watkins (1993) point out, the innovatory element of pregnancy regulation within marriage may not take the form of new information about the biology of procreation but a more moral one of thinking (and then doing) the hitherto unthinkable. This concept of "unthinkability" is a familiar one and appears under a number of terms: Coale's (1973) "calculus of conscious choice"; Rotter's (1966) "locus of control"; and "active agency," as used, for example by Carter (1995).

What then is the evidence that pregnancy prevention was a cognitive or an ideational innovation? For historical Europe, the evidence is largely indirect. The literary material is generally positive (van de Walle, 1992). Analysis of marital age-specific fertility rates certainly demonstrates that parity-specific control became very much more common in Europe between 1880 and 1930, though this evidence does not rule out the possibility that minority groups may have practiced family limitation long before the fertility transition itself nor that deliberate regulation of birth spacing may have been common. The single most telling piece of evidence to support the view that pregnancy prevention was indeed an innovation is the fact that illegitimate fertility fell in parallel with marital fertility (Knodel and van de Walle, 1986). It requires considerable sophistry to explain this trend without coming to the conclusion that individuals in Europe were putting to effective use new forms of behavior that were previously denied to them.

Evidence with regard to developing countries comes mainly in the form of the direct testimony of the actors themselves, gathered in structured interview surveys or by ethnographic techniques. The results of early fertility and family planning surveys strongly suggest that there are indeed societies where almost no one attempts to prevent or delay pregnancy within marriage (or, alternatively, is prepared to report such behavior). If, as some have claimed, traditional methods are always available when needed, this is an astonishing finding that is compatible only with extreme forms of pronatalism or the existence of more attractive methods of control. As mentioned earlier, it is implausible to characterize historical societies as strongly pronatalist, nor do most of the alternative control mechanisms appear to be intrinsically superior. Reported awareness of methods of contraception—either traditional or modern—can also be very low. Majorities of women canvassed in the World Fertility Survey reported ignorance of all methods in Yemen, Cameroon, Benin, and Nepal, for example. There is little evidence that coitus interruptus was widely known, let alone practiced.

Qualitative or ethnographic evidence, on occasion, has raised serious questions about the validity of standardized survey results with regard to contraceptive knowledge and use (e.g., Stone and Campbell, 1984; Bleek, 1987). There also is no doubt that women are reluctant to admit their familiarity with male methods such as coitus interruptus and condoms, presumably because of shyness or shame. Yet much of the ethnographic evidence is entirely consistent with the impression given by survey results. In North India (Jeffery et el., 1989), Bangladesh (Maloney et al., 1981), Thailand (Knodel et al., 1984), Mali (van de Walle and van de Walle, 1991), and early twentieth-century Prussia (Lee et al., 1994), to cite but a few examples, there is convincing testimony that the idea of fertility regulation was unthinkable and/or the means to achieve it unknown. A few quotations give the flavor of responses.

> "Truly the number I wanted was four, but going on to ten was God's work." (Mali)
> "We didn't think about how many (children] we should have. [My husband] felt sorry for me when I had lots of children but no one knew what to do." (Thailand)
> "In the old days, no one used medicines to stop having children. They would say it was bad to stick out your leg to trip up God in his work. However many children were in a person's fate, that many would certainly be born." (India)
> "It is very hard with more than two children, but if they are given by dear God, one must be satisfied." (Prussia)
> "The number of children to be born is indicated in the woman's childbearing tube. Only God knows this, and no one can foretell it." (Bangladesh)

The constant reference to religion need not be interpreted literally. In my interpretation, these statements reflect a distrust of an alien idea that appears unnatural, rather than a carefully considered rejection on the basis of religious doctrine. In societies where religious sentiments permeate every aspect of life, the easiest way to express this distrust is to resort to familiar religious terminology.

To sum up, the case that the idea of marital fertility regulation was a true innovation both in Europe and elsewhere remains robust despite widespread skepticism.

Does the Idea of Fertility Regulation and Methods Initially Evoke Feelings of Uncertainty, Ambivalence, and Fear?

In some developing countries the advent of modern contraceptive methods was greeted enthusiastically. In the 1960s, many Taiwanese and Thai women, for example, traveled long distances to have Intrauterine Devices (IUD) fitted. In other settings it is clear that marital birth control and its methods is initially greeted with suspicion, ambivalence, and fear. Both surveys and more indepth investigation in many parts of the developing world point to the same verdict. Fear of side effects or more serious damage to health are among the most commonly cited reasons for nonuse. Religious objections and fear of social disapproval figure in some settings but not in others. Much of the early evidence is summarized in Bogue (1983). Recent studies document more fully the anxieties, fears, and sometimes even outrage that can be evoked by the introduction of modern contraception into a social system. Simmons et al. (1988) describe the initial uproar caused by the advent of female family planning workers in Bangladesh. Casterline and Sathar (1997) conclude from their detailed study of unmet need in the Punjab province of Pakistan that the three decisive obstacles to contraceptive use are fear of side effects; concerns about social, cultural, and religious acceptability; and perceptions of husband's disapproval. The most vivid evidence comes from the studies by Watkins and collaborators in South Nyanza, Kenya (e.g., Watkins et al., 1995). The ambivalence, fear, and anguish with which women view modern contraception is unmistakably portrayed.

The reaction to the idea of birth control in Europe was also hostile. It was condemned by politicians, the medical profession, and church alike. Birth control was seen as a threat to health, a potential drain on national vitality, and an invitation to promiscuity. The trial of Charles Bradlaugh and Annie Besant in 1877 gives the flavor of the times. Their crime was to have printed and distributed a rather mild pamphlet on birth control called the Fruits of Philosophy. The indictment accused them of "inciting and encouraging the subjects of the Queen to indecent, obscene, unnatural and immoral practices and bring them to a state of wickedness, lewdness and debauchery."

The conclusion is clearcut. Contraception is not seamlessly incorporated into reproductive strategies, whenever the need arises. On the contrary, in many though not all societies, it encounters serious resistance, the most common expression of which takes the form of concerns about health. But just like the potato in Europe, the articulation of health concerns probably reflects more profound disquiet about a radical innovation that goes to the heart of one of life's central preoccupations.

One of the great mysteries of contraceptive diffusion is why the topic caused so little fuss in Thailand and Taiwan but met such hostile reactions in other parts of the world. One obvious explanation is that the need for birth control determined its reception. However, survey evidence on desired family sizes or unmet need lends little support to this obvious factor. For instance, desired family sizes in Pakistan or Bangladesh in the 1960s were little different from those in Taiwan and Thailand. The level of education or literacy appears to exert a major influence but this link has many possible interpretations.

Is the Evidence Concerning the Timing of Fertility Transitions Across Societies More Consistent with Expectations Derived from the Innovation-Diffusion Framework or with Those Derived from Economic Theories?

Acceptance, rejection, or modification of the pure variant of the innovation-diffusion explanation depends to a large extent on the answer to this multifaceted question. In this short paper, it cannot be addressed adequately but at the same time it is too important to be ignored.

The salient features of the European fertility transition lend more support to an innovation-diffusion framework than to economic theories of changing demand for children. One of its more striking characteristics is that it occurred more or less simultaneously in overseas colonies of European stock. This simultaneity, despite big differences in macroeconomic conditions and in population density, is most plausibly interpreted as testimony to the power of shared ideas, values, and language in determining the timing of demographic change. Within Europe, the forerunner of fertility decline, France, was rather backward in terms of industrialization and urbanization, but arguably the most advanced state in terms of intellectual ideas. As noted earlier, the timing of the onset of decline across the provinces of Europe was more strongly related to language than to levels of development. The transition swept across most of Europe between 1880 and 1930, incorporating poor, agrarian societies such as Bulgaria, but was effectively stopped for several decades at the boundary between Christianity and Islam in the former Soviet Union and in the Balkans. Moreover, the relationships between improved survival and fertility change were highly variable (van de Walle, 1986).

The fertility transitions of Asia, Latin America, and Africa that started in the second half of the past century took place under very different circumstances from the earlier European transition. Without exception they were preceded by very steep decreases in mortality that gave rise to rapid growth of population, which in turn evoked the policy response of population control and official promulgation of newly developed methods of birth control. The determinants of fertility decline in developing countries has attracted intense empirical scrutiny over the past 30 years, and the evidence provides a degree of support to most explanatory frameworks. There is, for example, a moderate link between overall socioeconomic development (as measured by the Human Development Index) and the onset of decline, though this has weakened over time (Bongaarts and Watkins, 1996). Among development indicators, life expectancy and the level of adult education, or literacy, are the strongest predictors of fertility decline. The education-fertility linkage is compatible with both economic and diffusionist theories of change. The spread of formal schooling may create new opportunities to invest in children, thereby raising costs. It may also act to increase openness to new ideas and new models of behavior, including the use of modern contraceptive methods. Similarly the life-expectancy linkage may be interpreted in several ways.

The expectation, derived from innovation-diffusion theory, that fertility transition should precede earliest and fastest in developing countries with strong links to the rich industrialized world can muster only modest support. It provides a plausible explanation for the contrast between Tunisia and Algeria (Lee et al., 1995). It also accords with the observation that the fertility transition in Sub-Saharan Africa has been led by three countries with substantial settler populations of European descent: South Africa, Zimbabwe, and Kenya. But there are telling counter-examples. Fertility has also declined sharply in some of the most isolated countries of the world, such as North Korea, Mongolia, and Myanmar.

Some analysts (e.g., Cleland and Wilson, 1987) have interpreted differences in the timing of fertility transition between communities in terms of variations in resistance to the idea of modern birth control rather than in terms of contrasts in the microeconomics of families. The persistence of high fertility among the Moslem minority in Thailand (Knodel et al., 1999) and regional differences within Malaysia (Leete, 1989) are among many examples where a cultural explanation, invoking differential opposition to new ideas, appears more plausible than a narrowly economic one.

Evidence that policies of governments and other elites had a decisive impact on fertility trends would also tend to favor diffusionist explanations. Major research investments to assess the impact of antinatal policies and programs has led to disappointingly little consensus. The reason is obvious. The role of programs in fertility decline has been highly variable and context specific. In many countries, fertility decline was already established before organized state efforts were made to legitimize birth control and make available free or heavily subsidized contraceptive methods. This sequence applies to most of Latin America, to many Arab states, and to some Asian countries, such as Thailand and Malaysia. In these settings, government actions may have accelerated diffusion of information and behavior from urban, educated strata to rural, less privileged sectors but clearly played no role in the initiation of reproductive change. It is also true that fertility has fallen in settings where governing elites have been hostile to the mass provision of contraception (e.g., Myanmar, North Korea, Saudi Arabia). However, there are other countries where government actions may have been decisive in determining not only the speed of fertility change but the timing of its onset (e.g., Bangladesh, China, Indonesia, Kenya).

To sum up, analysis of the timing of the onset of marital fertility decline yields no simple generalizations, whether they be derived from an economic or demand perspective or from innovation-diffusion theory. Rather it appears that the timing of each societal transition is responding to a unique constellation of circumstances.

Once a Certain Threshold Is Reached, Does Contraception Spread Rapidly Throughout Homogeneous Social Systems?

One of the strongest expectations derived from the innovation-diffusion framework is that once a threshold level of uptake, or critical mass, is reached, subsequent spread is rapid until saturation is approached. Formal tests of this proposition would require careful definition of threshold (innovation theory offers no guidelines here), of speed, of homogeneity, and of saturation. This degree of precision is approximated most closely in the Princeton European Project (Coale and Treadway, 1986). Once a 10-percent threshold was reached, further declines in marital fertility were fast, essentially irreversible, and affected all economic strata. Fast, here, refers to an approximate halving of the index of marital fertility in 30 to 40 years (see Coale and Treadway, 1986:40). The analysis by Chesnais (1992) yields a similar picture. The two main exceptions are France, where the threshold was reached at an exceptionally early date—1827—and Ireland, which had a rather late threshold—1922.

An equivalent analysis has been performed for developing countries by Bongaarts and Watkins (1996). They also define the threshold in terms of a 10-percent decline but examine trends in total rather than marital fertility, which is a disadvantage for present purposes. While on average the pace of decline subsequent to the threshold point has been faster than in Europe, there is also greater variability. Some countries have recorded 30-percent declines per decade, others a mere 10 to 15 percent. The analysis also suggests that a high level of socioeconomic development at the threshold point is positively related to the pace of subsequent decline.

Of course, many of the countries examined by Bongaarts and Watkins are diverse in terms of ethnicity, language, and religion. The policy context in which declines are occurring is also immensely varied, ranging from near-coercive population control programs to pronatalist policies under which, for example, the import of modern contraceptives is banned. These factors greatly complicate interpretation. Nevertheless, the wide variability in the pace of fertility declines in developing countries is rather damaging to the diffusion explanation. For some countries, the principle of endogenous feedback documented at local level for Taiwan and Costa Rica (Montgomery and Casterline, 1993; Rosero-Bixby and Casterline, 1994) appears to hold. The higher socioeconomic strata form the vanguard of contraceptive uptake and fertility decline. Large socioeconomic differentials arise but subsequently disappear as change spreads from urban to rural populations and from higher to lower strata. The fertility transition is completed within a mere three decades or so. This process has been documented for many countries, including much of Latin America (Rodriguez and Aravena, 1991).

However, this model of rapid diffusion following the achievement of a threshold does not apply universally. In some countries the pace of change has been modest. In Jordan, for instance, contraceptive prevalence rose from 22 percent in 1972 to only 35 percent in 1990. In the Philippines, it grew from 15 to 32 percent between 1968 and 1983, but the pace of change in the next decade actually decreased rather than accelerated. In 1993, contraceptive prevalence was estimated to be 40 percent. None of the evidence suggests that the saturation point was exceptionally low in these two countries because of high demand for children. To the contrary, surveys indicate the existence of widespread unmet need. Moreover it is unlikely that diffusion variables, such as communication networks, can offer plausible explanations. Other forces must be at work that condition the speed with which fertility regulation spreads. It is unlikely that these forces relate to the economic utility of children. More likely they reflect the persistence of values that are antagonistic to the idea of smaller families, or of birth control, which flow from political or religious considerations.

Do Individuals Talk About Contraception and Related Topics?

As noted by Watkins et al. (1995), evidence of interpersonal conversation about reproductive change is a sine qua non for serious consideration of the role of diffusion. The evidence with regard to men is too sparse to permit confident generalization, but, for women, there is overwhelming evidence that family planning is the subject of discussion. This has been clearly demonstrated for the United States (Palmore, 1967; Watkins and Danzi, 1995), Taiwan (Freedman and Takeshita, 1969), Thailand (Rosenfield et al., 1973), Republic of Korea (Rogers and Kincaird, 1981), India (Marshall, 1971; Blaikie, 1975), and El Salvador (Lin and Burt, 1975), and in many other studies. Not only is it clear that family planning is a fairly frequent topic of conversation in many settings, it is also apparent that the decision of individuals to adopt a method is often public knowledge within their networks and communities. In Bangladesh, women tend to be aware of the contraceptive status of others in the same village (Mita and Simmons, 1995). In Thailand, village women could even identify the first users of contraception, the methods they chose, and the approximate date (Entwistle et al., 1996). In closely knit communities, the observability of modern contraceptive practice appears to be high, a feature that suggests, though does not prove, that this form of behavior, far from being the outcome of isolated decision making within families, is subject to social control and social pressures that constrain other forms of behavior.

What exactly do individuals talk about? What exactly is it that diffuses? One of the very few detailed accounts comes from the work of Watkins and collaborators in South Nyanza. Not surprisingly, perhaps, discussions of contraception among women are embedded in more general debates about family size and modern life. Everyday conversation makes no distinction between motives and means. Information exchange goes hand in hand with assessment and evaluation. The experiences of close friends, neighbors, and relatives appear to be of particular importance. What matters most is the direct testimony of those who have actually tried a method. The deep ambivalence about family planning methods lends credence to disquieting stories about babies born with disease or deformity as result of their mother's contraceptive habits. There was little evidence that women explicitly seek information and advice from high-status or highly educated individuals. Formal health care providers are valued sources of technical information but they are socially distanced in a way that erodes complete trust (Rutenberg and Watkins, 1997). The metaphor used by Watkins et al. (1995:51) aptly sums up the general impression from their work: "Women in these areas are not navigating the domain of uncertainty alone, but rather in flotillas, convoys in which the topics of conversation are relevant, the debates widespread and sometimes intense." And the substance of the diffusion is a bundle of interrelated topics: the idea of birth control, characteristics of particular methods, and ideas about family size.

Are the Decisions of Individuals to Adopt Contraception and the Method Chosen Influenced by the Behavior of Those Around Them?

The evidence reviewed in the previous section suggests: that contraception is part of everyday conversation in many settings; that in some societies at least, it is regarded with ambivalence, uncertainty, and fear; and that the use of modern methods of contraception by individuals tends to be a socially observable form of behavior. It is but a small leap to postulate that the reproductive behavior of individuals is influenced by the behavior, or perceived behavior, of those with whom they interact daily. Indeed it would be astonishing if the social learning that clearly takes place partly though communication networks is not accompanied by a degree of social influence.

The illusion of rational decision making is a powerful influence on self-presentation in all societies. Whatever the topic of inquiry, the response "I behave in this way because everyone/no one that I know behaves in that way" is never heard. In noncontracepting communities, women may explain their own nonuse in terms of lack of knowledge or husband's disapproval but rarely in terms of the behavior or example of others in the same community. It appears difficult for individuals to accept that their beliefs and decisions may be influenced by those of immediate others. Moreover such influences are often subtle, indirect, quickly internalized, and thus impossible to identify and articulate. For these reasons, the evidence for social influence in the reproductive domain rarely takes the form of direct testimony but has to be inferred indirectly from observed patterns of behavior. Each strand of evidence, taken in isolation, is inconclusive. Taken together, however, they represent a powerful case in favor of social influence.

One of the weaker strands of evidence is the finding that a woman's perception that others in the community or village approve of family planning and/or are using family planning is predictive of her own contraceptive use (see Retherford and Palmore, 1983, and Beckman, 1993, for discussions of the evidence; and Valente et al., 1997, as an empirical case study). The evidence is relatively weak because it is usually impossible to ascertain whether contraception adoption of an individual preceded and then influenced her reported perception of others (following the principle of cognitive dissonance) or vice versa.

This simple approach can be extended to a formal network analysis, where individuals are asked to specify by name those with whom they interact most (in general or on particular topics). Perceived use status and attitudes of these network members can be gathered and in certain circumstances, it may be possible to contact and gather parallel information from these named friends. Such data were obtained in a remarkable 1973 Korean study, initially analyzed by Rogers and Kincaird (1981) and reanalyzed more recently by Montgomery and Chung (1999). The results of the latter analysis suggest that the extent of perceived use of contraception, advice giving, and perceived favorable attitude among network contacts were predictive of use. However, the estimates of the effect of actual contraceptive use among network contacts were ambiguous and, as the authors accept, the cross-sectional of the inquiry further erodes confidence. Prospective studies are clearly needed to demonstrate beyond doubt the effect of interpersonal influences at the micro level.

In view of the general lack of data to test diffusion, or social influence, at the micro level, the search has switched to the aggregate level: 361 townships in Taiwan and 100 counties in Costa Rica (Montgomery and Casterline, 1993; Rosero-Bixby and Casterline, 1993, 1994). The general approach in both these studies is to identify spatial-temporal patterns of fertility decline that are suggestive of social influence. Specifically, they assess evidence of endogenous feedback, whereby the fertility decline in a community is in part a function of past fertility decline in that community and adjacent communities. Although the idea is relatively straightforward, specification of an appropriate model to test the central hypothesis is a formidable undertaking, and a degree of faith in the methodology is required. In both countries, evidence of strong feedback mechanisms is found. In Taiwan, within-township diffusion effects were stronger than across-township effects and there was no evidence of an influence of lagged fertility in nearby larger towns. In Costa Rica, intercounty effects are estimated to be stronger than intracounty ones, which is surprising and remains unexplained.

These results are entirely consistent with the fact that fertility decline, and levels of overall or method-specific contraceptive use vary sharply between otherwise similar rural communities. This feature has been observed for German villages by Knodel (1986), for Korea by Rogers and Kincaird (1981), and for Thailand by Entwistle et al. (1996). There is more than one possible explanation for such disparities, but the obvious one, mentioned by analysts in all three studies, hinges on the role of social influence. At national levels, there is also evidence of social influence or social imitation in the choice of modern contraceptive method. In the average country (developed and developing), 50 percent of modern method use is accounted for by one type of method (Ambegaokar, 1996). One obvious explanation concerns biases in contraceptive provision; this factor is certainly important in some settings. However, there is no relationship between the skewness of method mixes in developing countries and method-access scores derived by Ross and Mauldin (1996). It seems unlikely, therefore, that supply factors can offer a convincing explanation and correspondingly likely that strong social influences operate to tilt individual choices.

As mentioned at the start, most of the direct evidence concerning social influences on reproductive behavior is fragmentary and indirect. A heavy penalty has been paid by excessive reliance on World Fertility Survey/Demographic and Health Survey (WFS/DHS) data in fertility research, because the sampling strategy used by these programs is ill suited for analysis of the spread of new reproductive habits within communities. The most powerful argument in favor of the view that individual decisions and behavior are indeed influenced by the behavior of friends, relatives, and neighbors remains the simple and obvious one of the speed with which behavior can change. It is unconvincing to explain rapid marital fertility transition solely in terms of the spread of knowledge. Knowledge of contraceptives and supply source is often well established long before changes in behavior. Nor is it plausible to conclude that couples, independently of each other, perform the same calculations and come to the same conclusion about family size and fertility regulation within a short span of time. The principle of Occam's razor should apply: give the simplest explanation that is consistent with the evidence. The simplest explanation for rapid rises in contraception and declines in fertility is that people are influenced by one another. Not only is it the simplest explanation, it is also the most compelling. Copying is a far more common influence on human behavior than calculation. The latter is fine for choices of minor significance, but individuals rarely make big decisions on the basis of cost-benefit calculations.

Do Falls in Demand for Children Precede, Accompany, or Follow Widespread Adoption of Contraception?

One strong expectation derived from economic theories is that falls in parental demand for children will precede widespread changes in reproductive behavior. Conversely the innovation-diffusion framework allows for the possibility that the advent of new means of regulating fertility may bring about radical reappraisals of desired family size. Apart from Sub-Saharan Africa, and to a lesser extent the Arab states, demand for children, as indicated by survey responses, typically have been modest. The very earliest surveys suggest that three or four children were considered sufficient by large majorities of women surveyed (Mauldin, 1965). It is, of course, possible that substantial declines in desired family sizes took place before the era of survey research, but our growing knowledge of pre-transitional reproductive regimes makes this proposition unlikely. There are rather few countries where fertility preferences have been monitored reliably over a prolonged period of time, but in many, if not most, of these cases, declines in fertility preceded drops in desired fertility. This holds true, for example, in Taiwan, Republic of Korea, Thailand, and Costa Rica. In these and many other settings, the early stages of fertility decline took the form of reductions in unwanted births rather than in declining demand for children.

For Sub-Saharan Africa, the indications are rather different. Desired family sizes are generally high, ranging from 6 to 8.3 children in WFS enquiries, with substantial numbers of respondents giving nonnumerical responses. More recent DHSs show a widespread downward drift in preferences: from 8.3 to 6.2 or 6.3 in Senegal and Nigeria; from 6 to 4.7 in Ghana; from 6.5 to 5.6 in Uganda. Thus it is fair to conclude that, in this region, falling demand for children will precede rather than accompany or follow actual changes in reproductive behavior. An intriguing exception is Kenya, where on the eve of fertility transition, fertility aspirations remained extremely pronatalist. In this country, the drop in desired family size from 7.2 to 3.9 accompanied the spread of fertility regulation.

Does Contraception Supercede Previous Methods of Managing Fertility and Family Size?

One reasonable, though not strong, expectation of innovation-diffusion theories is that contraception will supercede or displace prior ways in which the problems of human numbers were managed or mitigated. The evidence is, on the whole, negative. In developing countries, at least, there has been no increase in nuptiality. Breastfeeding durations remain surprisingly resilient. In West Africa, postpartum abstinence has actually increased in length. The incidence of induced abortion appears to increase, at least in the earlier phases of transition. To be sure, infanticide has declined but there are many obvious reasons for this trend and, in any case, rises in sex-selective abortion in East Asia may be seen as a modern equivalent of infanticide. In short, the advent of fertility regulation within marriage coexists with older ways of fertility or family size moderation rather than replacing them.

CONCLUSIONS

To sum up briefly, there is extremely strong evidence that fertility declines of the past 200 years have been conditioned by diffusion processes. The spread of new ideas about fertility regulation and new information about methods must form part of any convincing overall explanation. Moreover, the indirect evidence is very strong that changes in reproductive habits, like most other changes in human behavior, are a social transformation, heavily influenced by the climate of opinion and perceptions of how others are behaving. The transition from high to low fertility is not characterized by a shift from societal mechanisms of control to individualistic control. Social influences are just as strong in transitional and posttransitional societies as in pretransitional ones.

Rejection of both blended and pure variants of the innovation-diffusion explanations, as outlined earlier, is thus to ignore both common sense and a large body of evidence. However, the pure variant is rather implausible in the case of the developing world. I find it impossible to believe that the fertility transitions of the past 50 years would have occurred without the massive prior declines in mortality. These improvements in survival make a fertility response inevitable because no society can sustain for long a doubling in numbers every 25 to 30 years. The international family planning movement was one part of the response. Government efforts to popularize fertility regulation also stem directly from mortality decline. Fertility decline in the developing countries is essentially a lagged response to improved survival, but the length of the lag probably depends on cultural and political factors that condition the ease with which, and the speed with which, new methods of regulating fertility are incorporated. Transformations in the economic value of children are of secondary importance to the sheer increase in the numbers that have to be nurtured.

The causal role of prior mortality decline is an element of most classical statements of fertility transition and was asserted most emphatically by Davis (1963) in his theory of the multiphasic response. In his view, mortality decline constitutes both a necessary and a sufficient stimulus for fertility decline because, for the family, improved survival represents severe disadvantages, both in agrarian and industrial settings. The costs of child bearing rise steeply because more survive beyond infancy and early childhood. Inheritance of family resources is fragmented and delayed because of longer parental survival. These pressures on families invoke an inevitable response: out-migration, marriage postponement, and/or fertility control within marriage.

It is inappropriate in this chapter to review all the evidence that supports Davis's view of fertility to transition. This may be found elsewhere (Macunovich, 2000; Cleland, in press). Suffice it to say that the relatively rapid spread of fertility decline throughout Asia, Latin America, and Africa in the past 50 years surely implies that there is some common underlying cause; improved survival is the most plausible candidate as this common cause. The absence of any straightforward mechanical relationship between mortality and fertility simply reflects the complexity of the real world. A host of factors—social, political, cultural, and economic—mediate the inevitable fertility response to radically improved survival.

This scenario offers a less convincing explanation for the European transition. If new forms of parity-specific control had originated in countries with pronounced prior declines in mortality and subsequently spread to other countries within Europe, it could be argued that, in this part of the world, fertility decline was also essentially a response to improved survival. But of course it did not. It originated in France in the eighteenth century. Chesnais (1992:142), determined to assert the general principle that mortality decline must be temporally prior to fertility decline, notes that infant mortality in France fell "appreciably" from 296 per 1,000 births in the 1740s to 278 in the 1780s. Few other demographers would attach much significance to such a modest change. Moreover the subsequent spread of marital fertility control from France throughout the rest of Europe does not appear to be linked to mortality conditions. The pure version of the innovation-diffusion explanation remains compelling for this region of the world.

REFERENCES

Ambegaokar, M.A.
 1996 From Method Choices to Methods Used: Towards a Population-Level Indicator for Evaluating Family Planning Quality. Unpublished master's thesis, University of London.
Beckman, L.J.
 1993 Communication, power and the influence of social networks in couple decisions on fertility. Pp.415–443 in *Determinants of Fertility in Developing Countries, Volume 2*, R.A. Bulatao and R.D. Lee, eds. New York: Academic Press.
Blaikie, P.M.
 1975 *Family Planning in India: Diffusion and Policy.* London: Edward Arnold.
Bleek, W.
 1987 Lying informants: A field work experience from Ghana. *Population and Development Review* 13(2):314–322.
Bogue, D.
 1965 Family planning research: An outline of the field. In *Family Planning and Population Programs*, B. Berelson, R.K. Anderson, O. Harkavy, J. Mayer, W. Parker Mauldin, and S.J. Segal, eds. Chicago: University of Chicago Press.
 1983 Normative and psychic costs of contraception. Pp. 151–192 in *Determinants of Fertility in Developing Countries, Volume 2*, R.A. Bulatao and R.D. Lee, eds. New York: Academic Press.
Bongaarts, J., and S.C. Watkins
 1996 Social interactions and contemporary fertility transitions. *Population and Development Review* 22(4):639–682.
Bulatao, R.A., and R.D. Lee, eds.
 1983 *Determinants of Fertility in Developing Countries.* New York: Academic Press.
Carter, A.T.
 1995 Agency and fertility: For an ethnography of practice. In *Situating Fertility*, S. Greenhalgh, ed. Cambridge, Eng.: Cambridge University Press.
Casterline, J., and Z. Sathar
 1997 *The Gap Between Reproductive Intention and Behavior.* Islamabad, Pak.: Population Council.
Chesnais, J.-C.
 1992 *The Demographic Transition.* Oxford: Oxford University Press.
Clair, C.
 1965 *Kitchen and Table: A Bedside History of Eating in the Western World.* New York: Abelard-Schuman.
Cleland, J.
 1985 Marital fertility decline in developing countries: Theories and the evidence. Pp. 223–254 in *Reproductive Change in Developing Countries*, J. Cleland and J. Hobcraft, eds. Oxford: Oxford University Press.
 in Restating the obvious: The effects of improved survival on fertility. *Population and*
 press *Development Review.*
Cleland, J., and C. Wilson
 1987 Demand theories of the fertility transition: An iconoclastic view. *Population Studies* 41(1):5–30.
Coale, A.J.
 1973 The demographic transition reconsidered. Pp. 53–72 in *International Population Conference, Volume 1.* Liège, Belgium: International Union for the Scientific Study of Population.

Coale, A.J., and R. Treadway
    1986   A summary of the changing distribution of overall fertility, marital fertility and
            proportions married in the provinces of Europe. Pp. 31–181 in *The Decline of Fer-
            tility in Europe*, A.J. Coale and S.C. Watkins, eds. Princeton: Princeton University
            Press.
Coale, A.J., and S.C. Watkins, eds.
    1986   *The Decline of Fertility in Europe*. Princeton: Princeton University Press.
Davis, K.
    1963   The theory of change and response in modern demographic history. *Population
            Index* 29:345–366.
    1969   Population policy: Will current programmes succeed? *Science* 158(November 10):
            730–739.
Easterlin, R.
    1975   An economic framework for fertility analysis. *Studies in Family Planning* 6(3):54–
            63.
Entwistle, B., R.R. Rindfuss, D.K. Guilkey, A. Chamratrithirong, S.R. Cuvran, and Y. Sawangdee
    1996   Community and contraceptive choice in rural Thailand: A case study of Naag
            Rong. *Demography* 33(1):1–11.
Freedman, R., and Y. Takeshita
    1969   *Family Planning in Taiwan: An Experiment in Social Change*. Princeton: Princeton
            University Press.
Granovetter, M.
    1973   The strength of weak ties. *American Journal of Sociology* 78:1360–1380.
Hammel, E.A.
    1995   Economics 1, culture 0: Fertility change and differences in the northwest Balkans,
            1700–1900. Pp. 225–258 in *Situating Fertility: Anthropology and Demographic Inquiry*,
            S. Greenhalgh, ed. Cambridge, Eng.: Cambridge University Press.
Hauser, P.H.
    1967   Family planning and population programs: A book review article. *Demography*
            4:397–414.
Jeffery, P., R. Jeffery, and A. Lyon
    1989   *Labour Pains and Labour Power*. London: Zed Books.
Kertzer, D., and D. P. Hogan
    1989   *Family, Political Economy, and Demographic Change: The Transformation of Life in
            Casalecchio, Italy 1861-1921*. Madison: University of Wisconsin Press.
Knodel, J.
    1986   Demographic transitions in German villages. Pp. 337–389 in *The Decline of Fertility
            in Europe*, A. Coale and S. Watkins, eds. Princeton: Princeton University Press.
Knodel, J., R.S. Gray, P. Sriwatcharia, and S. Peracca
    1999   Religion and reproduction: Muslims in Buddhist Thailand. *Population Studies*
            53(2):149–164.
Knodel, J., N. Havanon, and A. Pramualratana
    1984   Fertility transition in Thailand: A qualitative analysis. *Population and Development
            Review* 10(2):297–328.
Knodel, J., and E. van de Walle
    1986   Lessons from the past: Policy implication of historical fertility studies. Pp. 390–
            419 in *The Decline of Fertility in Europe*, A. Coale and S. Watkins, eds. Princeton:
            Princeton University Press.
Kohler, H.-P.
    1997   Fertility and Social Interaction: An Economic Approach. Unpublished Ph.D. dis-
            sertation, University of California at Berkeley.

Lee, K., G. Walt, L. Lush, and J. Cleland
1995 *Population Policies and Programmes: Determinants and Consequences in Eight Developing Countries.* London: London School of Hygiene and Tropical Medicine and United Nations Population Fund.

Lee, R., P.R. Galloway, and E.A. Hammel
1994 Fertility declines in Prussia: Estimating influences on supply, demand and degree of control. *Demography* 31(2):339–373.

Leete, R.
1989 Dual fertility trends in Malaysia's multi-ethnic society. *International Family Planning Perpectives* 15(2):58–65.

Lesthaeghe, R.
1977 *The Decline of Belgian Fertility, 1800–1970.* Princeton: Princeton University Press.

Lightbourne, R.E.
1985 Individual preferences and fertility behaviour. Pp. 165–198 in *Reproductive Change in Developing Countries,* J. Cleland and J. Hobcraft, eds. Oxford: Oxford University Press.

Lin, N., and R.S. Burt
1975 Differential effect of information channels in the process of innovation diffusion. *Social Forces* 54:256–274.

Macunovich, D.J.
2000 Relative cohort size: Source of a unifying theory of global fertility transition? *Population and Development Review* 26(2):235–261.

Maloney, C., K.M.A. Aziz, and P.C. Sarker
1981 *Beliefs and Fertility in Bangladesh.* Monograph No. 2. Dhaka: International Centre for Diarrhoeal Disease Research.

Marshall, J.F.
1971 Topics and networks in intra-village communication. Pp. 160–166 in *Culture and Population: A Collection of Current Studies,* S. Polgar, ed. Chapel Hill: Carolina Population Center, University of North Carolina.

Mason, K.O.
1997 Explaining fertility transition. *Demography* 34(4):443–454.

Mauldin, W.P.
1965 Fertility studies: Knowledge, attitude and practice. *Studies in Family Planning* 7:1–10.

Mita, R., and R. Simmons
1995 Diffusion of the culture of contraception: Program effects on young women in Bangladesh. *Studies in Family Planning* 26(1):1–13.

Montgomery, M.R., and J.B. Casterline
1993 The diffusion of fertility control in Taiwan: Evidence from pooled cross-section time-series models. *Population Studies* 47:457–479.

Montgomery M.R., and W. Chung
1999 Social networks and the diffusion of fertility control: The Republic of Korea. Pp. 179–209 in *Dynamics of Values in Fertility Change,* R. Leete, ed. Oxford: Oxford University Press.

Palmore, J.A.
1967 The Chicago snowball: A study of the flow and diffusion of family planning information. Pp. 272–363 in *Sociological Contributions to Family Planning Research,* D.J. Bogue, ed. Chicago: University of Chicago Press.

Pollack, R.A., and S.C. Watkins
1993 Cultural and economic approaches to fertility: Proper marriage or mésalliance? *Population and Development Review* 19(3):467–495.

Pyke, M.
   1968   *Food and Society*. London: John Murray.
Retherford, R.D.
   1985   A theory of marital fertility transition. *Population Studies* 39:249–268.
Retherford, R.D., and J.A. Palmore
   1983   Diffusion processes affecting fertility regulation. Pp. 295–339 in *Determinants of Fertility in Developing Countries*, Vol.2, R.A. Bulatao and R.D. Lee, eds. New York: Academic Press.
Rodriguez, G., and R. Aravena
   1991   Socio-economic factors and the transition to low fertility in less developed countries: A comparative analysis. Pp. 39–72 in *IRD/Macro International, Proceedings of the Demographic and Health Surveys World Conference*, Vol.1. Columbia, MD: IRD/ Macro International, Inc.
Rodriguez, G., and J. Cleland
   1981   Socio-economic determinants of marital fertility in twenty countries: A multivariate analysis. Pp. 337-414 in *World Fertility Survey Conference 1980: Record of Proceedings*, Vol.2. Voorburg, Neth.: International Statistical Institute.
Rogers, E.M.
   1983   *Diffusion of Innovations*. New York: Free Press.
Rogers, E.M., and D.L. Kincaird
   1981   *Communication Networks: Towards a New Paradigm for Research*. New York: Free Press.
Rogers, E.M., and F.F. Shoemaker
   1971   *Communication of Innovations: A Cross-Cultural Approach*. New York: Free Press.
Rosenfield, A.G., W. Asavasena, and J. Mikhanova
   1973   Person to person communication in Thailand. *Studies in Family Planning* 4(6):145– 149.
Rosero-Bixby, L., and J.B. Casterline
   1993   Modelling diffusion effects in fertility transition. *Population Studies* 47:147–167.
   1994   Interaction diffusion and fertility transition in Costa Rica. *Social Forces* 73(2):435– 462.
Ross, J., and W. Mauldin
   1995   Family planning programs: Efforts and results, 1972–94. *Studies in Family Planning* 27(3):137–147.
Rotter, J.
   1966   Generalised expectancies for internal versus external control of reinforcement. *Psychological Monographs 80*.
Rutenberg, N., and S.C. Watkins
   1997   The buzz outside the clinics: Conversations and contraception in Kenya. *Studies in Family Planning* 28(4):290–307.
Salaman, R.
   1949   *The History and Social Influence of the Potato*. Cambridge, Eng.: Cambridge University Press.
Simmons, R., L. Baqee, M.A. Koenig, and J.F. Phillips
   1988   Beyond supply: The importance of female family planning workers in rural Bangladesh. *Studies in Family Planning* 19(1):29–38.
Stone, L., and J.G. Campbell
   1984   The use and misuse of surveys in international development: An experiment from Nepal. *Human Organization* 3:27–37.

United Nations
  1985   Women's employment and fertility. In *Population Studies* 16. New York: Department of Economic and Social Affairs.
Valente, T.W., S. Watkins, M.N. Jato, A. Van der Straten, and L.M. Tsitsol
  1997   Social network associations with contraceptive use among Cameroonian women in voluntary associations. *Social Science and Medicine* 45:677–687.
van de Walle, E.
  1992   Fertility transition, conscious choice and numeracy. *Demography* 29(4):487–502.
van de Walle, E., and F. van de Walle
  1991   Breastfeeding and popular aetiology in the Sahel. *Health Transition Review* 1(1): 69–81.
van de Walle, F.
  1986   Infant mortality and the European demographic transition. Pp. 201–233 in *The Decline of Fertility in Europe*, A.J. Coale and S.C. Watkins, eds. Princeton: Princeton University Press.
Visser, M.
  1993   *The Rituals of Dinner*. London: Penguin.
Watkins, S.C.
  1991   *From Provinces into Nations: Demographic Integration in Western Europe 1870–1960*. Princeton: Princeton University Press.
Watkins, S.C., and A.D. Danzi
  1994   Women's gossip and social change: Childbirth and fertility control among Italian and Jewish women in the United States, 1920–1940. *Gender and Society* 9(4):469–490.
Watkins, S.C., N. Rutenberg, and D. Wilkinson
  1997   Orderly theories, disorderly women. Pp. 213–245 in *The Continuing Demographic Transition*, G.W. Jones, R.M. Douglas, J.C. Caldwell, and R.M. D'Souza, eds. Oxford: Oxford University Press.
Wilson, C., and P. Airey
  1999   How can a homeostatic perspective enhance demographic transition theory? *Population Studies* 53(2):117–128.

3

Diffusion in Sociological Analysis

ALBERTO PALLONI

OBJECTIVES

There are a number of very lucid, thorough, and authoritative reviews about the nature and applications of theories and models of diffusion in sociology (see, for example, Rogers, 1962, 1973, 1988, 1995; Valente, 1995). However, this literature is neither geared to deal with problems in the explanation of demographic phenomena nor does it indicate how to take advantage of new developments in economic and social network theories and methodological innovations for the study of dynamic processes. This paper is designed to fill this gap. In particular, I have four interrelated goals:

(1) To identify the backbone of diffusion models and theories in sociology, and to show that recent formulations and applications require robust, well-specified theories about social systems and about the positions that individuals exposed to diffusion occupy within the social structure;

(2) To illustrate recent applications of diffusion models and theories in two key areas of sociology, social movements and social organizations;

(3) To define conditions ("identification conditions") for testing new hypotheses and conjectures that invoke diffusion processes. These conditions are strict, are difficult to satisfy, and have implications for issues ranging from data collection to selection of estimation procedures. I argue that unless these conditions are met, we will not be able to identify

Alberto Palloni is professor of sociology at the University of Wisconsin, Madison.

diffusion processes from among other processes producing similar observable outcomes.

(4) To argue that until very recently at least, applications of diffusion models in demography have not taken advantage of innovations identified in goal 1, and have not adhered to the formal conditions identified in goal 3. Thus, these applications are unlikely to be of much help to improve our understanding of demographic phenomena.

The organization of the paper is as follows: the first sections deal with goals 1 and 2, respectively, middle sections focus on goal 3, the next section discusses material related to goal 4 and, the last section contains a summary and concluding remarks.

THE BASIC MODEL OF DIFFUSION IN SOCIOLOGY

In this section I show that sociological theories of diffusion have evolved from fairly simple propositions regarding average or aggregate behavior into complex formulations about how individuals define preferences and make decisions to realize those preferences. In this section I argue that in order to be analytically useful, diffusion models require theorizing about social structures, about the positions that individuals occupy in them, about individual decision-making processes that accompany adoption of a behavior, and about the constraints these individuals face. I conclude that it is unilluminating to confront diffusion theories with competing explanations that regard behaviors as responsive to "structural" factors, such as socioeconomic positions or social class membership, as if diffusion processes did not require or could proceed independently of structural factors that characterize the environment where individuals act and where behaviors take place. Similarly, it is misleading to cast diffusion models or theories against alternative ones on the grounds that the latter are usually erected on a foundation of assumptions about rational actors and well-defined decision-making processes, as if diffusion processes did not require making assumptions about preferences, costs, and a rational calculus. Well-defined diffusion hypotheses and models must be built on assumptions about social and economic conditions that constrain individual actors' preferences and resources, and rely on these assumptions no less than alternative hypotheses and models often pitted against them. This is not to say that diffusion models or theories do not have a specificity of their own. They do, and it will be the task of the next sections to identify what this specificity is. In the end, however, my message is somewhat pessimistic because the conditions for identification of a diffusion process from observables are fairly hard to meet, much harder than what is normally implied in traditional applications of diffusion theories and models to sociological and demographic analyses.

Diffusion Explanations and Structural Explanations

"Structural" explanations of behavioral changes seek their cause in the alteration of preferences and opportunities that result from either changes in positions that individuals occupy (individual social mobility) or from reshuffling of resources associated with a given social position (structural social mobility or redistribution of wealth). Diffusion explanations or models, on the other hand, attempt to identify a cascading mechanism that leads to cumulative adoption of behaviors by some individuals, even while their social position, or the resources associated with them, changes only trivially or remains unaltered. In diffusion models, the behavior "spreads" and is adopted by individuals irrespective of their socioeconomic positions, even among those whose social or economic positions are hypothetically associated with cost-benefit calculations that do not necessarily require the new behavior. Adopting the new behavior occurs as a result of reevaluation of one's own choices in light of other people's behavior, not as a strategic response or accommodation to a realignment of resources associated with one's social position in the social system. To use the terminology Coleman (1990) coined for the study of collective behavior, diffusion models are built on the central idea that individuals transfer partial or total control of their own behavior to others. As I will show later, this requires a decision process as complicated (or uncomplicated) as the ones that are normally associated with structural explanations.

Diffusion processes do not always involve adoption of new behaviors. In fact, they may include abandonment of a recently adopted behavior or resistance to change. For example, it has been observed that, contrary to expectations, class-based political alignments do not always take hold at a pace that is commensurate with advances of industrialization. Instead, traditional political allegiances, based on language or ethnic identities, may remain dominant long after industrialization has created the structural conditions for class-based politics. This type of phenomenon has been studied widely in political sociology to understand the stubborn persistence of nonclass-based allegiances and ethnic enclaves (Hechter, 1975). In these cases observed individual political behavior (voting behavior) is at odds with what is expected by virtue of an individual's position or ranking in the social system. Failure of individuals to act according to class positions—an expectation derived from a "structuralist" explanation of political behavior—occurs as a result of adherence to practices that were consistent with positions occupied prior to the social and economic transformations that accompanied industrialization. What is diffused or adopted here is the individual resistance to act according to class-based principles (the new behavior), and the reinforcement of traditional political alignments (the old behavior). If political sociologists were able to gather information on collective protests against British rule, rather than just on voting patterns, they would observe waves of protests extending across and confined within the boundaries of the British fringe, much as they observe waves of protests in the United States during the 1960s (Myers, 1997).

Similarly, we know all too well that fertility decline in Europe did not always follow a trajectory consistent with social and economic transformations that accompanied industrialization. Instead, the course of the decline revealed a marked tendency to proceed along or be halted by ethnic, language, and religious boundaries. The resulting geographic and territorial clustering of fertility levels and patterns has been construed as evidence against a structural explanation of fertility decline, and as support for the hypothesis that fertility changes were strongly associated with ideational or cultural changes and diffusion mechanisms.[1] The existence of strong clustering of fertility levels along cultural lines could be evidence of either diffusion of a new behavior (adoption of contraception and a low fertility norm) in areas with lower than expected fertility (structural changes), or of resistance to the new behavior (rejection of birth control and adherence to a high fertility norm) in areas with higher than expected fertility.

The foregoing examples share two features. The first is that in both cases we establish a contrast between an explanation that infers an expected behavior from a reading of individual socioeconomic positions (the structuralist explanation) with an alternative explanation that infers a pattern of expected behavior from the likely adherence of actors to ethnic, religious, or cultural prescriptions or beliefs shared by others in the same community, including individuals belonging to different social classes or occupying different socioeconomic positions. In the latter case, the likelihood of adherence to prescriptions increases as a function of others' adherence to it (or others' resistance to the novel behavior). The definition of what is included in "others" is and must be a key element of the theory, as should the identification of the mechanisms that reproduce efficiently adherence to prescriptions and beliefs.

The second common feature shared by these two examples is that the structuralist or socioeconomic explanation and the diffusion explanation offered to account for the phenomena rest on the idea that individuals are decision makers, acting in uncertain environments; sorting through limited information on prices, utilities, constraints, and potential outcomes of alternative behaviors; elucidating their own preferences; and ultimately taking some course of action. But, whereas investigators are normally careful to produce a thorough definition of the decision process associated with the structuralist explanation, they all too often fail to specify the decision-making process associated with diffusion, to the point that this appears, in many instances, as a result of passive contagion and the irrational or at least a-rational adoption of a behavior. This is a situation not unlike the one found until recently in the study of collective actions that could be explained only through recourse to the irrationality of actors (Coleman, 1990). The exceptions to this lack of attention to decision-making processes embedded within diffusion are precisely the most recent studies and formulations of diffusion processes in sociology, economics, and demography (Montgomery and Chung, 1994; Montgomery and Casterline, 1993; Valente, 1995; Marsden and Friedkin, 1993; Burt, 1987).

Lack of theoretical specificity is not the only problem we face as we try to identify diffusion processes. In fact, most of the evidence produced in sociology and demography to distinguish between explanations based on diffusion arguments from those attributing the primary role to socioeconomic or structural changes is carved out of aggregate, not individual, data. Because the individual adoption process is never defined, the aggregate process is also ill conditioned: there is rarely a way to determine what kind of aggregate evidence one would expect when the individual adoption process is left unspecified. This leads to the very generalized practice of using residual evidence or, equivalently, to infer the validity of a diffusionist explanation from the failure of the structural explanation: the explanatory power assigned to the diffusion argument is always directly proportional to the magnitude of the inconsistency between observed outcomes and those expected from a competing structural explanation. Handling only aggregate and residual evidence leads to the central problem in this literature—both in sociology or demography— namely, the inability to identify the key process from observables.

The Elements of an Explanation Based on Diffusion Processes

A classic definition of diffusion is the following: "(Diffusion) is the process by which an innovation is communicated through certain channels over time among the members of a social system. It is a special type of communication, in that the messages are concerned with new ideas" (Rogers, 1983:19). There are a number of essential elements contained in this definition: the innovation, the population of potential adopters, those who adopt, and the mechanisms through which adopters and potential adopters communicate with each other. The classical problem in diffusion models is to understand who adopts the innovation, and how fast they do so. Thus, Rogers (1995) distinguishes different types of adopters depending on how early during the adoption process occurs. To these groups one could add a category including those who never adopt, much as in social mobility we recognize movers and stayers. Delays in adoption or resistance to adopt are explained by inadequate information or by uncertainty about the results or outcomes associated with the innovation. As the process advances and more individuals adopt, and as the outcomes of adoption by others become observable, more individuals' resistance to adoption crumbles as the information is enriched and their uncertainty about risks, costs, and benefits diminish.

Although later in the paper I will introduce a more complex notion of diffusion, in the remainder of this section I will focus on the classic definition just given. I will use it as a reference to identify elements of a diffusion process that should be important in model building but that many applications overlook. The simplicity of the classic definition is deceiving, for it contains explicitly or implicitly a number of key elements that are important to identify at the outset. First, diffusion occurs through an individual decision-making process in which there are costs and benefits (and implicitly preferences) associated with adoption (or its obverse, resistance to adoption), as well as information and ignorance about prices, costs, outcomes, and alternatives. In their influential work on cultural transmission, Cavalli-Sforza and Feldman (1981) stress the importance of decision making as the factor that distinguishes cultural from biological evolution. Whereas the latter is driven by natural selection (or genetic drift), the former is characterized by the influence of individual decision making that may reinforce or offset the pressures of natural selection: "In cultural evolution, however, there is in addition [to natural selection] a second mode of selection, which is the result of the capacity of decision making" (Cavalli-Sforza and Feldman, 1981:10).

Diffusion only occurs because individuals decide to adopt after observing others do so, and after updating their information by including observed outcomes associated with others' adoption into their own decision-making process. There may be a variable number of stages in this decision-making process (Rogers, 1983), but what is important is that its core is an individual who is making cost-benefit calculations under uncertainty about whether to join others in adopting a behavior or, alternatively, resisting. A diffusion model rests on assumptions and imageries not dissimilar to the ones that prevail when, for example, we refer to individuals changing their fertility behavior as a result of socioeconomic changes that affect them (the so-called demand theories of fertility). The vast majority of applications of diffusion models in both demography and sociology neglect this very simple tenet of diffusion models: adopters and nonadopters are rational decision makers and adoption is the outcome of a rational decision-making process. These issues have been confronted head-on in only a handful of applications. For example, in a recent study Montgomery and Casterline (1996) define three distinctive elements of a diffusion process—social learning, social influence, and institutional constraints—which operate to determine and shape individual decision making about adoption of behaviors. Similarly, Erbring and Young (1979) and Marsden and Friedkin (1993) carefully elaborate on the types of social relations that are relevant for processes whereby behaviors of one individual are affected by consideration of behaviors of other individuals belonging to the same group or social system. Coleman's (1990) study of collective action and those involving or generating trust reveal the fundamental elements of the decision-making process on which every diffusion process depends. Even in the study of organizations and organizational diffusion (DiMaggio and Powell, 1991), there is explicit consideration of actors who imitate organizational features adopted by successful organizations as a device to minimize uncertainty.

Second, given conditions defining their preferences and opportunities, individual decision makers may be more or less resistant both to adopt innovations and, if they adopt, more or less reluctant to jettison the innovation from the menu of practices and behaviors they normally employ. That is, after one accounts for all elements entering in the decision to adopt or to resist, there might be individuals who are more (less) risk averse and adopt more (less) easily than others. These will be forerunners (laggards) in the diffusion process (Rogers, 1983). As stated by Cavalli-Sforza and Feldman (1981:39),"It seems very likely, a priori, that there is variation between individuals in their capacity both to learn of an innovation and to decide for adoption. Many factors contribute to such variation, including social and economic stratification, geographic conditions such as means of transportation, availability of communication networks, and, last but not least, individual differences in the behavioral characteristics that govern both awareness and eventual adoption." This acknowledges that after accounting for a number of social and economic factors, we are likely to face the existence of "unmeasured heterogeneity" or the inability to include all elements that contribute to the individual's decision regarding the innovation. It is a concept analogous to frailty in the analysis of mortality and induces the same empirical patterns: as individuals who are more resistant to adopting become a larger fraction of the pool of nonadopters, the overall risk of adoption will tend to decrease. But this is not a reflection of a risk profile of adoption that decreases over time. Rather, it is an artifact of the changing composition of the pool of nonadopters as the process progresses over time. To my knowledge, the traditional literature on diffusion processes in sociology or demography has not addressed the problem created by the unmeasured resistance to adoption, except insofar as the study of forerunners and the conditions that determine their appearance is indeed a way to identify factors influencing unmeasured resistance.[2] In general, however, we neglect the issue altogether. This practice is explained by one of two factors: either the assumption is made that all relevant factors were well measured (including those affecting awareness and propensity to adopt), or the focus of attention is on aggregate patterns of adoption. It is only recently, mainly through the influential work of Granovetter (1978) and Valente (1995), that the concept of individual (or group) thresholds has been introduced as a way to handle the problem, but still without deriving the full consequences for model testing. Later I will provide an interpretation, by no means unique, of unmeasured resistance to adoption.

Equally important for the successful progression of diffusion are processes that may undermine continued practice of the new behavior. To the extent that these acquire some dominance, individuals are more likely to abandon the new practice or behavior some time after adoption. Despite the fact that this is a rather key part of a diffusion process, it is rarely mentioned and almost never explicitly modeled or studied.[3]

Third, the decision-making process underlying adoption of new behaviors occurs within a social structure composed of formal and informal elements. Individuals occupy positions within these social structures, perform certain roles, and are connected formally and informally to a number of other individuals within them through relations of authority, functional rapports, respect, and trust. They adhere to values and norms that shape preferences, constrain the field of feasible behaviors, and alter the information they may receive about prices, utilities, and ultimately about what others are doing. Despite the fact that often it is difficult to tell so from actual empirical research involving diffusion models, diffusion processes are affected by the social structure of systems within which they are occurring. Social structures determine the content and shape of the repertoire of feasible behaviors ("Is the behavior within the realm of conscious choice?"), individual's preferences ("Is the behavior advantageous at all?"), and individual's resources ("Can individuals adopt at low costs?"). The questions within quotes describe Coale's well-known desiderata for fertility change (Coale, 1973; see also Lesthaeghe and Vanderhoeft, this volume) and could be utilized equally well by an explanation resting on diffusion as an alternative mechanism involving adjustment to structural changes. I will elaborate on this in later sections.

The importance of social structure appears to weigh more heavily when the diffusion process is suspected to be under the control of internal sources rather than external sources of diffusion. However, even the idea that external sources of diffusion have an impact independent of individuals' position in the social structure is acceptable only as a tool to render the algebra of models tractable, but it is woefully inadequate for analytic purposes. Some of the best original work on diffusion processes emphasizes that social diffusion is an analytically sterile construct if not cast against a social structure: "It is as unthinkable to study diffusion without some knowledge of the social structure in which potential adopters are located as it is to study blood circulation without adequate knowledge of the structure of veins and arteries" (Katz, 1961; cited in Rogers, 1983:25). Similarly, in their influential study on use of hybrid corn among farmers in two Iowa communities, Ryan and Gross (1943) argue that it is the social structure that may explain the delay with which certain technologies are adopted. They reason that, if all individuals act as rational actors, adoption of an advantageous technological innovation must occur instantaneously and simultaneously. Delays and lags in the process and the emergence of laggards in the population of potential adopters can only be explained by institutional constraints and by sociocultural and psychological factors that influence the diffusion process. In this case, social structure is taken to be an obstacle rather than a facilitator. Structure accounts for the slow progress of diffusion rather than diffusion undermining the constraints fabricated by social structures.

   Although emphasis on the importance of social structure for diffusion processes is hardly new, and even despite the fact that there are good examples demonstrating careful attention to social structure (Rogers and Kincaid, 1981; Coleman et al., 1966; Burt, 1987), it has seldom been systematically incorporated into actual empirical research. It is only recently that sociologists interested in diffusion have begun to pay close attention to it and accounting for it explicitly in the formulation of models. In a recent paper, Strang and Soule (1997:1) make the point that while diffusion studies inquire about how practices spread, they also "provide an opportunity to locate and document the social structure, where we consider how patterns of apparent influence reflect durable social relations." Furthermore, because these models involve individual decision making subjected to constraints imposed by a social structure, they may " . . . verge on the one hand towards models of individual choice, since diffusion models often treat the adopter as a reflective decision maker . . . [or] verge on the other [hand] towards a broader class of contextual and environmental processes, where conditions outside the actor shape behavior" (Strang and Soule, 1997:2).

   Fourth, once innovations are adopted, they could be abandoned and replaced by other technology, instruments, or behaviors. Thus, in addition to understanding who adopts and how fast they do so, models of diffusion should specify the obverse process, the persistent use of the innovation. This aspect of a diffusion process is of importance in applications to social behaviors that are inherently reversible or unstable. For example, participation in mass protests usually involves increased risk of participation followed by increased risk of withdrawal from the pool of protesters. Withdrawal from protest is as much a diffusion process as is participation in it (Myers, 1997), and could be triggered and encouraged by external reprisals. Discontinuation is also relevant for situations where what is at stake is the adoption of an innovation such as contraception. Contraceptive discontinuation is an obvious illustration that has become a staple of empirical studies of contraception, but so is the possibility that certain groups may adopt contraception and then abandon altogether the very ideal of family limitation. If one succeeded in providing a convincing explanation of fertility decline in Western Europe entirely based on diffusion arguments, we should also explain why the decline turned out to be irreversible. Although this seems an obvious requirement, I have seen no systematic evidence indicating that the issue has been raised, much less treated systematically (for an exception, see Kohler, 1997). Note that this is not a requirement that applies to explanations invoking adaptation to new social and economic conditions. Whenever possible and nontrivial, an ideal diffusion model ought to specify the conditions for the persistence of adoption.

Fifth, the social and economic environment may be modified by the process of adoption itself, and may involve feedbacks accelerating or retarding the process. The adoption of some computer technologies, for example, becomes unavoidable once a critical mass of users has adopted because the incentive structure for all users is altered, becomes more favorable for adoption of the technology, and creates niches for the introduction of even newer technology. The adoption of operating systems for PCs proceeds in this fashion, with software production being the element that induces interdependence among consumers in the market. Similarly, changing prices of a product induced by partial adoption of a technological innovation in agriculture will alter the elements that enter into the calculus of nonadopters (Ryan and Gross, 1943; Hagerstrand, 1967). Adoption of organizational features such as civil service reform may begin to occur for reasons that have more to do with the establishment of legitimacy of the practice than with associated increases in efficiency (DiMaggio and Powell, 1991). Adoption of a practice may accelerate as organizations that have not yet adopted find it advantageous to mimic what others have done successfully as a way to sharpen their competitive edge in the new environment created by a handful of forerunners (Fligstein, 1985). DiMaggio and Powell's "mimic processes," whereby organizations imitate what other organizations do, refers to processes whereby the linkage between a practice and its net benefits is subject to less variability, but also to processes where the institutional environment is so changed by early adopters that adoption simply becomes more cost effective. Only the latter is an example of endogenous feedback.

Similar processes may be at work in fertility behavior: forerunners who first adopt fertility control not only generate an environment with reduced uncertainty for others to follow, but may also create emulation conditions. This can happen, for example, if with fewer children they are able to support higher or better educational standards and if, in the long run, this enhances their power and prestige. To the extent that this is so, nonadopters pursuing power and prestige will be better off if they imitate fertility limitation. As the process evolves, the institutional context to satisfy the demand for more and better education also evolves, thus changing the context in which fertility decision making is taking place.

In the case of organizational adoption, the pool of means to attain some ends is changed by adoption of newer procedures or strategies, and so is the ranking of those that are preferred among all organizations in the field, not just those who initially adopt. In the case of fertility, the connection between fertility limitation and power and prestige via children's education converts the adoption of contraceptive behavior from an oddity to a useful and productive behavioral strategy.

In these examples taken from sociology of organizations and fertility, there is endogenous feedback since the spread of the behavior changes the elements that enter into the decision-making process of everybody, including nonadopters. Surely, there must be considerable empirical variability in the lags with which the feedback operates, and in their actual significance for individual decision makers. Thus, endogenous feedback need not be an inherent nor a uniform characteristic of all diffusion processes. But, when it is, it will alter individual probabilities of adoption for individuals who have not yet adopted at a certain time in the process.[4]

The combination of some of these five elements of a diffusion process may produce lightning-fast spread of innovations. By the same token, though, particular constellations of the elements may lead to excruciatingly slow adoption, to innovation processes that begin rapidly but then taper off without ever reaching near saturation, or to those that fail altogether and are then relegated to the pool of diffusion processes that we will never be able to study.[5] An immediate corollary of this inherent variability is that it is not necessarily correct to infer the existence of a causal mechanism (diffusion mechanisms versus structural mechanisms) only from observation of the relative speed with which a behavioral change occurs. It is as much an error to believe that when a process of behavioral change is quick and swift it must have been due to diffusion as it is to think that no diffusion process could be responsible for slow changes. The observed rate of change in the prevalence of a behavior by itself will generally be of limited help to identify a diffusion process because the effects of the basic elements of a diffusion process may lead to outcomes that can also be produced by mechanisms not associated with diffusion at all. Rapid rates of change in a behavior in the absence of changes in structural condition may be a reflection of diffusion, but it surely should not be taken as prima facie evidence of its existence or predominance.

These five elements are strategic for a proper formulation of a diffusion model. But, needless to say, they are not always taken into account. In one subsequent section, I show that this oversight leads to shortcomings in sociological applications. In another section, I revisit these elements and use them to define more formally the nature of a diffusion process and the mechanisms through which it operates.

DEVELOPMENT OF DIFFUSION MODELS IN SOCIOLOGY

In this section I discuss developments in the formulation and application of diffusion models in sociology. I start with early models that mimic those used for the study of the spread of diseases and focus on narrow aggregate outcomes. I then discuss some of the most novel applications in the areas of collective action and organizations.

Early Studies and Formulations

The main territory of diffusion theories and models is the innovation. Innovations by their very nature require communication and information for adoption. They are also risky because their outcomes are for the most part uncertain or unknown, thus requiring an agent engaged in a decision-making process. It is not surprising, then, that diffusion processes have been mostly used to study adoption of innovations. The most influential works include Ryan and Gross's (1943) analysis of the diffusion of hybrid corn, Hagerstrand's (1967) investigation of the diffusion of tuberculosis tests in Sweden, Coleman et al.'s (1966) study of the adoption of tetracycline among Midwestern doctors, Katz and Lazarsfeld's (1955) celebrated formulation of the two-step flow of influence process, and Rogers' and Kincaid's (1981) analysis of contraceptive behavior. The main goal of all these studies is to assess the effects of the mass media, the degree of influence of individuals located at the top of the community hierarchy (agents of change), and the relative contribution of interpersonal interactions within the boundaries of the community where the innovation is spread. In all these applications, the empirical evidence gathered to demonstrate the existence of diffusion includes individuals, and their characteristics and interactions. In only one study was the evidence restricted to observation of aggregate outcomes such as proportion of adopters. With the exception of the works by Hagerstrand and Ryan and Gross, these studies placed emphasis on interpersonal relations and channels of influences as the mechanisms fostering or impeding diffusion. In this sense they anticipated some of the most useful work on social influences in general and diffusion in particular (Bandura, 1986; Moscovici, 1985; Marsden and Friedkin, 1993; Erbring and Young, 1979). However, besides these handfuls of very consequential empirical studies of diffusion, the bulk of the tradition in the area rests on the formulation of models that are testable with aggregate information about behaviors, such as the total numbers of adopters or proportions of a population who are adopters. These formulations mimic contagion models for the spread of disease and had the unfortunate consequence of portraying the social diffusion process as one where individuals are either passive carriers of information and innovations or passive "susceptibles," rather than actors engaged in real interactions. Furthermore, these models almost always require the rather strong and frequently unacceptable assumption of temporal and spatial homogeneity. Stochastic versions of these early models make room for some types of heterogeneity, but have proved to be mathematically intractable and have stimulated little empirical research (Bartholomew, 1982; Bailey, 1975). New deterministic formulations of contagion models with explicit consideration of limited types of social heterogeneity have had little impact in sociological analysis (Anderson and May, 1992; for an exception, see Morris, 1993).

As shown in the review by Mahajan and Peterson (1985), conventional formulations of aggregate diffusion incorporate external sources and social interaction among individuals, and result in testable hypotheses about the progression of the number or proportion of adopters in the population over time. The classic representation with a logistics cumulative distribution (the "S-shaped" curve of adoption) is, in fact, a very general result, and holds up well under a number of formulations. The reasoning behind this formulation is that, if diffusion is mediated by interactions between individuals, it must be the case that the rate of change in the proportion P(t) of adopters is given by:

$$\frac{dP(t)}{dt} = [r_o + r_1 P(t)](A - P(t)) \qquad (1)$$

where A is the ultimate fraction of the population that will adopt, r_0 is the number of new adopters that results from interaction with external forces, and r_1 is the number of new adopters that results from interactions between adopters and potential adopters in a small interval of time, dt (the "diffusion yield" of social interaction). When r_0 is 0 we have a simple case of pure social interaction effects, and when r_1 is 0 we have a case of pure external effects and no social influence to speak of. This formulation does not distinguish between types of external sources nor between classes of social contacts as all interactions are considered the same, and all are thought to be equivalent in terms of their diffusion yield. Admittedly, one can complicate the formulation in a number of ways (see Mahajan and Peterson, 1985) to include the influence of several external sources and, more generally, to represent limited social heterogeneity.

For the most part, these modifications preserve the main advantage of the logistic process, simplicity, but do not supercede its main shortcomings, a result of the fact that the structure modeled is not complex enough to enable us to distinguish empirically among alternative processes. For these reasons, improvements in models that focus on aggregate outcomes are unlikely to generate significant progress. Thus, logistic and related aggregate representations of diffusion processes are increasingly relegated to the camp of fragile descriptions.[6]

About a decade or so ago, sociological analyses of diffusion moved in two different directions, away from conventional contagion models. The first and, as suggested above, perhaps least promising route was to reformulate logistic models to enrich the complexity of the structure being represented. The second and most promising was to reshape the object of study: rather than targeting aggregate parameters, such as the overall adoption rate, researchers began to focus on individual processes. This type of model shifts focus toward individual behaviors and individual adoption, and redirects attention to actors who are decision makers, to the processes of social influence that shape decision making, and, lastly, to the constraints to which these are subjected. The models eschew discourses about aggregate trajectories but formulate quite precise conditions for individual decision making that underlie a diffusion process. These models enable the researcher to fully incorporate complexities of the adoption process itself (interagent communication, external sources, barriers, agents of change, etc.) and the social conditions of interaction between actors who are adopters and potential adopters.

New Models for Aggregate Outcomes:
Examples from Collective Action

An important step forward in the formulation of new diffusion models is the work on collective violence carried out by Pitcher et al. (1978). Their formulations were part of a more general effort to produce fruitful applications of diffusion models (Hamblin et al., 1973). The main notion behind their model is that the observed expression of collective violence depends on both imitation and inhibition processes determined by outcomes of prior events. Individuals learn from others' behavior, including those participating in and those repressing violence, and are able to understand when and how collective violence occurs and what tactics seem to work best. As in all other aggregate diffusion models, however, it is the number of past events that determines decisions about adoption of violent behavior. Similarly, individuals are assumed to be homogeneous with respect to the relevant behavior (or characteristics determining the behavior), and events in the past influence current events in like manner (there is time homogeneity of outcomes). With these simplifying assumptions, the authors formulate a model for the rate of change of acts of collective violence and the rate of change of repression acts. The model rests on two equations representing respectively the rate of new acts of violence and the rate of inhibition of acts of violence:

$$\frac{dP(t)}{dt} = \alpha \frac{P(t)}{I(t)}$$

$$\frac{dI(t)}{dt} = \beta I(t) \tag{2}$$

where P(t) is the cumulated number of acts of violence at time t and I(t) is the cumulated number of inhibited acts of violence. The algebra to solve for P(t) is transparent but tedious and results in the following function:

$$P(t) = P_o \exp(\delta/\beta) \exp[(-\delta/\beta) \exp(-\beta t)] \tag{3}$$

a model that represents the cumulated number of events (acts of violence), P(t), as a Gompertz's distribution function. A Gompertz function is better suited to fit processes that lack the symmetry embedded in a logistic formulation, namely, those where the adoption process drags on through initially long and protracted stages before finally taking off. Asymmetry suits well most processes of collective violence studied by Pitcher et al. (1978). But although this curve fits the data better (see endnote 6), the most important innovation introduced here is that the aggregate model is derived from an ideal individual decision-making process whereby actors decide whether to participate in, abandon or avoid altogether acts of violence.

Modifications to the model introduced by Pitcher et al. (1978) that include an explicit definition of the growth process of repressive acts leads to an even better representation of the trajectory of collective violence (Myers, 1997). Not only does this formulation enable us to model the decision-making process of individuals who are potential adopters of the behavior but also the responses of those who are charged with the function of preventing those actions from occurring at all. The idea of formulating jointly two diffusion processes, one that fosters the behaviors of interest and one that inhibits their realization, should be of interest to those studying social process where the innovation, such as fertility control, may generate resistance on the part of central authorities or among influential members of the community (such as community elders, the church, provincial authorities, or even the state). This is, in fact, an elegant way to treat one element of the diffusion process, namely, the phenomenon whereby individuals cease to embrace or adopt a behavior. Yet, although from the point of view of the theory of collective action this is much richer material, it continues to lead to a model for the aggregate number of collective acts of violence. And this is its main limitation.

A second type of diffusion models estimated with aggregate data relies on a more subtle representation of how individuals experience transitions from the state of nonadopter to the state of adopter (Rosero-Bixby, 1991; Rosero-Bixby and Casterline, 1993, 1994). Although the models are estimated from aggregate information (pooled cross-section and time series data on mean levels of fertility), their very nature (a close kin of compartment models) makes them suitable as representations of individual processes. Thus, the linkage between aggregate outcomes and individual behavior is more explicit here than what normally is in conventional diffusion models or even in the modified diffusion models for collective violence reviewed before. It is from this property that the model derives its superiority because it facilitates a richer formulation of the process than some of the models proposed by Pitcher and colleagues. The disadvantage of the compartment model formulation is that it is somewhat difficult to estimate from data normally available to us and, as other aggregate models of the same type, does not identify sufficient evidence to determine whether a diffusion process or something else explains the behavior under study (see, for example, simulations carried out in Rosero-Bixby and Casterline, 1993).

Models of Social Influence in Collective Action and Organization Theory

Somewhat paradoxically, an important part of the drift toward individually based models of diffusion occurs within areas traditionally reserved for the study of macrosocial processes, such as social movements and social organizations.

Collective Action

Initially, studies of common forms of collective action (e.g., protests and lynching), sprung from the idea that individual participation in such movements is a result of spontaneous and irrational imitation of antisocial behavior (LeBon, 1897). A contagion process was thus clearly justified as the best representation. This was replaced in the late 1960s and early 1970s by theories with an economic foundation that viewed collective action as the result of an atomized, individual decision-making process within a given social context and social environment (Olson, 1965). The overwhelming preoccupation in these formulations was centered in the so-called free-rider problem: to the extent that collectivities did not suppress the tendency of individuals to stay at the margins of actions, thus avoiding the costs of participation but reaping potential benefits, individual participation could simply be an irrational act. Reactions to Olson's atomistic theory came from many camps but mainly from those who saw the absence of a role for social institutions and social interactions as a fatal flaw. Soon new theories were built around conceptual frameworks emphasizing economic and demographic conditions external to the movement or action (Olzak, 1992; McAdam, 1982); facilitation, repression, or channeling from the state or societal elites (Jenkins and Eckert, 1986; Tilly, 1978; Piven and Cloward, 1979; Pitcher et al., 1978); competition among protest groups (Tarrow, 1994); internal resources (Obershall, 1989); and the role of internal social processes and heterogeneity among actors or groups of actors that frustrate or promote the smooth organization of collective action (Marwell and Oliver, 1993; Myers, 1997).

Perhaps the most interesting developments in collective action theory take place with the introduction of the idea that the decision to participate in collective actions may depend to some extent on conditions associated with the individual's position (e.g., individual costs or access to resources that facilitate action) and on the individual's interpersonal relations. A sophisticated paradigm emerges, one that poses the existence of a diffusion-like or social influence process mediated by "the network structures of everyday life" (McAdam, 1995; cited in Strang and Soule, 1997:20). This change of focus is accompanied by a parallel displacement of the object of study: it is no longer sufficient or desirable to account solely for aggregate properties of the process (e.g., the proportion or number of protesters at a particular time or the rate of growth of protesters at the onset of the process). Instead, verification of richer theoretical specification of social influence requires modelling individual decisions and individual actions (Myers, 1997; McAdam, 1995; Valente, 1995; Laumann et al., 1977; Granovetter, 1973).

It is incorrect to think that recent theories in this area reduce the complicated processes that lead to collective action and determine its success or ultimate disappearance to diffusion or social influence processes. It is equally incorrect, though, to overlook the fact that it is in actors' interactions and mutual social influence where one will find the essential features of collective action. This explains why, as indicated in the conclusion to a comprehensive overview of collective action theories and models, that "recent development in collective action models has centered on the problem of the interdependence of individuals within collectivities" (Marwell and Oliver, 1993:292). To be sure, there are other determinants and factors that should be examined, but without attention to social influence there is little hope of fully understanding how collective action develops.

Not surprisingly, modeling actor interdependency in collective action requires concepts and tools that are suitable for modeling diffusion of behaviors. This is clearly evident in a number of recent models, from simple threshold models where actors' decisions at one point in time are affected by the prevalence of participation or adoption among other relevant actors (Granovetter, 1973; Marwell and Oliver, 1993) to more complex constructions where an individual's decision making evolves as a learning process or as a function of decision making among members of networks to which individuals belong (Marwell and Oliver, 1993; Laumann et al., 1977; Marsden, 1998). Threshold models, social learning models, and models of mutual influence are at the core of reformulation and representation of diffusion processes.

New theories of collective action (Coleman, 1990) rest on an assumption about an individual decision maker facing alternative action paths (adopting or not adopting a behavior also contemplated by other actors in the system). In doing so actors consider what others are doing. Who the relevant others may be and the exact influence they may exert on an individual's behavior is possibly variable, and will depend on the actor's position within the collectivity, his channels of communications, and the type and frequency of relations to others. It is at this juncture where the investigation of contextual effects and its connections to social networks becomes strategic for understanding collective action. Because these are also the foundations on which new diffusion theories and models rest, it is worth reviewing them in some detail. To do so I will begin from and then extend the Erbring and Young formulation of contextual processes.

According to Erbring and Young's (1979) important contribution, contextual effects only make sense if they lead to the specification of a model where actors' responses are a well-defined function of other actors' responses. Assume, for example, one is studying a response for individual i, y_i , and that we observe a vector of responses Y containing the values y_1, y_2, ... y_k, that is, all the information on responses for all relevant actors (1 through k) in the system. A proper model in Erbring and Young formulation requires that we define Y as a function of a transformed vector of responses:

$$Y = \alpha WG(Y) + \beta X + \epsilon \qquad (4)$$

where Y is the observed vector of responses, ϵ is vector of errors, W is a matrix of weights, G is a well-defined functional form, X is a matrix of covariates, and β is a vector of associated effects. The central components in the model are W and α. The matrix of weights W, the "contiguity" matrix, specifies the importance attached to other actors' responses by any one actor in the system. This matrix is what informs the nature of the network within which individuals participate, and the form in which their decision-making process influences all other members. The ith row of the contiguity matrix contains elements that identify the weight that individual i assigns to the influence of the response of another member of the system. We could think of these quantities as measures of the degree of "infectiousness" of other members of the system (if they are infected) or social distance. In most cases one normalizes these quantities so the sum over all j is identical to 1 (Marsden and Friedkin, 1993). Clearly, the definition of **W** will vary depending on the mechanisms that generate or govern social influence. As they strive to understand achievement or aspirations among students of various classes in a school, Erbring and Young (1979:411) express the nature of the dependency of **W** on various social processes: "In the case of a contagion process, contiguity may be based explicitly on the amount of face-to-face interaction specific to each pair of students; whereas in the case of comparison or competition processes, contiguity may be defined as fixed and equal for all pairs of students in a given class room and zero for all pairs of students of different class rooms." In the following examples, **W** is defined in a number of distinct ways.

The parameter α reflects the strength of the feedback from the group or collectivity. If this parameter drifts to 0, it is an indication that there is no social influence process affecting actors' responses, and that these are only a function of structural characteristics (contained in **X**). One could generalize the formulation above by converting α into a vector, so that each individual in the system reacts differently to social influence and adoption by other members. In such case, the elements of the vector are equivalent to what individual infectiousness would be in contagion models.

As a consequence of this formulation, a necessary condition to prove the presence of diffusion of responses within the collectivity is that α (scalar or vector) be significantly different from zero. To the extent that **W** is misspecified, however, the estimates of α will be biased and incorrect inferences about social influences will be drawn. Thus, our ability to identify processes of social influence rests heavily on a proper specification of **W**. It is the task of general social network theories to specify what the nature of **W** ought to be, and what modifications we must introduce in (4) to capture better the social context which it is intending to represent. It is telling that social network theorists utilize formulations that are analogous, identical, or simple extensions of those proposed by Erbring and Young (see Valente, 1995; Marsden, 1998). I will show later that researchers in demography have also turned to variants of (4) to test new diffusion models for understanding fertility decline.

Note that model (4) is very flexible and that a number of variants could be tested. For example, suppose that **Y** represents responses at some time t and that **G** is the identity function. This simply means there is a contemporaneous social influence. But if **G** is a lag operator so that **G(Y)** represents a vector of lagged responses, the model suggests that the process of social influence requires some time to be triggered and to exert significant effects on individual behaviors. Another useful extension is one where we postulate different matrices **W** for each lagged form of the vector of responses to reflect the possibility that actors' mutual influence varies over time. Thus, for example, we can define matrices $\mathbf{W}_1$ and $\mathbf{W}_2$ to be associated with vectors of responses of lags 1 and 2 respectively, $\mathbf{Y}_{(t-1)}$ and $\mathbf{Y}_{(t-2)}$. Similarly, while the response variable y can stand for a dichotomous indicator at time t (actor adopts a response or not at time t), it is probably more informative to follow a sequence of values for y over time. Rather than modeling an actor's response directly, one could choose to model the actor's risk of adopting the response at some time t, $\mu(t)$, as a function of a transformation of actual responses of other actors in the system, **G(Y)**. Finally, we could expand (4) to make **Y** a function not just of whether or not other responses have occurred but also of their observed outcomes. Thus, if adoption of a behavior by an actor could be classified as leading to "success" or "failure," we could augment model (4) as follows:

$$\mathbf{Y} = \alpha\mathbf{W}\ \mathbf{G(Y)} + \delta\mathbf{W'G'(O)} + \beta\mathbf{X} + \boldsymbol{\epsilon} \qquad (5)$$

where **W'** is a modified contiguity matrix, **G'** is a modified functional transform, and **O** is the vector of outcomes associated with positive (adopt) and negative (does not adopt) responses. In this model, evidence of diffusion or social influence must be retrieved from the estimates of α as well as from δ. And, as before, α and δ need not be scalar quantities but could be vector valued.

In what follows I briefly discuss an example from collective action research that makes use of these reformulations, and where the key empirical test is designed to identify the magnitude and direction of effects of social influence. My objective here is only to highlight the adoption of model (4). The technical difficulties in estimating its parameters is a theme discussed later.

The last example of diffusion models in collective action is the spread of trade unions in Sweden (Hedström, 1994). In this example, spatial relations are determinants of networks and networks participation, and these are the main factors determining the outcome of a mobilization effort. The main thesis is that spatial contagious processes exerted a decisive influence in the growth of the Swedish union movement.

Hedström's analysis starts from a critical review of Olson's theory and his unilateral attention to the free-rider problem and consequent inattention to social networks that generate dependency between actors' decision making. In the case of Swedish trade unions, the claim is that decisions to join the union movement are influenced not only by individual characteristics (the structural conditions) but also by the nature of their real or potential interrelations. The latter are in turn a function of spatial contiguity.

Hedström formulates a model for the hazard of a first union in a particular district. This model depends on (a) district-specific (structural) factors that are likely to promote (inhibit) the formation of unions and (b) an indicator of the network exposure to union formation. Because the data are in a discrete (year) period, the author chooses to estimate a logit model, rather than a continuous time hazard model, of the following form:

$$\ln(p_{it}/(1-p_{it})) = \alpha_t + \Sigma_k \ (\gamma_k X_{ikt}) + \beta Z_{i,t-1}$$

where p_{it} is the probability that the first union will be formed in district i in the year (t,t+1), X_{ikt} is a characteristic k in district i at the beginning of year t, and $Z_{i,t-1}$ is the weighted sum of union members in other districts in the year before t. The weights chosen represent the inverse of the distance between district i and all others. Note that with these weights, the variable $Z_{i,t-1}$ is a simple function of the product of a contiguity matrix and a matrix of lagged responses in other units or districts. Indeed:

$$Z_{i,t-1} = \Sigma_j \ \pi_{ij} \ n_{jt-1}$$

where π_{ij}'s are the reciprocal of the distance between district i and district j and n_{jt-1} is the total sum of union members in district j during the year (t–1,t). Thus this model has the classical form of other models for the spread of collective action. The evidence for (against) the existence of a diffusion process depends on the sign and magnitude of β. Hedström finds strong evidence that the onset of a first union is dependent on the spatial networks even when other factors accounting for structural conditions and national trends are considered. His conclusion is "the spread of information through the social or geographic landscape was of decisive importance for the formation of trade unions" and "the spread of the Swedish union movement was caused by a combination of local factors operating within districts and a contagious process operating between districts" (Hedström, 1994:1176). Or, translated in our jargon, the emergence of the Swedish trade union movements owes to both structural conditions as well as to diffusion processes.

Organizations

The formulation of diffusion or contagion-like processes and their application in organizational analysis is relatively new. Its most explicit and fullest development takes place within the so-called new institutionalism framework. In what follows I discuss central elements in this framework and identify exactly where and for what purpose diffusion-like processes are invoked and utilized. I will attempt to show that these formulations are amenable to an analytic treatment very similar to those in collective action and that, as these do, they permit identification of all the definitional elements of a diffusion process.

Modern theorists of organizations have long been intrigued by the diversity of organizations and preferentially sought to explain heterogeneity in organizational structure and behaviors. Yet, proponents of the new institutionalism reverse the question and ask instead about the startling homogeneity in organizational forms and behaviors. The latter position is, of course, a revisionist version of the classic Weberian bureaucratic perspective that seeks to explain organizational uniformity by invoking the need to adopt rationalization to stay competitive and efficient. In some analyses of organization survival, the demise or failure of organizations is seen as a result of a selection process that weeds out the least competitive and efficient forms (Hannan and Freeman, 1977). According to the new institutionalism, this is only partially correct. Indeed, homogeneity in the organizational field is a result of two processes, one of which is driven by mechanisms of selection and competition (survival of the fittest or competitive isomorphism), whereas the other is one of institutional isomorphism. Its most distinctive characteristic is to be a result or consequence of adjustment in an environment populated by other organizations.

In an influential paper, DiMaggio and Powell argue that competitive and institutional isomorphism are applicable in general but that different fields of organization may be more or less prone to one or the other of these two processes. Thus, they suggest that "[competitive isomorphism] is most relevant for those fields in which free and open competition exists. It explains parts of the processes of bureaucratization that Weber observed, and may apply to early adoption of innovation, but it does not present a fully adequate picture of the modern world of organizations . . . ." As Aldrich (1979:265) has argued, "The major factors that organizations must take into account are other organizations" (DiMaggio and Powell, 1991:62).

There are three mechanisms of institutional isomorphism: coercive isomorphism, normative, and mimetic. It is only the last that involves processes of social influence whereby organizations act and react to each other by adopting (rejecting) organizational features and behaviors, much as individuals are assumed to do in models of social contagion applied to collective action. Organizational mimicry could be construed as a diffusion-like process where the actual actors are not individuals but organizations themselves or key units within an organization.

The fundamental factor driving mimetic process is uncertainty. Ac-

cording to DiMaggio and Powell (1991:69), "when organizational technologies are poorly understood (March and Olsen, 1976), when goals are
ambiguous, or when the environment creates uncertainty, organizations
may model themselves on other organizations." Just as in the case of
individual actors, there are organizations that innovate and others that
follow and imitate. Innovations are sometimes the result of imperfect
imitations by one or more organizations of features observable in another
that result in a modified feature that turns out to be beneficial for organizations in a particular field. As in individual processes of social influence,
organizations are more likely to imitate those organizations in the field
perceived to be legitimate or successful.

Isomorphism attributable to mimetic process is more likely to occur
under a variety of conditions characterizing the organizational field or the
organizations themselves. Thus, for example, to the extent that the connections between means and ends of an organization are unclear or uncertain, the more likely these organizations will be to adopt behaviors or
features from other organizations in the field. Similarly, organizations
with ambiguous goals will tend to imitate successful organizations in the
field. Imitation can also be the result of threshold effects in the sense that
adoption proceeds at a faster rate once the total prevalence of the feature
exceeds a threshold value.

The propositions of interest with regard to organizational mimicry
are very similar to the case of collective action, and the new models introduced to falsify them are, not surprisingly, also very similar. I will now
illustrate these parallelisms of propositions and models with an example
drawn from the recent literature in organizations.

The multidivisional form is a decentralized management organizational
structure overwhelmingly preferred by those large firms that dominate the
U.S. economy. Under this organizational form, "firms are organized into
product divisions and each division contains a unitary structure. There also
exists a central office where the long-range planning and financial alloca-
tions are located" (Fligstein, 1985:378). This organizational form could be
considered a central feature of firms within an industry that adopt it. An
interesting question is the following: what are the mechanisms that lead to
the "spread" of this organization feature? Is it simple adaptation to conditions set by the U.S. market (of goods and employment), transportation
technology, and the legal environment, or are there also imitation processes
that trigger adoption of the form? This question was posed by Fligstein in
an important article about ten years ago. To be fair, his effort was much
broader, for he attempted to discriminate between several alternative theories, all of which could account for the multidivisional form, but only one of
them involves a mimicking process.

Fligstein explicitly models the adoption of the organizational feature with simple logit models, each of which is defined for one decade during the entire period under observation (1929–1979). Each logit model is for a dependent dichotomous variable that indicates whether the feature in a firm is adopted or not. Several independent variables capture essential features of the mechanisms postulated by competing theories (structural factors). He then includes in the model the percentage of firms in a given industry that adopted the feature before the beginning of the decade under observation. This is the variable that represents the crucial feature of a mimicry mechanism. For each period we have (t, t + 10):

$$\ln (p_t/(1-p_t)) = \beta_t X_t$$

where β_t and X_t are vectors of covariates and effects for the period.

Although in a very simplified form, the model used by Fligstein is an example of the relational model for social influences introduced before. Indeed, the indicator of prevalence of the organizational form in a given industry is a summary indicator of the information contained in a lagged response matrix (Y) combined with the identity matrix as a contiguity matrix.

Fligstein's findings suggest that there is evidence indicating that mimicry does operate in the transmission of the multidivisional form. This evidence is not overwhelming as there is also support for the existence of other mechanisms of isomorphism. Inferences about the existence of a diffusion process, however, are somewhat weak, not just because the evidence is less strong than desirable, but also for two other reasons. First, as formulated the model cannot identify exactly how the imitation process proceeds, that is, it does not shed light on the micromechanisms (at the level of sections or units or single individuals in a firm) that sustain the imitation process. Second, there are a number of statistical problems that the author cannot resolve with the data available to him, and they all involve issues of proper (inconsistent) estimation of parameters. These will be reviewed more thoroughly in the next section. Despite these shortcomings, however, Fligstein's work represents the first attempt to explicitly test DiMaggio and Powell's mimetic mechanism.

NEW MODELS OF DIFFUSION: PROBLEMS AND UNRESOLVED ISSUES

The discussion and review of recent sociological applications above provide elements for identifying essential characteristics of diffusion models and for testing propositions that seek to identify their relevance in empirical cases. Unlike conventional diffusion models, the new models applied in sociological analysis formulate explicitly the mechanisms through which diffusion occurs and provide an environment for testing their empirical relevance.

In this section I will identify the main characteristics of these models, establish the advantages gained by adopting them, note important short-comings, and discuss possible improvements. Throughout, the discussion is focused on the following query: how can we empirically identify a diffusion model, that is, how can we tell it apart from altogether different mechanisms? This discussion will furnish a "golden" standard that will be used later to assess diffusion models applied to demographic problems.

A Simple Representation of Diffusion Processes

In light of our previous discussion, we introduce a modified version of the definition given earlier. A diffusion process is one in which selection or adoption (rejection) of a behavior or practice depends on an individual decision-making process that assigns significant influence to the adoption (rejection) behavior of other individuals within the social system. There are a number of ways to define who the other individuals are, and there are alternative mechanisms through which their social influence may affect an individual's decision-making process. In what follows I briefly identify the most significant social relations and three mechanisms that drive diffusion processes.

I start from a simplified version of the decision-making process worked out by Montgomery and Chung (1994) (see also Montgomery and Casterline, 1996) and assume that we are dealing with the adoption (rejection) of behavior B_0 and that individuals may choose among a repertoire of alternative behaviors contained in the set $\{B_j\}$, of which B_0 is a member. Each of these behaviors is associated with expected costs and expected benefits. Assume that individuals associate each behavior B_j with a distribution of net benefits, NB_j. Let us say for simplicity that NB_j is continuous, can attain values in the interval $(-\tilde{n}, +\tilde{n})$, and is associated with probabilities $P_j(x)$, where x is a given level of net benefits. Each individual assigned to behavior B_j receives a net benefit, $NB_j = x$ with probability $P_j(x)$. This is what we will refer to as linkage between behavior and net benefit. That is to say, for any behavior B_j, there is an expected net benefit given by:

$$E(NB_j) = \int_x (NB_j(x))P_j(x)\, dx.$$

The decision-making problem is simply to choose the behavior within the set $\{B_j\}$ that maximizes $E(.)$.

In the absence of a diffusion process, the inclusion (exclusion) of B_0 from the set of alternative behaviors, the actual configuration of the set of equivalent behaviors itself, and the probabilistic association of net benefits depends on the actors' position in the social system or, rather, on the bundle of resources (including information) associated with or available to the actor. This is what a structural explanation points to: the selection of behavior is solely dependent on characteristics associated with the individual, not with what others do regardless of whom they may be. Instead, a diffusion process exists when either the inclusion of B_0 in the set of alternative behaviors, the linkage between behavior and net benefits, or the actual calculus of costs and benefits depends also on conditions dictated by social contacts with other members of the system, however tenuous or formal these may be. That is, these social contacts or social influences are effective mechanisms of diffusion in that they have an effect on (a) information about the feasibility of B_0, (b) knowledge about net benefits associated with B_0, or (c) assessment of net benefits associated with B_0 given a nonzero prevalence of B_0 in the social system.

To make the above definition unequivocal, a number of issues require clarification. First, we need precision in the timing of the individual calculus. Thus, we need to know the time horizon for the calculation of net benefits and, more importantly, the time lags required to establish an association between a behavior and its net benefits. If there is no diffusion at all, the time lag may be instantaneous, very short, or quite long, but if there is diffusion individuals will surely require some time to learn from others' experiences about rewards and costs associated with B_0. And if this is the case, how long does it take for the association to become established from observation of others' behavior?

Second, it was assumed that decision makers are only interested in the mean of the distribution of net benefits, and that issues such as higher risks imposed by higher variances are irrelevant. This assumption may be inadequate both when there is diffusion and in the absence of it, but more so in the first case (Montgomery and Chung, 1994). In fact, when there is diffusion and individuals purposely take into account others' behavior, it is likely they will have only sparse information on rewards and costs of adoption of B_0, particularly at the onset of the process. In such cases, the distribution of net benefits will have higher variances, and risk-averse individuals will have a harder time adopting the behavior, regardless of what the mean net benefit is. This may be one explanation for the phenomenon of resistance to adopt, which is especially relevant at the onset of the diffusion process. We elaborate on this below.

Third, to identify the diffusion process from observables, one needs to know with precision about which social networks are relevant and which relations are key within them. This is the material informed by network theory; it is discussed briefly below. In addition, we should consider two additional difficult issues. First, the formation of an individual's reference networks may be endogenous to the process being studied. This means that the selection of social networks or of relevant relations within them could be influenced by the same factors that affect decision making about adoption of a behavior. For example, suppose that individuals in a given social position tend to choose a behavior B_0 based on maximization of net benefits purely as a function of their position in the social system, and that there is no influence of others' behavior in their decision-making process. If, to avoid social friction, social rejection, or complete isolation, they decide to choose social networks (and relations within them) whose members have also chosen B_0, the empirical process will appear as though individual adoption of B_0 was associated with prevalence of B_0 in relevant networks. The incorrect inference is that there is a diffusion process because the probability of adoption of the behavior will be associated with the relevance of B_0 in the individual's network. But in this example membership in a network follows adoption of behavior, not the other way around. The only way to avoid an incorrect inference is to have full information about the timing of the adoption and the timing of effective membership in networks.

The second and related issue is of great relevance for current processes in this volume of diffusion of contraceptive (and other) behaviors via the influence of television (Potter et al., 1998). As suggested by Montgomery and Chung (1994), television creates fictional networks with which individuals identify and participate. The television program communicates the existence of alternative behaviors (plausibility of contraception, for example), but also transmits information about the connection, usually spurious, between the behavior and desirable rewards. Thus, admired couples in soap operas may have no more than two children, live in a mansion, and drive red Ferraris. To the extent that these are desirable objects, they will be associated with two children at most. This may introduce, reaffirm, or consolidate the idea that children are costly. Thus, although television is an external source, it can operate much in the same way as membership in social networks does and, therefore, raises the same issues of selectivity alluded to before.

Fourth and last, the preconditions for the existence of a diffusion process stated above refer to mechanisms through which social networks affect individual choice of behavior. Montgomery and Chung (1994) suggest that there are two mechanisms: one is by altering knowledge about the elements of the set of plausible behavior and the other is by establishing a linkage between the behavior and its net benefits. There is a third mechanism through which costs and benefits associated with adoption are changed by the diffusion process itself. An example that shows this type of effect is the spread of a technological innovation, such as an operating system. The adoption of the innovation changes the conditions for everybody else, whether they are adopters or not. For example, adoption of an operating system among some users prompts the creation of software designed for the operating system, but the software may be useful to the entire collectivity of PC users. The immediate effect should be to increase the likelihood of adopting the operating system simply as a way to access the software. Examples such as these are easy to identify in the area of technology, and they are not altogether absent in the area of social behaviors. Thus, the social costs of refusal to participate in collective action may grow steeper as members of a reference group increasingly adopt the new technology. Similarly, the adoption of contraceptive behavior may become more plausible if social and economic conditions emerging after and as a result of the initial adoption of contraception impose steep costs among large families.

This third mechanism acts by speeding the spread of the behavior, but is the result of a feedback and operates through adjustments that individuals make to changes in costs or benefits, not as direct response to others' adoption. It is a mechanism that augments (inhibits) the diffusion or spread of the behavior by activating the structural factors that affect behaviors. The feedback mechanism operates through influence of others' adoption on costs and benefits associated with known behaviors, not by altering awareness about a set of options nor by establishing a new connection between behaviors and net benefits. Furthermore, the influence of the feedback effect on an individual's adoption may be exerted by diffuse and distant social networks, not necessarily by any specific social network to which the individual belongs.[7]

Below I describe in more detail some of the problems we encounter in the definition and treatment of relevant social influences and individual resistance and thresholds. I then discuss considerations for model building.

Relational and Structural Models

The most recent diffusion models that explicitly incorporate the effects of social network do not neglect the existence of traditional elements altogether. Insistence on the influence of external sources remains an important feature, and the new formulations may even include nontraditional external sources (e.g., those that regulate the environment within which decisions are being made). What is novel in these models is a more detailed treatment of the mechanisms through which external sources affect the adoption process. It becomes relevant, for example, to formulate precisely whether a televison show or a particular radio program affects values or preferences, whether it facilitates communication of information among individuals in different social positions, or whether it alters the costs of certain alternatives. The task of model formulation becomes a more taxing one because we must hypothesize in advance the mechanisms through which external sources are thought to affect the adoption process.

The mainstay of these models is attention to the sources of social influence and the attempt to model these as precisely as possible. Classical formal models of diffusion assume spatial and social homogeneity, that is, they rest on the assumption that members of the population do not differ in terms of the chances of affecting others or being affected by others. Sociologists now postulate that there are at least four different mechanisms of interpersonal relations that shape the social structure within which adoption decisions are made. Each of them requires a different modeling strategy. First, relational linkages refer to the set of relations an individual may establish with others within a particular setting or network. What matters here is the density of individual connections, as well as the type of connections that some actors in the network have with others outside it. These relations can be represented by an individual, vector-valued function. Each individual is characterized by a vector-valued function, the contiguity matrix introduced above, that reflects all social connections considered to be relevant. To the extent that relations maintained by others in the network with individuals outside it are relevant for the process, they can be incorporated into the matrix in the form of weights. For example, a set of weights might distinguish the relative importance of strong and weak ties for a given individual in the population (Granovetter, 1973).

Second, structural linkages refer to relations with structurally equivalent actors. More generally, they are relations between individuals evaluated as a function of similarity of structural positions occupied within a given network or in the wider social system (Burt, 1987). Application of this idea is fairly common in recent studies of organizational diffusion. Thus, it is thought that structural equivalent relations promote imitation through competition among individuals in a firm. But it can also be the case that competition with structurally equivalent actors may spur not imitation but divergence of behavior (that is, resistance to adoption). This is an empirical matter and can be settled only if we are able to associate with each individual a matrix-valued function of relations to individuals who are structurally equivalent (or dissimilar). The empirical estimates associated with such matrix-valued function will enable us to determine the direction and magnitude of effects.

Third, the new models incorporate and account explicitly for the degree of influence accorded to others within a network. Influence attributable to a position or member will usually be a function of the relative ordering of individuals in the network according to some relevant metric (Valente, 1995).

Fourth, the models include consideration of influence exerted by culturally bounded groups (Strang and Soule, 1997). These refer to relations maintained with individuals based on definitions of actions, status, and purpose. For example, the influence of individuals who consider themselves as activists (McAdam and Rucht, 1993) was singled out as an important factor in the spread of activists' tactics. An interesting but somewhat puzzling type of cultural influence might be one generated by the innovation itself. Thus, individuals may align themselves around the notion of being or not being adopters. This could influence continuation of adoption and attract (or even repel) nonadopters.

Fifth, and finally, spatial proximity can be incorporated into the analysis. A common finding in classic diffusion research is that spatially proximate actors are more likely to influence each other. The difficulty is that spatial proximity is an open concept in the sense that many mechanisms can operate to render it an effective means to promote (or resist) adoption. In most cases, spatial proximity is used as a proxy, albeit imperfect, of network connections and potential social influences originated in either structural, relational, or cultural connections as defined before.[8] Ideally, the use of spatial proximity should be justified a priori by defining the precise mechanisms through which it may affect the process. Some of these mechanisms are easiness of communication, social and economic homogeneity, and frequency of interactions.

For the most part, the study of effects of spatial proximity has been monopolized by geographers (Brown, 1981), but the development of tools for statistical inference from spatial statistics (Cressie, 1991) and the rapid adoption of accessible software (Anselin, 1988) has promoted the use of spatial models of diffusion (see, for example, Hedström, 1994; Bocquet-Appel, 1997).

Resistance and Thresholds

An important innovation introduced in recent formulations of diffusion models is the notion of individual thresholds. According to this idea, individuals may resist adoption up to a certain point as the process proceeds within the group. In theory at least, individuals may be carriers of different thresholds and thus be characterized by a unique, individual-specific value identifying the percent of total adoption below which efficient individual resistance to adoption will be exerted. This is, of course, an unmeasured quantity, in much the same way as frailty in the literature on health and mortality is an unmeasured quantity. If all variables affecting the individual decision-making process were known, it would be pointless to speak of thresholds, in much the same way as the notion of individual frailty would be empty if all conditions for survival were known. For example, one mechanism promoting (slowing) adoption that requires the notion of individual threshold also requires invoking the notions of variance of the distribution of net benefits associated with the behavior to be adopted (see above) and of risk aversion. A high variance of net rewards will prompt risk-averse individuals to delay or reject adoption. In this interpretation, individual resistance and thresholds are a function of (a) perceived variance of net benefits and (b) whether or nor an individual is risk averse. Neither of these are readily measurable quantities.

Initially at least, proponents of the notion of threshold have made it equivalent to the effect that levels of prevalence of adoption within the relevant group has on the individual risk of adopting (Valente, 1995). But this is a conceptually different idea and it creates relatively serious identification (Manski, 1995) and interpretational (Erbring and Young, 1979) issues that have not yet been addressed satisfactorily. Because the notion is quite promising, however, it is hoped that work toward the development of better measurement and modeling strategies will continue.

SEARCHING FOR DIFFUSION: THE IDENTIFICATION PROBLEM

The Ideal Test

The only way to conclusively prove whether a diffusion or a structuralist theory is correct is an unrealizable experiment, namely, the observation of patterns of behavior under conditions that hold constant the distribution of individuals by social positions and the distribution of resources associated with positions while allowing variations in conditions that trigger the spread of the behavior (e.g., participation in social networks). If the prevalence of the behavior grows, it cannot possibly be because of structural factors (they are being kept constant) but because of diffusion. The key issue, however, is to remember that at least one of the three mechanisms of diffusion identified above mimics the effects of structural changes, namely, when social positions or resources associated with them change *as a result of the process of diffusion itself*. Put otherwise, if we are to identify diffusion effects, the ideal experiment cannot allow the diffusion feedback mechanism to operate and simultaneously maintain invariance in individual characteristics. Thus, even under ideal conditions, it is difficult to sort out precisely how much of the ultimate change in behavior is due to all diffusion mechanisms and how much to secondary changes in the social structure induced by diffusion itself. In the case of the study of fertility or of the bulk of social sciences problems, where conventional study conditions are far from ideal, it will be virtually impossible to make the relevant distinctions. This limitation is, of course, irrelevant when the feedback mechanism is weak or if its operation requires long time lags.[9]

Testable Models

The recent literature in diffusion models is very rich in suggested formal representations (Strang, 1991; Strang and Tuma, 1993). I will borrow freely from these but tailor the discussion to capture useful features for demographic analyses. My purpose is not to suggest what the true models are, but rather to provide an indication of the degree of complexity that the models ought to have, and to point to the problems one is likely to face when a diffusion model is misspecified.

A diffusion model must represent individuals choosing among a set of alternative behaviors under a set of constraints. It must also account for the persistence of the adoption or selection over time. This can be done in a number of ways, but perhaps the most efficient one is to construct a system of two states, one representing adoption of the target behavior and the other adoption of a different behavior (or refusal to adopt). Individuals may move between these two states as a function of individual characteristics associated with social and economic conditions (costs and utilities), external characteristics acting as constraints (or facilitators), influence of external sources of ideas, or influence of individual social networks. To capture the dynamic of this two-state system, we can formulate a pair of equations for the risk or hazard of transitions between the two states:

$$\mu_{12i}(t)=\mu_{o12}(t)\ \exp(\beta X_i(t)+\gamma Z_i(t)+\alpha W_i(t)G(Y(t))+\varepsilon_{12i})$$

$$\mu_{21i}(t)=\mu_{o21}(t)\ \exp(\beta^* X_i^*(t)+\gamma Z_i^*(t)+\alpha W_i^*(t)G^*(Y^*(t))+\varepsilon_{21i}^*)$$

(6)

where $\mu_{12i}(t)$ refers to the risk of moving from state 1 (nonadopter) to state 2 (adopter) for individual i at time t, $\mu_{o12}(t)$ is a baseline hazard, X_i is a vector of structural characteristics of individual i, Z_i is a vector-valued function containing information on external sources of information that may influence i[th]'s choice, W_i is a contiguity vector for individual i containing the weight assigned to the influence from contacts with individuals j=1, . . . N, where is N is the total number of members in the system, G is a functional transform, and Y is a vector of responses for members j=1, . . . N. Finally, ε_{12i} is an error term. The second equation defines the risk of moving from state 2 to state 1 (abandoning the new behavior). It is analogous to the first, but I have allowed for the possibility of different baselines, different effects, and different matrices of covariates. The contiguity vector is time dependent to allow for changing influences derived from social networks during the process, and so are the vectors of responses Y and Y^* to allow for updating of information about members of the system.

Problems with Formulation of the Model

Before reviewing estimation problems, let us examine the anatomy and functionality of this formulation. Suppose this two-state model is correct. Under fairly general regularity conditions, there will be a steady state and a stable proportion of the population that will be in each of the two states. It is not difficult to show that those proportions or their logarithms are NOT a simple linear function of the vector of covariates, as the logarithms of the risks are. This statement is important: it means that if model (6) is the true representation of the diffusion process, aggregate linear models for quantities such as the proportion of adopters are misspecified. In addition because the model is misspecified, it is totally meaningless to estimate its parameters and to attribute to diffusion the part of the variance in the dependent variables (proportion of adopters) that remains unexplained by measured covariates.

Furthermore, let us say that variables are scaled in such a way that α and γ are positive. It follows that if diffusion is effective, the adoption process will proceed faster than it would otherwise (the risk of adoption will be higher and the probability of staying in state 1 will be lower). But this does not mean that one is correct in inferring the existence of diffusion if the change in the aggregate proportion of adopters is "rapid" or "fast" (relative to some standard). This is because (a) we assume that the second transition is nonexistent and (b) we assume that all relevant structural covariates are contained in X. Even if the second transition was irrelevant (all adopters remain adopters for life and beyond), lack of appropriate control for structural conditions that change rapidly and that have strong effects on the risk of adoption will end up concealing the extent to which the processes is structurally driven and mislead the investigator into believing that the whole process is the work of diffusion. Note that this will occur even if one is estimating model (6) rather than an aggregate variant of it, regardless of whether X's are unrelated to Z's.

A number of difficulties are associated with any possible extensions of model (6). First, we have not justified well the nature of the term associated with social networks. In particular, there is no reason why it should include all members of an individual network. An alternative representation would be to split the term into two components in the following way:

$$\alpha W_i(t)G(Y(t)) = \alpha_1 W_{1i}(t)G_1(Y_1(t)) + \alpha_2 W_{2i}(t)G_2(Y_2(t))$$

where each vector now refers to individuals in the network relevant for the ith individual according to their response, and collects all those who have not adopted in W_{1i} and all those who adopted in W_{2i}. This partition will enable us to distinguish the effects of attraction toward the new behavior (exerted by those who adopted the behavior) from the potential resistance effects exerted by those who have not yet adopted.

A second problem is whether the model must be multiplicative at all, that is, one where the diffusion component and the structural component enter as multiplicative terms. Strang and Tuma suggest pursuing an additive model because this has some desirable properties (Strang and Tuma, 1993). Because estimates and implications associated with each of these formulations will be different, the researcher must think through the assumptions made when adopting one or the other form.

Third, effects of diffusion operating through external sources should be captured by γ, whereas effects of social influence will be captured by α. Both γ and α can be allowed to be vector valued, that is, individuals may have different susceptibility to be influenced by others, depending on who the other individual is. If one considers this an important extension, then problems of identification will emerge. Whether α and γ are scalar quantities or vector-valued functions, their magnitude and sign will only reflect two mechanisms of diffusion: one whereby social influences change the set of plausible choices for the individual, and the other whereby social influences modify the linkage between the new behavior and expected net benefits. These effects will not capture the influence of the diffusion process via the feedback mechanism. To capture the feedback mechanism, model (6) must be extended to reveal the relation between prevalence of the new behavior and structural conditions contained in X_i. Alternatively, if the feedback mechanism requires a long time to operate relative to the speed of diffusion to be significant, one could simply dismiss it.

Fourth, there is no need to have a unique contiguity vector, W_i. In fact, one could partition the vector to reflect several (partially related) networks or to attempt to represent functional and structural influences (see discussion above). Furthermore, one could introduce a vector representing the success associated with the adoption of the behaviors by members of relevant networks (see above). These two modifications increase the richness of the social network representation, but they also pose additional data demands.

Problems of Estimation

If we insist on the existence of two transitions, the first problem that emerges is that of the relation between the two error terms. Without assuming a joint distribution for the errors (and, inevitably, this will be arbitrary), the parameters are not estimable. Of course, the easiest but least appropriate solution is always on hand, namely, to assume that the two error terms are independent.

But even a simplified, one-equation form of model (6) creates estimation problems of considerable import. Assume the simplified form that results when the transition from state 2 to state 1 (abandoning adoption) is insignificant. That is, we assume that once adoption occurs, it is irreversible. This is consistent with the process of fertility decline in general, although it may not be with other diffusion processes or with some examples of local fertility decline. Also, to simplify even further, assume there is no relevant feedback mechanism. The parameters of the simplified model that remain will be estimable only if we have available considerable amounts of information, and if we make some strong assumptions along the way.

The required information includes (a) nature of several types of networks relevant to all individuals in the population during the trajectory of the process, (b) information on outcomes associated with adoption of the new behaviors by members of the networks in which all individuals participate, (c) nature of the sources of external influence to which each individual is susceptible throughout the duration of the process, and, finally, (d) structural conditions that determine either individual positions or external constraints to take into account in individual decision making. Needless to say, there are very few datasets in sociology or demography that contain all this information, and even fewer social scientists who will be able to discern what all the relevant variables are. As a result the researcher faces the problem of unmeasured heterogeneity whereby estimated effects are inconsistent even if the omitted variables are unrelated to the included variables. It is not difficult to design scenarios where omission of a structural characteristic could impart an upward bias on some estimates thus misleading the researcher into believing there is a nontrivial diffusion process. Note that, unlike most cases where generalized linear models apply, the biases or inconsistencies will occur regardless of whether the omitted variable is related to those included in the model. Earlier we identified one potential culprit of unmeasured heterogeneity, namely, information on the appraisal of the risk to which an individual is exposed when connecting the new behavior to net benefits. If risk-averse individuals perceive a larger variance than others, they are likely to delay adoption. This will lead to a well-known artifact: the risk of adoption will look like a decreasing function of time. The most likely consequence of this will be to bias downward the effects of diffusion.

Unmeasured heterogeneity can be modeled, and one of the most effective ways of doing so is to postulate that each individual is characterized by a resistance (or susceptibility) to innovation or a "threshold" for innovation. This unmeasured individual characteristic is postulated to be a random variable with a known distribution. The assumption just made leads to calculations that result in a marginal risk that is not dependent on the unmeasured characteristic. Thus, the formulations of diffusion process or collective actions that invoke the existence of individual resistance or individual thresholds are really designed to interpret the existence of unmeasured characteristics that either promote or delay the adoption of the behavior. The hazard model formulation offers a framework showing where to include them.

Finally, a more troublesome feature of a diffusion process is that its own progress may affect the likelihood of reducing, eliminating, or inventing new social networks. Maintaining social networks that are not responsive to the new behavior may force adventurous individuals to seek new social attachments among those better prepared to embrace the new behavior. Although this avoids friction and possible penalties, it is associated with new costs, and individuals will need to weigh the advantages of leaving current social networks perceived to be unfavorable against the cost of creating new relations in newer and more receptive networks. Ultimately, however, what matters is that such endogenous change will produce the appearance that networks do have an influence on choice of behavior when actually they may have none. Naturally, the only way to handle this problem is to model separately network formation as a function of past behavior. This imposes more information constraints and generates new estimation difficulties.[10]

DIFFUSION MODELS THAT ACCOUNT FOR FERTILITY CHANGES

The history of applications of diffusion models to the study of fertility proceeds through a succession of intellectual stages, each characterized by a paradigm. These paradigms serve to conceptualize the nature of the process of diffusion, to identify the criteria for deciding empirically among competing explanations, and, finally, to define the opposition between two types of explanations for fertility decline, one relying on diffusion and the other on structural changes. The initial dominant paradigm is characterized by a naive conception of diffusion, undemanding methodological desiderata, and a simplistic contrast between diffusion processes and structural changes. This paradigm gradually gives way to more sophisticated and subtle views that include models closer to the ideal set forth above, adhere to strict principles of empirical inferences, and represent better the contrast between diffusion and alternative explanations in a more elaborated form. The limitation faced by this more recent paradigm is not conceptual but empirical, for its inferential principles require more information than what is normally available to us.

The Origins of the Contrast Between
Structuralist and Diffusionist Explanations

The dichotomy between structuralist and diffusionist explanations of fertility change was first formulated and translated into testable hypotheses in a seminal paper by Carlsson (1966). In it the author establishes a rather misleading contrast between processes of adjustment, rather than structural transformations and diffusion. Carlsson argues that fertility decline in Sweden could have been triggered by one of two processes. The first was an adjustment process whereby families tinkered heavily with their fertility targets to accommodate higher levels of child survival. Alternatively, fertility changes could have been the result of a diffusion process whereby a few forerunners introduce controlled fertility, and were subsequently imitated by others who adopted the innovation. The adjustment hypothesis is a corollary of a classic formulation of demographic transition theory that assigns importance to mortality decline as a precursor to fertility decline (Davis, 1963; Notestein, 1945; Knodel and van de Walle, 1967).

Carlsson's dichotomy is misleading for two reasons. The first is that the adjustment hypothesis is indeed one possible version of a structuralist argument, and in presenting it as a sharply different, competing explanation to a diffusion mechanism, it falls into the trap that has had us confused for years. The confusion is that we reify diffusion as a process that involves at best a-rational individuals, whereas the structurally based explanation invokes rational decision makers. I have pointed out that this interpretation is incorrect, and that the difference between one and the other has nothing to do with actors' rationality, and everything to do with the existence of two distinct rationalities: one where others' opinions and actions count for fertility decisions, and another where they exert no influence on the calculus of fertility.

Carlsson's distinction is misleading for another reason as well. This is that the main mechanism through which the process of adjustment is assumed to work involves improvements in child survival. If there is anything we learned from evidence gathered in Western Europe and in developing countries, it is that, in most regions of the world, mortality decline had little to do with fertility decline, and none of the three main mediating mechanisms linking mortality and fertility—biological, replacement, and hoarding—are powerful enough to amount to a full explanation (van de Walle, 1986; Preston, 1978; Cohen and Montgomery, 1998; Palloni and Rafalimanana, 1997). Few among us would argue that failure of this particular (Carlsson's) version of the structuralist argument is reason enough to sponsor the diffusion hypothesis.

Carlsson's formal representation and testing of a diffusion model is fraught with other problems as well. The most important among these, and a consequence of the simplistic notion of diffusion adopted, is that there is no model connecting individual fertility decision-making and social influences. Although the author does refer to geographic proximity, there is no effort to include it explicitly in a model and it is, instead, introduced as an ad hoc variable.

Finally, Carlsson (1966:173) reduces diffusion to a simple flow of information from an external source to individuals. Indeed, he represents his work as an effort to induce a shift from "innovation to adjustment theory [which] leads to *less emphasis on information about birth control and its means, and more emphasis on motivation and social situation*" (emphasis added). As we showed before, this reduction of diffusion to supply of information is misguided. Interestingly, he anticipates potential reversals in the diffusion process when he recognizes the possibility of individuals rejecting the new behavior after it has been adopted, but draws the wrong conclusion from it. Indeed, he speculates "One reason why it may be more misleading than helpful to regard the fertility decline and the wider adoption of birth control as an innovation process is that the latter designation often carries with it the idea that the process is bound to run its course to complete or near-complete adoption in a regular way. The notion of an adjustment over time to a new equilibrium level, on the other hand, keeps open the possibility of fertility staying neither fully controlled in the modern sense, nor completely uncontrolled, and this for an appreciable period" (Carlsson, 1966:172). This quote suggests that despite identifying the problem of rejection (and reversals) as a central one, he does not conceive of a solution within the boundaries of a diffusion model, as we did earlier using a two-state hazard model.

The Princeton Fertility Project and Its Aftermath

There is widespread agreement that the results of the Princeton project cast doubts on the validity of classical explanations of fertility changes. These results led and encouraged formulations of more refined interpretations of the diffusionist models. By far the most damaging empirical evidence produced by the Princeton project against a paradigmatic version of the structural explanation, conventional demographic transition theory, is that fertility decline appears to occur along territorial boundaries reproducing ethnic, language, and religious cleavages (Lesthaeghe, 1977; Livi-Bacci, 1971, 1986; Knodel, 1974; Coale and Watkins, 1986). Conventional regression analyses reveal that the explanatory power of variables measuring industrialization, urbanization, state centralization, bu-reaucratization, and others to predict the onset and the pace of fertility decline turns out to be modest at best. This evidence led to a more refined representation of how diffusion and resistance to diffusion may operate in societies sharply divided along linguistic and ethnic cleavages. Yet, with the exception of work by Lesthaeghe on Belgium's fertility decline (Lesthaeghe, 1977), the contrast between the structuralist and diffusion theories is always resolved by estimating conventional linear regression models on aggregate indicators of fertility, then resorting to residual analyses as a tool to assess the degree of failure of the structuralist theory. This failure is automatically considered as a sort of reverse measure of the degree of success of the diffusion model. Thus, although most studies in the Princeton project attempted to conceptualize more precisely the pro-cess of diffusion, adding the idea of cultural and ethnic boundary and refining the conceptualization and measurement of structural conditions, the rules of inference remained quite primitive.

The paradigm that characterizes the Princeton fertility project has been subsequently modified along three lines of research. The first intro-duces more fine-tuned analyses of the same or moderately augmented data used in the Princeton study without significantly changing the theo-retical discourse (see the work by Galloway et al., 1994; Bocquet-Appel, 1997). The second line of research focuses on different measures of fertil-ity, correctly arguing that the proper measures to test diffusion models ought to be measures of prevalence of the new behavior (contraception) that are only poorly correlated with the indirect measures of fertility nor-mally used by demographers (Okun, 1994).

Finally, the third line of research is more theoretical because it refines the conceptual scheme and brings to the forefront the discussion of the nature of mechanisms whereby individual adoption of new behaviors takes place. This occurs in reaction to overwhelming evidence of the failure of conventional, structuralist explanations of fertility changes. At the end of the 1990s, de-mographers had already surveyed extensive territories in addition to West-ern and Eastern Europe. The World Fertility Survey, the Demographic and Health Survey, and a handful of other more localized data collection under-takings produced a large amount of evidence regarding fertility decline in developing nations. In a sweeping and controversial summary of this evi-dence, Cleland and Wilson (1987) suggest that any version of demand theo-ries of fertility, that is, economic theories invoking the need for structural changes in individual's positions as a precondition for fertility changes, can-not account for the onset, pace, and geographic location of fertility declines throughout the developing world. Instead, these changes appear to be driven by ideational changes riding on the back of a diffusion process. Much the same conclusion had been reached by Caldwell in some of his writings where he assigns importance to the onslaught of an ideational change ("Westerniza- tion") that precedes and is partially independent of changes in forms of production and distribution (Caldwell, 1982).

However persuasive their argumentation may be, the formulation put forward by Cleland and Wilson runs into two problems, one theoreti- cal and the other methodological. First, there is a conceptual confusion that takes ideational changes as equivalent to diffusion processes. If fertil- ity declines because individuals change ideas about the advantages of having children, even though their social and economic positions remain apparently the same, one cannot automatically infer the existence of a diffusion process. For this to be a proper inference, one must find evi- dence that the new ideas or the change of ideas are driven by imitation of others' ideas. Second, the evidence that Cleland and Wilson use to sup- port their claims belongs to a type we identified before as insufficient. Indeed, they examine the speed of changes in fertility and compare them with what would be expected given observed changes in structural condi- tions or, alternatively, they verify that the main cleavages created by fer- tility changes are drawn by ethnic or language distinctions. This contrast between ideational changes and demand-driven changes at the core of Cleland and Wilson and Caldwell's formulations are reminiscent of the coarse contrast between adjustment and diffusion already contained in the older paradigm used by Carlsson. More recently, Bongaarts and Wat- kins (1996) review aggregate empirical evidence regarding the timing and pace of recent fertility declines. As Cleland and Wilson do, they too reach the conclusion that much of what we observe during the past twenty or thirty years is attributable to the transmission of information and ideas regarding fertility control. Their conceptualization of what is being trans- mitted and how it is transmitted is broader and perhaps more precise than Cleland and Wilson's because it includes both micro-level diffusion processes (at the level of local networks and peers) as well as macro-level diffusion (global and national networks). But their inferences are based on linear shifts analysis, a device that rests on the unverified assumption that the magnitude of unexplained variance accounted for by shifts is associated with mechanisms facilitating diffusion. This may be sugges- tive but it is not the kind of proof we require to verify the existence of diffusion processes.

Robust Theoretical Formulations

The paradigm that characterizes the third stage in the history of ap- plication of diffusion processes to the study of fertility rests on three different and somewhat independent developments. In all three cases, the most important contribution is the introduction of conceptual precision and ex ante identification of the mechanisms promoting (inhibiting) diffusion of new behaviors.

An Integrated Theory

In an attempt to grapple with the proper identification of the nature of diffusion processes and adjustment behaviors in fertility, Retherford (1985) formulates an integrated theory that contains many of the advances we singled out as necessary for a testable theory of diffusion. In particular, the author assumes a unique decision-making framework whereby behavioral adjustments (structural factors) and emulation of others' behaviors (diffusion) may occur in tandem, the latter being more likely in highly integrated communities where psychic costs of deviant behavior are minimized. An important limitation of Retherford's theory is that it does not contain much elaboration of mechanisms of social influence and only indirect reference to feedback mechanisms.

Coale's RWA Framework

In a much-cited statement, Coale formulated three preconditions for fertility decline, "ready, willing and able" (RWA). This statement can be the basis for an alternative integrated framework. First, fertility control must be within the field of conscious choice or, equivalently, the new behavior, B_o, must be a member of the set of feasible behaviors among which the individual can choose. A necessary condition for this readiness to exist is that there should be information flowing from members of an individual's network or from external sources of information. The idea of a new behavior must appear from somewhere. When we refer to ideational change, we seem to have in mind at least this dimension of the process. If so, and as indicated above, ideational change and diffusion should not be used as equivalent concepts because ideational changes may also depend on structural changes. The second and third conditions can be considered simultaneously because they are two parts of a model of rational decision making. Individuals must be willing to engage in the new behavior and they must be able to do so. Being willing refers to the ability to detect net benefits associated with the new behavior—what we referred to earlier as the linkage between net benefits and behavior. Being able simply refers to the accessibility to means to engage in the behavior and to the ability to bypass institutional constraints that impede the practice of the behavior.

Coale's RWA framework is agnostic regarding the nature of forces that may erode or develop support for each of the three preconditions. In particular, changes in any one of the three components could involve both ideational changes as well as nonideational changes, and all three of them could be affected by diffusion processes to different degrees.

Coale's integrated framework has been recently operationalized in a number of developing countries by Lesthaeghe and Vanderhoeft (this volume). They assess the status of these three conditions and estimate their influence on the onset and speed of observed fertility changes (Lesthaeghe and Vanderhoeft, this volume). The limitation of this kind of work is that, in order to test diffusion models, one needs to estimate the effects of social influences (and feedbacks) on the level and patterns of each of the three components. Only then could one assess the overall contribution of diffusion to observed fertility changes, and to estimate the relative weight of the influence of the diffusion mechanisms across the conditions contained in the RWA set.

Social Learning, Feedbacks, and Institutional Constraints

Finally, recent developments in model formulation and in empirical analyses have led to important improvements on two fronts. The first consists of defining explicitly an individual-based decision-making process that acknowledges the operation of social influences, and then formulating a model of such a process whose parameters are estimable from available data. Once parameters are estimated, hypothesis testing is carried out to determine if the estimates are what we would expect if social influences were indeed part and parcel of the decision-making process. The bulk of this work has been carried by a few researchers but mainly by Casterline, Montgomery, and Rosero-Bixby in various publications (Rosero-Bixby, 1991; Casterline et al., 1987; Rosero-Bixby and Casterline, 1993; Montgomery and Casterline, 1993, 1996; Montgomery and Chung, 1994). Although this work utilizes different types of models, some more data demanding than others, it derives from a unified framework (see earlier sections) that makes it comparable to other attempts to tease out social influences from observed behaviors either in organizational contexts (Erbring and Young, 1979; Marsden and Friedkin, 1993) or in social movements (Liao, 1994).

One of the shortcomings of these models is that they do not specify the network dynamics in detail, although they allow simplified representation of what social influences are. In a second line of improvements, researchers focus much more rigorously on the actual configuration of networks in which adopters and nonadopters may participate. In particular, the models are formulated to understand the dynamic interplay between individual decision making and the aggregate properties of the system, notably the continuous reshuffling of network connections that take place as the diffusion process advances (Kohler, 1998; Durlauf and Walker, this volume).

SUMMARY AND CONCLUSIONS

The main task of this paper has been to derive explicit rules for testing the existence of diffusion processes and their mechanisms or, equivalently, to formulate conditions for the empirical identification of diffusion processes.

I begin by recognizing the opposition between structural and diffusion-based explanations and confirm that this contrast is pervasive in demography and sociology. Furthermore, I also verify that, in most cases, the contrast is ill posed, ill defined, and poorly resolved through empirical analyses. In particular, I suggest that the opposition between the two types of explanations tends to undermine and overlook the decision-making process that is at the root of every diffusion process.

Using previous discussions and elaborations on the subject, I introduce a preliminary, minimal definition that enables identification of key elements of a diffusion process. These are decision making, resistance and thresholds, social influence, rejection, and feedbacks. Armed with this minimal definition, I undertake the task of reviewing broad areas of application of diffusion models in sociology and demography in general, and identify several stages in the history of sociological applications. I discuss recent applications in collective action and organizational theory as examples of what would be near-to-ideal conditions for model formulation and testing of diffusion processes. This review leads me to the elaboration of a much refined definition of diffusion, one that highlights what is unique to a diffusion process, namely, the salience of social influence in decision making, and three mediating mechanisms through which social influence modifies individual behavior. This leads to the formulation of a golden standard or ideal model to uniquely represent and distinguish among various mechanisms of diffusion. Finally, I state fairly precise conditions for empirical identification of such processes.

The paper ends with a brief review of diffusion research in the area of fertility. This review reveals that only very recent applications and hypotheses verification meet the stricter conditions set forth in the previous section's discussion. Paradigms used in the past are simply too loose, too unspecific, and ultimately too far removed from the golden standard to be considered as anything more than useful suggestions. The most promising areas of research are those that rest on integrated formulations, where changes via diffusion and structural adjustments are viewed as results of individual decision-making processes that include individuals' social and economic characteristics and individuals' ties to significant others in a set of relevant social networks. We need refinements in the identification of how individuals choose and remain members of social networks, on the nature of feedback mechanisms, and on the existence of institutional constraints and their effects on individual choices.

The most important conclusion we draw from this review, and one that should guide future efforts in the area of fertility and other social behaviors, is that the sharp divide established between processes of structural adjustment and diffusion may be a good didactic tool and part and parcel of a respectable intellectual tradition, but it is seldom an accurate way of portraying the mechanisms that shape the behaviors they are intended to explain.

NOTES

1. An important idea that I will defend later is that one should not conflate the notions of cultural or ideational explanation with the notion of diffusion. They are simply not equivalent, and many confusions could be avoided if we kept them separate.

2. An interesting example of a case study of forerunners is Livi-Bacci's (1986) description of apparent practices of fertility control among elites and other selected social groups in Western Europe.

3. Potter (1998) addresses the problem explicitly, though devoting more attention to what he calls "pernicious aspects" of social interactions that end up imparting inertia in the adoption of contraceptive technology and locking populations into a restricted menu of contraceptive choices, and less attention to mechanisms of outright abandonment of an adopted practice. Sinding and Mason (1998) also addresses the problem of rejection and, finally, Kohler's new work (Kohler, 1997) provides an opportunity for rigorous formal treatment of it. This problem has been better formalized in the literature on collective violence (Myers, 1997).

4. See the paper by Durlauf and Walker (this volume) for a formal treatment of some aspects of the endogenous feedback mechanism.

5. The selection issues arising from devoting overwhelming attention to diffusion processes that more or less succeed in taking hold, while neglecting those where diffusion never takes off or dies out shortly after its onset, are presumably quite important but, to my knowledge, have not been studied seriously.

6. An important aspect of the weaknesses of these models to identify underlying processes is that researchers who employ them usually assess the fit between observed and expected outcomes by examination of cumulative occurrence (proportion of the population who has adopted, for example). It is well known that a good fit of a cumulative distribution can conceal complete failure to predict associated densities (frequencies of new adopters during a small time interval).

7. This third mechanism is associated with a number of interesting formal and substantive problems regarding the possibility of unstable equilibria and the relation between small changes at the individual level that may translate into large changes at the aggregate level (see Durlauf and Walker, this volume). As formulated here this mechanism includes what Arthur (1989) identifies as sources of increasing returns that emerge as an adoption process gets under way. Increasing returns can occur due to coordination externalities, advantages associated with learning, and advantages associated with increased information flows. These are all sources of positive feedback. The formulation I suggest here, however, leaves the door open for the possibility that feedback also can be negative.

8. See examples of the use of spatial proximity in the previous discussion of applications to collective action and organizations.

9. Needless to say, controlled experiments, though close to this ideal, are not close enough.

10. For a review of processes of network formation, see Doreian and Stokman (1997).

REFERENCES

Aldrich, H.E.
  1979   *Organizations and Environments.* Englewood Cliffs, NJ: Prentice-Hall.
Anderson, R.M., and R.M. May
  1992   *Infectious Diseases of Humans.* Oxford: Oxford University Press.
Anselin, L.
  1988   *Spatial Econometrics: Methods and Models.* Boston: Kluwer.
Arthur, B.W.
  1989   Competing technologies, increasing returns, and lock-in by historical events. *Economics Journal* 99:116–131.
Bailey, N.T.J.
  1975   *The Mathematical Theory of Infectious Diseases and Its Applications.* London: Charles Griffen.
Bandura, A.
  1986   *Social Foundations of Thought and Action.* Englewood Cliffs, NJ: Prentice-Hall.
Bartholomew, D.J.
  1982   *Stochastic Models for Social Processes.* New York: Wiley.
Bocquet-Appel, J.-P.
  1997   Diffusion Spatiale de la Contraception en Grande-Bretagne, a l'Origine de la Transition. July, Institut National d'Etudes Demographiques. Seminaire Demodynamiques.
Bongaarts, J., and S.C. Watkins
  1996   Social interactions and contemporary fertility transitions. *Population and Development Review* 22(4):639–682.
Brown, L.
  1981   *Innovation Diffusion: A New Perspective.* London: Methuen.
Burt, R.S.
  1987   Social contagion and innovation: Cohesion versus structural equivalence. *American Journal of Sociology* 92:1287–1335.
Caldwell, J.
  1982   *Theory of Fertility Decline.* New York: Academic Press.
Carlsson, G.
  1966   The decline of fertility: Innovation or adjustment process? *Population Studies* 20: 149–174.
Casterline, J.B., M.R. Montgomery, and R.L. Clark
  1987   Diffusion Models of Fertility Control: Are There New Insights? PSTC WP 87-06. July, Brown University.
Cavalli-Sforza, L.L., and M.W. Feldman
  1981   *Cultural Transmission and Evolution: A Quantitative Approach.* Princeton: Princeton University Press.
Cleland, J., and C. Wilson
  1987   Demand theories of the fertility transition: An iconoclastic view. *Population Studies* 41:5–30.
Coale, A.J.
  1973   *The Demographic Transition.* Liège, Belgium: Ordina.

Coale, A.J., and S.C. Watkins
   1986   *The Decline of Fertility in Europe.* Princeton: Princeton University Press.
Cohen, B., and M. Montgomery
   1998   Introduction. Pp. 1–38 in *From Death to Birth: Mortality Decline and Reproductive Change,* M. Montgomery and B. Cohen, eds. Committee on Population, Commission on Behavioral and Social Sciences and Education. Washington, DC: National Academy Press.
Coleman, J.S.
   1990   *Foundations of Social Theory.* Cambridge, MA: Harvard University Press.
Coleman, J.S., E. Katz, and H. Menzel
   1966   *Medical Innovation: A Diffusion Study.* New York: Bobbs Merrill.
Cressie, N.
   1991   *Statistics for Spatial Data.* New York: Wiley.
Davis, K.
   1963   The theory of change and response in modern demographic history. *Population Index* 29(4):345–366.
DiMaggio, P.J., and W.W. Powell
   1991   The iron cage revisited: Institutional isomorphism and collective rationality in organization fields. In *The New Institutionalism in Organizational Quantitative Analysis,* P.J. DiMaggio and W.W. Powell, eds. Chicago: University of Chicago Press.
Doreian, P., and F.N. Stokman, eds.
   1997   *Evolution of Social Networks.* Amsterdam: Gordon and Breach.
Erbring, L., and A.A. Young
   1979   Individuals and social structure: Contextual effects as endogenous feedback. *Sociological Methods and Research* 7(4):396–430.
Fligstein, N.
   1985   The spread of the multidivisional form among large firms, 1919–1979. *American Sociological Review* 50(June):377–391.
Galloway, P., E.A. Hammel, and R.D. Lee
   1994   Fertility decline in Prussia, 1875–1910: A pooled cross-section time series analysis. *Population Studies* 48(1):135–148.
Granovetter, M.
   1973   The strength of weak ties. *American Journal of Sociology* 78:1360–1380.
   1978   Threshold models of collective behavior. *American Journal of Sociology* 83:1420–1443.
Hagerstrand, T.
   1967   *Innovation Diffusion as a Spatial Process.* Chicago: University of Chicago Press.
Hamblin, R.L., R.B. Jacobsen, and J.L.L. Miller
   1973   *A Mathematical Theory of Social Change.* New York: Wiley.
Hannan, M.T., and J.H. Freeman
   1977   The population ecology of organizations. *American Journal of Sociology* 82:929–964.
Hechter, M.
   1975   *Internal Colonialism: The Celtic Fringe in British National Development, 1536–1966.* London: Routledge and Kegan Paul.
Hedström, P.
   1994   Contagious collectivities: On the spatial diffusion of Swedish trade unions 1890–1940. *American Journal of Sociology* 99(5):1157–1179.
Jenkins, C.J., and C.M. Eckert
   1986   Channeling black insurgency: Elite patronage and professional social movement organizations in the development of black movement. *American Sociological Review* 51:812–829.

Katz, E.
    1961   The social itinerary of technical change: Two studies on diffusion of innovation.
            In *Studies on Innovation and of Communication to the Public,* W. Schramm, ed.
            Stanford: Stanford University.
Katz, E., and P.F. Lazarsfeld
    1955   *Personal Influence: The Part Played by People in the Flow of Mass Communications.*
            New York: Free Press.
Knodel, J.
    1974   *The Decline of Fertility in Germany.* Princeton: Princeton University Press.
Knodel, J., and E. van de Walle
    1967   Breast feeding, fertility, and infant mortality. *Population Studies* 21(2):109–131.
Kohler, H.
    1997   Learning in Social Networks and Contraceptive Choice. *Demography* 34(3):369–
            383.
Kohler, H.-P.
    1998   Social Interactions and Fluctuations in Birth Rates. Unpublished manuscript. Uni-
            versity of California at Berkeley.
Laumann, E.O., P.V. Marsden, and J. Galaskiewicz
    1977   Community-elite influence structures: Extension of a network approach. *Ameri-
            can Journal of Sociology* 83:594–631.
LeBon, G.
    1897   *The Crowd.* London: Unwin.
Lesthaeghe, R.J.
    1977   *The Decline of Belgian Fertility, 1800–1970.* Princeton: Princeton University Press.
Liao, T.F.
    1994   A theoretical framework of collective action for the evaluation of family planning
            programs. *Population Research and Policy Review* 13:49–67.
Livi-Bacci, M.
    1971   *A Century of Portuguese Fertility.* Princeton: Princeton University Press.
    1986   Social-group forerunners of fertility control in Europe. In *The Decline of Fertility in
            Europe,* A. Coale and S. Watkins, eds. Princeton: Princeton University Press.
Mahajan, V., and R.A. Peterson
    1985   *Models for Innovation Diffusion.* Newbury Park, CA: Sage Publications.
March, J.G., and J.P. Olsen
    1976   *Ambiguity and Choice in Organizations.* Bergen, Norway: Universitetsforlaget.
Marsden, P.
    1998   Diffusion Through Social Networks. Unpublished paper presented at Workshop
            on Social Processes Underlying Fertility Change in Developing Countries, Na-
            tional Research Council, January 29–30, 1998, Washington, DC.
Marsden, P., and N. Friedkin
    1993   Network studies of social influence. *Sociological Methods and Research* 22(1):127–
            151.
Marwell, G., and P.E. Oliver
    1993   *The Critical Mass in Collective Action: A Micro-Social Theory.* Cambridge, Eng.: Cam-
            bridge University Press.
McAdam, D.
    1982   *Political Process and the Development of Black Insurgency 1930–1970.* Chicago: Uni-
            versity of Chicago Press.
    1995   Initiator and spin-off movements: Diffusion processes in protest cycles. Pp. 217–
            239 in *Repertoires and Cycles of Collective Action,* M. Traugott, ed. Durham, NC:
            Duke University Press.

McAdam, D., and D. Rucht
    1993   The cross national diffusion of movement ideas. *American Academy of Political and Social Science* 528:56–74, July.
Montgomery, M.R., and J.B. Casterline
    1993   The diffusion of fertility control in Taiwan: Evidence from pooled cross-section, time-series models. *Population Studies* 47(3):457–479.
    1996   *Social Learning, Social Influence, and New Models of Fertility.* New York: The Population Council.
Montgomery, M.R., and W.S. Chung
    1994   Social networks and the diffusion of fertility control in Korea. In *Cultural and Temporal Variations in Values: Impact on Fertility Change,* Richard Leete, ed. Oxford, Eng.: Oxford University Press.
Morris, M.
    1993   Epidemiology and social networks: Modeling structured diffusion. *Sociological Methods and Research* 22:99–126.
Moscovici, S.
    1985   Social influence and conformity. *The Handbook of Social Psychology* 2:347–412.
Myers, D.J.
    1997   Diffusion Models for Riots and Other Collective Violence. Unpublished Ph.D. dissertation, University of Wisconsin.
Notestein, F.W.
    1945   Population—the long view. Pp. 36–57 in *Food for the World,* T.W. Schultz, ed. Chicago: University of Chicago Press.
Obershall, A.
    1989   The 1960s sit-ins: Protest diffusion and movement takeoff. *Research in Social Movements, Conflict and Change* 11:31–33.
Okun, B.S.
    1994   Evaluating methods for detecting fertility control: Method and cohort parity analysis. *Population Studies* 48:193–222.
Olson, M.
    1965   *The Logic of Collective Action.* Cambridge, MA: Harvard University Press.
Olzak, S.
    1992   *The Dynamics of Ethnic Competition and Conflict.* Palo Alto: Stanford University Press.
Palloni, A., and H. Rafalimanana
    1997   *The Effects of Infant Mortality on Fertility Revisited: Some New Evidence.* Center for Demography and Ecology Working Paper No. 96-27. University of Wisconsin-Madison.
Pitcher, B.L., R.L. Hamblin, and J.L.L. Miller
    1978   Diffusion of collective violence. *American Sociological Review* 43:23–35.
Piven, F.F., and R. Cloward
    1979   *Poor People's Movements: Why They Succeed, How They Fail.* New York: Vintage.
Potter, J., R.M. Assumcão, S.M. Cavenghi, and A.J. Caetano
    1998   The Spread of Television and Fertility Decline in Brazil: A spatial-temporal analysis: 1970–1991. Unpublished paper presented at Workshop on Social Processes Underlying Fertility Change in Developing Countries, National Research Council, January 29–30, 1998, Washington, DC.
Preston, S.H.
    1978   Introduction. In *The Effects of Infant and Child Mortality on Fertility,* S.H. Preston, ed. New York: Academic Press.

Retherford, R.D.
  1985   A theory of marital fertility. *Population Studies* 39:249–268.
Rogers, E.M.
  1962   *The Diffusion of Innovations.* 1st ed. New York: Free Press.
  1973   *The Diffusion of Innovations.* 2d ed. New York: Free Press.
  1983   *The Diffusion of Innovations.* New York: Free Press.
  1988   *The Diffusion of Innovations.* 3d ed. New York: Free Press.
  1995   *The Diffusion of Innovations.* 4th ed. New York: Free Press.
Rogers, E.M., and D.L. Kincaid
  1981   *Communication Networks: A New Paradigm for Research.* New York: Free Press.
Rosero-Bixby, L.
  1991   Interaction Diffusion and Fertility Transition in Costa Rica. Unpublished Ph.D.
          dissertation, School of Public Health, University of Michigan.
Rosero-Bixby, L., and J.B. Casterline
  1993   Modelling diffusion effects in fertility transition. *Population Studies* 47(1):147–167.
  1994   Interaction diffusion and fertility transition in Costa Rica. *Social Forces* 73(2):435–
          462.
Ryan, B., and N.C. Gross
  1943   The diffusion of hybrid seed corn in two Iowa communities. *Rural Sociology* 8:15–
          24.
Sinding, S., and K.O. Mason
  1998   Diffusion Theories and Population Policies. Unpublished paper presented at
          Workshop on Social Processes Underlying Fertility Change in Developing Coun-
          tries, National Research Council, January 29–30, 1998, Washington, DC.
Strang, D.
  1991   Adding social structure to diffusion models: An event history framework. *Socio-
          logical Methods and Research* 19:324–353.
Strang, D., and S. Soule
  1997   *Diffusion in Organizations and Social Movements: From Hybrid Corn to Poison Pills.*
          Technical Report 9702. Department of Sociology, University of Arizona.
Strang, D., and N.B. Tuma
  1993   Spatial and temporal heterogeneity in diffusion. *American Journal of Sociology*
          99:614–639.
Tarrow, S.
  1994   *Power in Movement.* Cambridge, Eng.: Cambridge University Press.
Tilly, C.
  1978   *From Mobilization to Revolution.* New York: McGraw-Hill.
Valente, T.W.
  1995   *Network Models of the Diffusion of Innovations.* Cresskill, NJ: Hampton Press.
van de Walle, F.
  1986   Infant mortality and the European demographic transition. Pp. 201–233 in *The
          Decline of Fertility in Europe,* A. J. Coale and S.C. Watkins, eds. Princeton: Princeton
          University Press.

4

Social Interactions and Fertility Transitions

STEVEN N. DURLAUF AND JAMES R. WALKER

INTRODUCTION

No topic in demography has received as much theoretical and empirical attention as the study of fertility transitions. Yet, as Mason (1997) notes in her presidential address to the Population Association of America (PAA), no single extant theory explains the historical record on transitions in a sufficiently comprehensive way so as to dominate its competitors. The empirical evidence is too varied and too rich to admit any of the current explanations: for every existing theory, there is a striking counterexample. For example, Coale (1986) documents one pattern exhibited by Western European countries whereas Bongaarts and Watkins (1996) show that Asia and Latin America follow quite a different one and the African countries yet another. Although conventional economic explanations play an important role in several of the primary theories, the historical experiences appear to be too disparate for fertility transitions to have been generated solely in this way. Cultural explanations thus appear to be a natural complement to the economic explanations. Yet, it also is true that "culture," unless defined so broadly as to render the explanation tautological, is insufficient to place the full range of transitions in a common framework.

Within demography, it seems fair to conclude that a consensus view of fertility transitions is slowly emerging through the combination of several traditional competing explanations—economic and cultural. This new

Steven N. Durlauf and James R. Walker are professors of economics at the University of Wisconsin, Madison.

literature finds a parallel within economic theory with the emergence of a theory of social interactions.[1] As described below, social interactions models apply neoclassical economic reasoning to environments that embody richer sociological structures than have been traditionally studied by economists. In this way, the core ideas of both economics and sociology are preserved as the role of individual incentives emphasized by economists is integrated with the social norms stressed by sociologists.

This paper is designed to introduce demographers to the social interactions approach in economics. We do this through the development of an analytical framework that shows how the rational-choice approach of neoclassical economics can be combined with social factors. We present models that are sufficiently rich (or at least complicated) to provide some qualitative insights into fertility transitions. We leave the actual task of formally implementing these models empirically to future research. Our goal in this paper is to communicate the basic ideas of social interactions models in a way that demographers can use in subsequent research.

The models we describe are complementary to that strand of the demography literature based on contextual effects in fertility. For example, Entwisle et al. (1986), and Entwisle and Mason (1985) provide analyses of how socioeconomic development levels within a society affect individual fertility decisions; Entwisle et al. (1989) provide complementary evidence on village-level influences. Further, Pollak and Watkins (1993) provide an interpretation of the role of interactions in demography, which is complementary to ours. We hope to add to this literature by emphasizing how these approaches can be embedded in a structural model of choices that embodies both contextual effects as well as feedbacks from the actual decisions of group members. This structural modeling approach will in turn have implications for statistical analysis.[2]

The second section of this paper provides a survey of the empirical evidence on fertility transitions that the social interactions model can help to explain. The third section provides some basic ideas concerning interactions. The fourth section develops a discrete-choice approach to interactions (due to Brock and Durlauf, 1999a, b), which seems useful for demographic analysis. The fifth section comments on the statistical obstacles that challenge the empirical implementation of these models. The sixth and final section concludes with implications for demographic research.

EMPIRICAL EVIDENCE ON FERTILITY TRANSITIONS

There are several recent summaries of the empirical descriptions of fertility transitions and we draw liberally on these.[3] We focus our discussion on a set of empirical observations, which suggest social interactions may be important.

With so many descriptions available in the literature, it is difficult to concisely characterize the fertility transitions experienced by countries during the last couple of hundred years. Nevertheless, we use two tables modified from Schultz (1997) to focus our discussion. Table 4-1 reports birth and death rates and natural rates of growth for high- and low-income countries for a 250-year period from 1750 to 2000. Definitions of high- and low-income countries are based on income levels in the second half of the twentieth century.

Europe experienced its demographic transition during the 60-year period from 1870 to 1930, with considerable variation in the timing of the transition for individual countries. All countries in Europe (including Russia and the other countries of the former Soviet Union) completed the transition by 1960.[4] European countries comprise an important share of the high-income countries of Table 4-1, and the influence of the European experience on the overall features of the table is in some respects evident. One such respect is the relative stability of the natural rate of population growth through the nineteenth century. By the end of the demographic transition in Europe (conventionally dated around 1960), the natural rate of population growth for high-income countries is only slightly higher than that reported a century earlier. Since 1960, the rate of natural population growth for high-income countries fell, and the medium variant forecast of the United Nations for 2000 suggests that it will fall further. Interestingly, the crude birth and death rates imply that the decline in the

TABLE 4-1 Birth, Death, and Natural Growth Rate By Income Group, 1750–2000

	High-Income Countries			Low-Income Countries		
	Birth	Death	Growth	Birth	Death	Growth
1750			6.5			4.0
1850			10.6			4.9
1900			9.9			6.7
1950	22.6	10.1	12.5	44.6	24.3	20.3
1960	20.1	9.0	11.1	41.9	18.3	23.6
1970	16.7	9.3	7.4	37.1	13.2	23.9
1980	15.2	9.6	5.6	31.7	10.6	21.1
1990	13.9	9.6	4.3	30.0	9.1	20.9
2000	13.1	9.7	3.4	25.3	7.8	17.5

NOTES: High-income countries include industrially advanced countries, such as Europe, North America, Asiatic USSR, Australia, New Zealand and Japan. Low-income countries include all other countries. Crude birth, death, and natural population growth rates in annual growth per 1,000 population in the 5-year period following the year reported from 1950 to 2000, for the 50-year period following the year reported in 1750, 1850, and 20-year period after 1900.
SOURCE: Schultz (1997:352–353). Reprinted with permission from Elsevier Science.

natural population growth rate for high-income countries stems from falling birth rates.

Consistent with the European transition, the population growth rate for the currently high-income countries increased in the initial stages of the demographic transition (around 1850) and then declined as a new equilibrium was reached. Admittedly, the highly time-aggregated nature of Table 4-1 and the baby boom following World War II make this difficult to see. The detailed analysis of the European Fertility Projects supports this claim. The common explanation for the surge in population is that mortality rates decline initially and then stimulate a decline in fertility rates. Table 4-1 does not, of course, report birth and death rates during the period of the demographic transition and so we rely on the extensive analysis of the European Fertility Project to support this conclusion.

The demographic rates of the low-income countries also are informative. Unsurprisingly, the rates of natural population increase for low- and high-income countries are low (about 1/2 percent) and close in magnitude (differing by only 2.5 per 1,000) at the onset of the Industrial Revolution (around 1750). Yet during the first half of the twentieth century, the natural rate of increase jumps by threefold for the low-income countries (from 6.7 to 20.3 per 1,000). Although Table 4-1 does not give a decomposition of the demographic components, it indicates that the huge increase in natural population growth rates for these countries stems from the reduction in mortality rates. These gains in life expectancy continued through the second half of the 1900s, so that by 1990 there is no difference in crude death rates between high- and low-income countries.[5] Notice, however, that while death rates fell by 67 percent, fertility rates only fell by 40 percent among low-income countries. If the currently developing countries had followed a demographic pattern even roughly consistent with the European demographic transition, birth rates among low-income countries would have fallen much more rapidly and be much lower than are actually observed. So, even the highly aggregated statistics of Table 4-1 illustrate the diversity of fertility transitions.

Grouping all low- and high-income countries together masks important differences among these countries. Table 4-2 reports (age-adjusted) period measures of fertility, mortality, and life expectancy as well as rates of change of these measures during 1950–2000. We separately report rates for various regions to highlight differences among developing countries.

Notice that all countries experienced large relative improvements in infant mortality rates—even Africa more than halved its rate of infant mortality, although the projected absolute level for 2000 exceeds that of the higher income countries in 1950. Gains in life expectancy mirror the improvements in infant mortality rates. The smallest relative gain occurred among the higher income countries (16 percent) while the lower

TABLE 4-2 Period Rates 1950–2000 by Region

	1950	2000	Percent Change
Higher Income			
TFR	2.84	1.91	–32.7
Infant Morality Rate	56.0	9.0	–83.9
Life Expectation	66.0	76.6	16.1
Lower Income			
TFR	6.19	3.20	–48.3
Infant Mortality Rate	180.0	57.0	–68.3
Life Expectation	42.2	66.5	57.6
Latin America			
TFR	5.87	2.81	–52.1
Infant Mortality Rate	126.0	37.0	–73.0
Life Expectation	51.9	70.4	35.6
South East and East Asia			
TFR	5.78	2.33	–59.7
Infant Mortality Rate	175.0	24.0	–86.2
Life Expectation	44.1	72.1	63.5
South and West Asia			
TFR	6.17	3.61	–41.5
Infant Mortality Rate	190.0	68.0	–64.2
Life Expectation	39.6	64.4	62.6
Africa			
TFR	6.65	5.31	–20.2
Infant Mortality Rate	188.0	77.0	–59.0
Life Expectation	37.7	58.1	54.1

NOTES: Rates refer to the 5-year period following the year reported. South East and East Asia extends from Myanmar to Mongolia excluding Japan and Asiatic USSR. Southern and Western Asia extends from Bangladesh to Turkey.
SOURCE: Schultz (1997:355). Reprinted with permission from Elsevier Science.

income countries as a group increased life expectancy by 58 percent. These relative increases translate into quite different absolute gains, from 10 years for the higher income countries to 20 and 25 years for the lower income countries. There is, however, only a weak relationship between reductions in infant mortality and reduced fertility. By this measure, Africa looks more like the high-income countries than other low-income countries. That is, in Africa fertility rates fell only 20 percent, about one-third the decline of infant mortality rates, while in the other regions the ratio of percent change of fertility rates to percent change in the infant mortality rate is closer to 2/3 to 3/4. Thus, as we know from other studies, the fertility transition in African countries is distinct.

Yet, it is still the case that fertility and infant mortality rates are linked. The relationship, as Mason (1997) notes, is that declines in infant mortality are necessary but not sufficient for fertility transitions. Indeed, the conceptual link between the two is at the very core of some theories of fertility transitions. To Notestein and other practitioners of classical demographic transition theory, modernization (development in modern parlance) and modern technology first decreased infant mortality rates, which as families realized that survivorship had improved, were translated into lower fertility rates. The direct causal link between mortality and fertility rates is based on the relative costs and benefits of children. Families are seen as caring about the surviving number of children. With lower infant mortality, fewer births are necessary to obtain the desired stock of surviving children. Moreover, modernization also is assumed to have shifted the relative costs of children; the net benefit of children declines through the increased housing prices in urban areas and restrictions on child labor reduce children's productivity.

It is interesting to note that in her presidential address to the PAA, Mason lists six theories of fertility transitions, four of which are premised on the economic costs and benefits of children. Thus, although the exact mechanism characterizing the role of individual (household) incentives is often disputed, there is general agreement on the importance of these types of incentives. However, if households were responding solely to economic conditions, it is difficult to understand why fertility transitions have been initiated at such different levels of development. Similarly, it is difficult to see why later transitions have occurred at much lower development levels than observed in the case of Europe. Although we fully accept that economic conditions are important, they do not appear to be the only determinant of transitions.

Indeed, as Bongaarts and Watkins (1996) neatly summarize in their review of the literature and their findings from an analysis of 62 developing countries during the period from 1960 to 1990, there is a "highly significant" negative correlation between fertility (as measured by the total fertility rate) and development (as measured by the Human Development Index[6]). A central feature of this analysis is that there is no tight link between development and fertility:

> The main implication of these findings, is that, as in Europe, at the onset of a fertility decline the level of development as measured by conventional socioeconomic indicators is highly variable and has very limited power to predict a country's transition timing. . . . There is apparently no fixed threshold of development for entry into the transition. In this respect, the contemporary record is a continuation of the historical one. (1996:647)

The weakness of this link is one factor that motivates our belief that social interactions may be an important component of a successful theory of demographic transition.

Bongaarts and Watkins (1996:651) also find that the relationship be-tween fertility and development is both nonlinear and shifting over time, "[there] is a clear reduction over time in the level of development associ-ated with transition onset. Transitions are observed first among the most developed countries within each macro-region, and later transitions are initiated at much lower development levels."

Indeed, various nonlinearities are an important feature of the histori-cal record of Europe. A primary finding of the European Fertility Project was a dynamic threshold effect in fertility decline; "once marital fertility had fallen by at least 10 percent—the decline is not reversed until marital fertility had fallen very far, by 50 percent or more" (Coale, 1986:21). Threshold effects (while not impossible) are difficult to generate from independent households. In contrast, this kind of threshold effect, that is, a situation where a change in a variable above or below some level pro-duces a qualitative change in the properties of a system, is one which social interactions models commonly generate.

The simple tabulation of aggregate statistics considered so far misses the spatial dimension of fertility transitions. The beautiful maps at the back of the Coale and Watkins (1986) monograph document a number of interesting patterns of spatial diffusion of fertility control across modern Europe. Bongaarts and Watkins (1996) summarize the literature:

> Examination of the historical evidence in Europe shows that regions (geographically proximate provinces with a common language and ele-ments of a common culture) tend to experience fertility decline at more or less the same time, largely independently of the level of development . . . (1996:647)

The link with language and a common culture, noneconomic factors, again highlights the importance of noneconomic factors and particularly a role for social interactions. As our discussion will illustrate, social interactions models, through social multipliers and multiple equilibria, have the fea-ture that small differences in the initial conditions between two popula-tions can lead to very large differences between the populations' respec-tive behaviors. Our argument is that it is precisely these features that allow social interactions models to usefully complement monocausal ex-planations of fertility transition in a way to accommodate the heteroge-neous experiences observed historically.

BASIC IDEAS

Before describing various formal models of social interactions, it is useful to define the basic notions of social interactions that underlie the algebra. Social interactions arise when actions by one or more individuals, which are not mediated through the market, affect the propensity of decisions made by another. Similar definitions of social interactions or diffusion in the context of fertility behavior have appeared in Montgomery and Casterline (1993), Chung (1994), and Bongaarts and Watkins (1996) among others.[7] The distinction between market and nonmarket influences is important. Market influences operate only through the price system and affect the resources and opportunities available to households. Social exchanges that occur in markets have long been studied by economists. Indeed, until recently this was the only form of social interactions studied by neoclassical economists who adopted independent and atomistic households as its unit of analysis. Alternatively, sociologists have seen social groups as the basic unit of society and have an equally long history of considering a wider range of social interactions. Some of the mechanisms giving rise to social interactions considered by sociologists include sanctions, social learning, and conformity.

The key feature of the social interactions of interest is that they are *endogenous:* the choices made by one individual depend on actions taken by others. It is important to note that not all social effects are endogenous, though we wish to reserve the term social interactions for endogenous effects. Manski (1993) classifies three types of social effects. The first type is an *endogenous* social effect, which we have labeled as social interactions. The classic example of an endogenous effect is a pure contagion effect from epidemiology whereby the probability of infection increases with the proportion of the population infected (Feller, 1971). The second type of effect, *contextual,* occurs when an individual's behavior is affected by exogenous characteristics of the group of which he is a member. So, the distribution of fertility choices within a community can affect the future behavior of children growing up there. Alternatively, contextual effects appear if fertility rates vary with the socioeconomic composition of the reference group. Finally, *correlated* effects occur when "individuals in the same group tend to behave similarly because they face similar institutional environments or have similar individual characteristics." A correlated effect would be present if households within the same group face the same costs and benefits of childbearing and therefore have similar fertility profiles.

The following example illustrates some of the subtleties involved in distinguishing these different explanations of inter-group differences in behavior. Consider a family planning program that successfully reduces fertility for a given group. Whether there is a social interaction depends on the mechanism involved. If the program operated solely through the direct cost or benefits of children, (e.g., distributing free contraceptives) then according to Manski's scheme there is a correlated effect but not a social interaction. However, if a woman's use of the modern contraceptive devices depends on the prevalence of use by her neighbors or village members, then a social interaction exists. Several mechanisms could give rise to the social interaction. It could be that social learning occurs as women communicate their experiences to one another on the effectiveness of the new technology. As more women adopt the new technology, each succeeding woman faces less uncertainty on the technology thereby lowering the cost of adopting and increasing the adoption rate. Alternatively, greater use by community members signals its acceptance and the lowering of social sanctions against the new technology. These conjectures are of course not exhaustive as yet other mechanisms may occur.

The distinction between endogenous and exogenous forms of social effects is important. Why? The answer is embedded in the family planning example above. Social interactions generate social multipliers,[8] which exogenous social effects do not. By social multipliers, we refer to the idea that the total change in individual incentives in a population leads, through interactions, to an effect in excess to that generated directly by the change in incentives. Stated differently, social multipliers exist when the cumulative social effect of an individual's decision on a population's behavior is larger than simply the direct effect of her choice. Consider the family planning example above. In the presence of social interactions, a woman's decision to reduce her fertility will, through one of the mechanisms described above, increase the likelihood of reductions by others. The size of the spillover effect depends on the timing of the decision, decisions by individuals early in the process may have large social multipliers (e.g., the decision by leaders); in some cases, their actions can even generate a new equilibrium, in a sense we formalize below. To understand the dynamics of the system, we need to distinguish between endogenous and exogenous effects because their dynamic paths will be different.

The difference between endogenous and exogenous effects also is important for evaluating the effects of public policies. As may be obvious from the family planning example, a program that spawns social interactions will have very different consequences than does a program that changes only the exogenous determinants. The exact nature of the effect will depend on the nature of the social interaction, but the presence of social interactions dramatically changes the policy landscape.

Within demography, there has been criticism of the use of social diffusion models to explain fertility patterns (see the summary in Bongaarts and Watkins, 1996) on the grounds that the diffusion process is not simply a mechanical "carrier" as occurs in models of this type. However, this criticism does not apply to the social interactions approach. The behavior or factors giving rise to the social interaction is an integral part of the theory that makes it impossible to separate the diffusion process from its sources. To study the process is to study behavior. The old criticisms of social diffusion processes do not apply to the economic models of social interactions.

To fix the basic ideas associated with social interactions models, we discuss two simple examples. Although the examples are extremely stylized, they are illustrative of issues that arise in observed behavior. We select these examples to capture the features of different equilibrium outcomes that arise when considering population issues.

Social Interactions as a Coordination Problem

For our first example, we make use of a standard example from non-cooperative game theory.[9] Consider a 2 by 2 game in which each player chooses between the action *low* and *high,* which we denote by 1 and 2 respectively. In the payoff matrix describing outcomes, the pair $p_{i,j}$ denotes the payoffs to players 1 and 2 when 1 chooses i and 2 chooses j. We focus on a particular payoff structure, which can be represented by a matrix whose elements (i, j) correspond to the $p_{i, j}$s we have defined.

$$\begin{bmatrix} (1,1) & (0,0) \\ (0,0) & (2,2) \end{bmatrix} \tag{1}$$

To see how to read this matrix, consider the (1,2) element. This says that if player 1 chooses low and player 2 chooses high, each receives a payoff of zero. For concreteness, we can think of the possible actions as levels of effort in using contraception. This payoff structure reveals that if both players exert low contraceptive effort, then each receives a payoff (e.g., in "utils") of 1. We can interpret the payoff as meaning that birth rates remain high and per-capita income low. If both exert a high effort (e.g., birth rates decline, per-capita income increases and welfare increases), then both players receive a payoff of 2.

Notice that the choice pairs *high-high* and *low-low* are both Nash equilibria, which means that at this pair of choices, neither player has an incentive to deviate from his respective choice. Therefore, when players act noncooperatively, they can each choose an individually rational strategy which leads everyone off track. That is to say, once individuals axe making *low-low* choices, they will continue to do so, unless there is some coordinating mechanism (e.g., a government intervention) that can induce individuals to change their behavior.

At the same time, the collectively efficient set of choices (in this case both players choosing *high)* is also sustainable as a Nash equilibrium. Therefore, the absence of any mechanism to coordinate individual decisions does not preclude the achievement of a first-best outcome. This feature is different from a Prisoner's Dilemma game. In that game, the payoff matrix has a form such as

$$\begin{bmatrix} (1,1) & (3,0) \\ (0,3) & (2,2) \end{bmatrix}$$

(2)

Here, the choice of high by both agents is not a Nash equilibrium, since each person has an incentive to deviate and choose low given that the other agent chooses high.

Social Interactions as Complementarities

The basic ideas of our two-person game with multiple equilibria have been elaborated in an important paper by Cooper and John (1988). In this model, they consider how each of a group of I individuals chooses an effort level e, which is constrained to lie in the interval $[0, \bar{e}]$. Each of the individuals makes this choice so as to maximize a payoff function

$$u_i = \phi_i(e_1, \dots, e_I)$$

(3)

What is important about this function is that the individual's payoff depends not just on his own effort level, but on the effort levels of others. Cooper and John distinguish between two types of such dependence. First, there is the property of positive spillovers, which means that $\partial \phi_i/\partial e_j >$ 0 for $j \neq i$. The second is that of complementarities, which means that, $\partial^2 \phi_i/ \partial e_i \partial e_j > 0$. Notice that positive spillovers is an assumption about payoff levels whereas complementarities is an assumption about marginal payoffs. Intuitively, complementarities are relevant for individual behavior in a noncooperative environment as an individual's maximal payoff is implicitly characterized by a first-order condition (see equation 6).

Without loss of any important ideas, we assume that the payoff function for each individual is identical and that the payoff for each individual does not depend on the identities of the others, only the set of effort levels. This means that we can restrict ourselves to considering symmetric Nash equilibria, that is, equilibria where each person makes the same effort choice. Hence we can rewrite the payoff function for individual i as

$$\phi(e_i, \bar{e}_{-i})$$

(4)

where $\bar{e}_{-i}$ denotes the average choice of everyone other than i in the population.

The first-order condition for payoff maximization by individual i is that

$$\frac{\partial \phi(e_i, \bar{e}_{-i})}{\partial e_i} = 0$$

(5)

Given concavity, this will be sufficient as well. A symmetric Nash equilibrium will exist if there is an $e^* \in [0, \bar{e}\,]$ such that

$$\frac{\partial \phi(e^*,e^*)}{\partial e_i} = 0. \tag{6}$$

There are two features of this model of interest to us. First, the Nash equilibrium can be inefficient. To see this, we can ask what common effort level would be agreed upon if individuals could coordinate their decisions. A common effort level e^{**} will represent a symmetric cooperative equilibrium if

$$\frac{\partial \phi(e^{**},e^{**})}{\partial e_i} + \frac{\partial \phi(e^{**},e^{**})}{\partial \bar{e}_{-i}} = 0. \tag{7}$$

Since $\partial \phi(e^*,e^*)/\partial \bar{e}_{-i} > 0$ in the presence of positive spillovers, it must be the case that at the cooperative effort level, $\partial \phi(e^{**},e^{**})/\partial e_i$ must be negative. Contrasting this with the first-order condition for a Nash equilibrium and recalling that ϕ is concave with respect to e_i, we can conclude that $e^{**} > e^*$ and everyone is worse off at a noncooperative equilibrium. Thus, as one expects in a model with externalities, there is a gap between the private and social benefits of individual behavior.

Second, there is a relationship between complementarities and the number of Nash or noncooperative equilibria. To see this, notice that from the perspective of an individual, there is an optimal response function of the form $e_i = r(\bar{e}_{-i})$ that describes his optimal-effort level given the average-effort level of others. If one were to graph the function r in $(e_i, \bar{e}_{-i})$ space, then it is clear that the intersection of this function in $(\bar{e},e_i)$ space with the 45° line will define a Nash equilibrium. Equally clearly, multiple intersections, and multiple Nash equilibria, can only occur if the function is upward sloping somewhere.

We can compute the slope of this function as follows. Rewrite the noncooperative first-order condition (6) as

$$\frac{\partial \phi(r(\bar{e}_{-i}),\bar{e}_{-i})}{\partial e_i} = 0 \tag{8}$$

and differentiate with respect to $\bar{e}_{-i}$. This yields

$$\frac{\partial \phi^2(r(\bar{e}_{-i}),\bar{e}_{-i})}{\partial e_i^2} \cdot \frac{\partial r(\bar{e}_{-i})}{\partial \bar{e}_{-i}} + \frac{\partial \phi^2(r(\bar{e}_{-i}),\bar{e}_{-i})}{\partial e_i \partial \bar{e}_{-i}} = 0 \tag{9}$$

which implies that

$$\frac{\partial r(\bar{e}_{-i})}{\partial \bar{e}_{-i}} = -\frac{\dfrac{\partial \phi^2(r(\bar{e}_{-i}), \bar{e}_{-i})}{\partial e_i \partial \bar{e}_{-i}}}{\dfrac{\partial \phi^2(r(\bar{e}_{-i}), \bar{e}_{-i})}{\partial e_i^2}}$$

Because $\partial \phi^2(r(\bar{e}_{-i}), \bar{e}_{-i})/\partial e_i^2 < 0$ the right-hand side of this equation implies that the function $r(\cdot)$ can be upward sloping over some region of $\bar{e}_{-i}$ values if and only if the model exhibits strategic complementarities, as we have assumed the denominator is negative. This condition is of course necessary rather than sufficient for multiple equilibria to actually exist.

Both this and the two-player game example illustrate key ideas in the social interactions literature. The first idea is that there is a deep relationship between multiple equilibria and the condition that the optimal decision of one agent is increasing in the choice levels of others. The potential for multiple equilibria gives scope for social norms to combine with individual incentives to determine aggregate population behavior, in the sense that these norms can act to coordinate behavior on one of the possible equilibria. The second idea is that there may be some sort of social welfare ranking between equilibria. This is important in considering policies which are designed to alter which equilibria characterizes a population, as it facilitates resolving the difficult issue of adjudicating benefits and losses.

In the presence of multiple equilibria, which one is selected? Dasgupta (1993, 1995) argues that selection occurs through one of two basic sources, either through the expectations that individuals have of one another or through history (i.e., evolutionary selection). Under the expectations mechanism, each equilibrium is self-consistent in that the beliefs of each actor are validated by actual behavior. Perhaps it is not surprising that the empirical evidence on fertility control suggests that the *perception* of others' behavior is more important than the actual behavior of others (Chung, 1994).

DISCRETE CHOICE WITH SOCIAL INTERACTIONS

This section develops a model of choice, which captures the basic intuitions of the simpler models of the previous section, and simultaneously seems appropriate for considering demographic issues. In our analysis, we follow a framework for studying social interactions, which is developed in Brock and Durlauf (1999a). This particular version of social interactions models has the advantage that the equilibria are in a form that corresponds to the various logistic likelihood functions, which are standard in discrete choice analysis. In fact, when social interactions do not exist, the equilibria and the standard likelihood functions are identical. Therefore, the econometric formulation of these types of social interactions can draw on a substantial existing literature. In addition, Durlauf (1997) shows how many social interactions models can be placed in our discrete choice framework without any reduction of the economic logic driving their main features, so we believe this analysis can be generalized to have wide application in demography.

As we have noted, one of the most important features of social interactions models is their capacity to generate multiple steady states and this feature will reappear in our stochastic model. In this case, multiplicity occurs because the *probability* that one person makes a choice is an increasing function of whether members of his reference group make the same choice. Mathematically, this multiplicity occurs because the models are nonergodic, so that the conditional probability measures describing individual decisions conditional on their information sets do not generate a unique joint probability measure over all choices. One difficulty in identifying nonergodicity in a data set is that there may be types of behavior that are consistent with the decisions of agents (or the conditional probability measures describing the decisions), yet are never observed in the history of the process. It is for this reason that some types of nonergodicity are not identifiable. However, our estimation strategy allows us to identify those parameters of individual decisions that are consistent with multiple equilibria and thereby infer their presence or absence. Specifically, the use of individual-level data allows one to identify the sensitivity of individual choices to aggregate behavior, from which one can calculate the number of equilibria for the population.

We consider a population of I individuals, indexed by i who each make a binary choice w_i whose support is $\{-1,1\}$. In its most general form, this choice is the solution to maximizing a payoff function $V(\cdot,\cdot,\cdot,\cdot)$

$$\max_{\omega_i} V(w_i, Z_i, m_i^e, \varepsilon_i(\omega_i)). \tag{10}$$

In this payoff function, Z_i denotes a vector of individual specific characteristics which are known to the modeller. The variable m_i^e is agent i's expectation of the value of the average choice of the population. Thus we modify the interactions studied in the previous section in that social interactions in this model are mediated by the beliefs individuals have about one another's choices. This assumption seems intuitively appealing when groups are large, such as those defined by ethnicity, gender, or age, so that the total behavior of one's reference group is not directly observable. (It also is of great mathematical convenience.) Finally, $\varepsilon_i(\omega_i)$

denotes payoff shocks, which are observable to agent i but are unknown to the modeler. As is standard, we assume that $\varepsilon_i(1)$ and $\varepsilon_i(-1)$ are distinct shocks. We will further assume that these innovations are independent across individuals.

To render the model amenable to formal analysis, a number of assumptions are placed on the structure of the payoff function. First, the payoff function is assumed to possess the linear structure

$$V(\omega_i, Z_i, \varepsilon_i(\omega_i)) = u(\omega_i, Z_i) - \frac{J}{2}(\omega_i - m_i^e)^2 + \varepsilon_i(\omega_i). \tag{11}$$

This formulation allows us to refer to $u(\omega_i, Z_i)$ as deterministic private utility, $-\frac{J}{2}(\omega_i - m_i^e)^2$ as deterministic social utility and $\varepsilon_i(\omega_i)$ as random private utility. Notice that if $J = 0$, V reduces to a standard discrete choice payoff function (compare Anderson, dePalma, and Thisse, 1992). This feature means that our social interactions model nests the standard model of choice as a special case, and so the logic of the analysis in no way deviates from standard economic reasoning.

Second, we assume that the random private utility terms are extreme-value distributed, so that their difference has the standard logistic distribution.

$$\text{Prob}(\varepsilon_i(-1) - \varepsilon_i(1) \leq z) = \frac{1}{1 + \exp(-z)}. \tag{12}$$

To solve the equilibrium mean-choice level of the model, we proceed as follows. The probability of a particular choice, given an individual's observable characteristics and beliefs, equals the probability that his payoff given the choice exceeds the payoff given the other choice,

$$\text{Prob}(\omega_i \mid Z_i, m_i^e) =$$
$$\text{Prob}(V(\omega_i, Z_i, m_i^e, \varepsilon_i(\omega_i)) > V(-\omega_i, Z_i, m_i^e, \varepsilon_i(-\omega_i))). \tag{13}$$

Equations (13) and (12) together imply that

$$\text{Prob}(V(\omega_i, Z_i, m_i^e, \varepsilon(\omega_i)) > V(-\omega_i, Z_i, m_i^e, \varepsilon(-\omega_i))) =$$
$$\frac{\exp(h_i \omega_i + J\omega_i m_i^e)}{\exp(h_i \omega_i + J\omega_i m_i^e) + \exp(-h_i \omega_i - J\omega_i m_i^e)} \tag{14}$$

where $h_i = \frac{1}{2}(u(1, Z_i) - u(-1, Z_i))$. Observe that h_i measures the difference in private deterministic utility between the two choices and is the only aspect of that utility term that is relevant to the decision problems. Each choice is of course Bernoulli distributed, (14) gives the probability in terms of the relevant structural parameters of the model, the h_i's and J.

A rational expectations solution to the model corresponds to any m^* which solves

$$m^* = \int \tanh(h + Jm^*)dF_h,$$
(15)

where dF_h denotes the empirical probability measure of h's within the population.[10]

The uniqueness or multiplicity of equilibrium average choice levels will depend upon dF_h. In the special case where $h_i = h \forall i$, it is possible to explicitly characterize the relationship between the structural parameters of the model, since the expected choice level is any solution to

$$m^* = tanh(h + Jm^*).$$
(16)

Brock and Durlauf (1999b) verify the following theorem.

Proposition 1. (Brock and Durlauf, 1999b). Existence of multiple average-choice levels in equilibrium

i. If $J > 1$ and $h = 0$, there exist three roots to equation (16). One of these roots is positive, one root is zero, and one root is negative.

ii. If $J > 1$ and $h = 0$, there exists a threshold H (which depends on J), such that

a. for $|h| < H$, there exist three roots to equation (16), one of which has the same sign as h, and the others possessing opposite sign.

b. for $|h| > H$, there exists a unique root to equation (16) with the same sign as h.

Intuitively, this theorem says the following. If the strength of social interactions, as measured by J is below 1, these interactions will be too weak to generate multiple equilibria. If the strength is such that $J > 1$, then the presence or absence of multiplicity will depend on the private incentives for one choice or another as measured by h. If these private incentives are strong enough, as measured by the magnitude of h, they will swamp the interactions effect and produce one equilibria. Observe that this theorem provides an example of threshold effects in group behavior. Small changes in private incentives, h, can alter the qualitative features of group behavior in the sense of altering the number of equilibrium expected average choice levels. By implication, in a dynamic model where h evolves, it is possible to generate a highly nonlinear path for the expected average choice.

Issues in Empirical Implementation

Estimating models with social interactions poses new challenges, challenges that for the most part are only beginning to be understood. This section highlights a few of the problems and offers some observations. The basic theme of this section is that models with social interactions require a tight integration of theory and application; in turn, empirical specifications motivated by loose appeals to theory will be largely uninformative.

We start our discussion of empirical implementation of social interactions models by considering the conditions under which the binary choice model of the previous section is identified. Therefore, we assume that the model is a correct specification of the structural determinants of individual and group behavior and consider whether the model parameters can be recovered from behavioral data. To do this, we take our original Z_i vector and split it into an r-length vector of individual-specific observables X_i and an s-length vector of exogenously determined neighborhood observables $Y_{n(i)}$ associated with each individual in the sample. The subscript $n(i)$ maps individuals into groups, so two people in the same group n must have the same $Y_{n(i)}$. Relative to the Manski classification we described in Section 2, the $Y_{n(i)}$ variables are contextual effects. Finally, we assume the errors $\varepsilon_i(\omega_i)$ are independent of the regressors.

For identification, we consider the likelihood function implied by the model, that is,

$$L(\omega_I \mid X_i, Y_{n(i)}, m_{n(i)} \forall i) =$$

$$\prod_{\omega_i} \mathrm{Prob}(\omega_i = 1 \mid X_i, Y_{n(i)}, m_{n(i)})^{\frac{1+\omega_i}{2}} \cdot \mathrm{Prob}(\omega_i = -1 \mid X_i, Y_{n(i)}, m_{n(i)})^{\frac{1-\omega_i}{2}} \sim$$

$$\prod_{\omega_i} (\exp(c' X_i, d' Y_{n(i)} + J m_{n(i)})^{\frac{1+\omega_i}{2}} \tag{17}$$

$$\cdot \exp(-c' X_i, d' Y_{n(i)} + J m_{n(i)})^{\frac{1-\omega_i}{2}}).$$

We take the expectation $m_{n(i)}$ as observable without loss of generality; Brock and Durlauf (1999b) discuss ways to construct instruments for this variable.

Identification of the baseline model therefore is a specific case of the general (and well studied) question of the identifiability of logistic likelihood coefficients for the regressor set $(\underset{\sim}{X}_i, \underset{\sim}{Y}_{n(i)}, m_{n(i)})$. Following the treatment in Manski (1988:730), the necessary and sufficient condition for identification in a logit model such as this one is that the covariance matrix of these regressors is nonsingular. To discuss this, we need some additional notation. For any r length vector $\underset{\sim}{A}$ and s-length vector $\underset{\sim}{B}$, let $V(\underset{\sim}{A}, \underset{\sim}{B})$ denote the variance-covariance matrix of the random variables $\{a_1,\ldots,a_r, b_1,\ldots,b_s\}$. Finally, let $\rho(V(\underset{\sim}{A}, \underset{\sim}{B}))$ denote the rank of $V(\underset{\sim}{A}, \underset{\sim}{B})$. Thus, identification will require that $\rho(V(\underset{\sim}{X}_i, \underset{\sim}{Y}_{n(i)}, m_{n(i)})) \, r + s + 1$.

To see what is necessary to produce identification in the binary-choice model, notice that there is a functional relationship between the distribution of the $\underset{\sim}{X}_i$'s, $\underset{\sim}{Y}_{n(i)}$ and $m_{n(i)}$ for each neighborhood, the form of which is determined by the theoretical model. At first glance, one might think that this means the model is not identified. However, notice as well that this relationship is nonlinear, since by our theoretical model

$$m_{n(i)} = \int tanh(c' \underset{\sim}{X} + d' \underset{\sim}{Y}_{n(i)} + Jm_{n(i)}) dF_{\underset{\sim}{X}} \tag{18}$$

where $F_{\underset{\sim}{X}}$ is the within-neighborhood $n(i)$ distribution of $\underset{\sim}{X}_i$'s. Nonidentification would require special restrictions on the cross-neighborhood distribution of the $\underset{\sim}{X}_i$'s and $\underset{\sim}{Y}_{n(i)}$'s to reduce the dimensionality of $H(\underset{\sim}{X}_i, \underset{\sim}{Y}_{n(i)}, m_{n(i)})$ below $r + s + 1$. Stated differently, so long as $\underset{\sim}{X}_i$ and $\underset{\sim}{Y}_{n(i)}$ possess a joint variance covariance matrix of full rank, the addition of the regressor $m_{n(i)}$ cannot affect nonsingularity except for pathological cases. Therefore, we can state the following theorem.

Theorem. Identification in the binary-choice model with interactions (Brock and Durlauf, 1999a, b)

In the logistic binary-choice model with interactions, if $\rho(V(\underset{\sim}{X}_i, \underset{\sim}{Y}_{n(i)})) = r + s$, then the model's parameters are identified.

Taking this model as a baseline, one can isolate several key features that are essential in empirical work. First, nonlinearity plays a key role. Manski's (1993) nonidentification results for social interaction models were obtained in the context of a linear model; as shown by Brock and Durlauf (1999a,b), nonidentification in the context can be overcome through a certain exclusion restriction concerning the $\underset{\sim}{X}_i$ and $\underset{\sim}{Y}_{n(i)}$ variables, which is not necessary for the binary-choice case.

Second, it is necessary that with respect to the individual-level determinants of behavior, $\underset{\sim}{X}_i$, neighborhoods are not perfectly segregated. To see this, notice that a violation of the rank condition means that there is a combination of individual characteristics which is perfectly collinear with some linear combination of group characteristics, that is,

$$\sum_{l=1}^{r} \alpha_l x_{i,l} = \sum_{k=1}^{s} \gamma_k y_{n(i),k}. \qquad (19)$$

One can interpret the left-hand side of this equation as a composite individual characteristic and the right-hand side as a composite neighborhood characteristic. Therefore, a violation of the rank condition would require that there is a composite individual characteristic that perfectly predicts a composite neighborhood characteristic. This is equivalent to saying that with respect to that composite individual characteristic, there is perfect segregation of neighborhoods. Partial segregation will affect standard errors, but not identification per se.

Alternatively, the assumption that the errors $E_i(\omega_i)$'s are independent of the regressors is not critical per se, in the sense that one can relax it to something, such as independence of the median from the regressors in order for identification to hold (Manski, 1985; Horowitz, 1998).

Turning from identification to specification, what is critical in empirical analysis of interactions is that the errors are uncorrelated with the regressors. A violation of this condition is a form of misspecification. This will only be plausible if one is confident that the individual and contextual regressor sets are rich enough to incorporate the full range of factors that determine individual behavior within the group.

At first glance, this would appear to be a standard problem with any statistical analysis, in that the omission of relevant variables will render estimates of a structural model inconsistent. However, it is particularly salient for interactions models when groups are endogenously formed. Because the factors that cause individuals to form a common group are plausibly correlated across the individuals and with the errors in the behavioral equation that describes what they will do once they are in the group. Although Brock and Durlauf (1999a) suggest ways of dealing with this problem, it is clear that empirical analysis of interactions will require careful specification of the determination of the sources of individual behavior as well as an understanding of the process of group formation to provide compelling empirical support for interactions. This in turn will, we believe, require attention to ethnographic and historical studies.

CONCLUSIONS

The "new economic demography" initiated by Gary Becker in 1960 focused on the choices of individual households. Much of our understanding of the determinants of the costs and benefits for childbearing and the tradeoffs that households face by having and raising children stem from this literature. It is a literature that focuses on individual decision making at the household level. Less is known about the aggregate consequences of these individual decisions. Indeed, in a real sense, until Boserup, economists had to look back to Malthus for a model of endogenous population and economic growth. Interest in the environment and an increasing recognition of the finiteness of the world's natural resources stimulated public debate on population growth. Spawned from this debate was an appreciation of the negative externalities generated by excessive population growth and the insight that understanding the determinants of individual decision making is not enough. As Paul Demeny stated in his 1986 presidential address to the PAA, "We must bear in mind that the workings of the invisible hand are not necessarily always for the better, not necessarily for improvement" (1986:477). In the presence of externalities, there can be substantial divergence between the individual's welfare and that of the society. To evaluate the consequences of population growth requires consideration of the whole not solely the individual.

The emerging literature on the economics of social interactions identifies other aggregate mechanisms that complement the negative externalities noted by Demeny. Unlike the literature on the population problem, the new models in economics concentrate on positive feedback mechanisms, including coordination failure, social learning, and social preferences. However, a commonality between these literatures is that both develop frameworks that generate multiple equilibria. The multiplicity of equilibria is central because it permits the same analytical framework to represent both the pre-and post-transition equilibria and thus provides a causal interpretation for a transition. An important implication of the new economic models on social interactions is that (in the presence of social interactions) small changes in individual behavior can have large changes on the observed equilibrium outcome. Behavior by interacting agents can reinforce one another that may serve to destabilize the system. Thresholds and rapid social change are common occurrences in these models as social processes may appear to "jump" from one equilibrium to another.

And yet, social interactions by themselves are not enough. A compelling causal interpretation requires some exogenous forcing variable or variables to generate change. Our perspective is that the economic conditions drive the process, which are then amplified by social interactions. Applied to fertility transitions, the insight of the social multiplier is that economic conditions need only change enough to get a few "leaders" to switch behavior. Then once in play, endogenous exchanges among agents (i.e., social interactions) ultimately drive the fertility transition. The context, characterized by the level and relative importance of economic and cultural factors, will vary from society to society (and across time) so there is no reason why a common level of economic development will initiate a fertility transition. Some cultures may possess strong proscriptions against fertility control or the economic benefit of children may be so large to mandate high levels of economic development to induce even a few individuals to change their behavior. The interplay between economic conditions and social interactions is important, if not obvious. In isolation of one another the empirical literature reveals that economic and cultural factors are unable to explain fertility transitions. However, when combined and employed in a structured way, economic determinants and social interactions offer a rich set of mechanisms by which to explain the process of fertility transitions. The daunting task for researchers is to harness the theoretical insights from these models and implement empirical representations that will help us understand sometimes elusive and always complex fertility behavior.

NOTES

1. Important precursors to this new literature include Schelling (1971) on the emergence of racial segregation and Föllmer (1974) and Pollak (1976) on interdependent preferences; Brock and Durlauf (1999b) provide an extensive survey of the recent research in this broad area.

2. As will become apparent, the statistical concerns that have arisen in the economics literature on interactions are quite different from those that have arisen in other social sciences. In particular, hierarchical linear models, which have become a standard approach to modeling interactions in sociology, education, and demography, have had no impact as far as we know on economics. Our guess is that this has occurred because of the interest economists have in structural modeling, which makes the random coefficient assumption, and is the hallmark of linear hierarchical models, relatively unnatural. See Bryk and Raudenbusch (1992) for an excellent discussion of the statistical issues that have arisen outside of economics.

3. For example, Coale (1986) (Introduction) and Watkins (1986) (Conclusion) summarize the findings of the European Fertility Project. Bongaarts and Watkins (1996) summarize the experience of currently developing countries. Schultz (1997) and Kohler (1997) take a longer view and attempt to synthesize the literature. Each summary also includes a particular interpretation of the processes generating the observed patterns. As Bongaarts and Watkins (1996) note, it is the interpretation of the observed patterns, not the facts that are in dispute.

4. As clearly described by Coale (1986), European societies moved from one locally stable (in time) equilibrium of moderate fertility and moderate mortality to another characterized by low fertility and low mortality. Pretransition fertility rates were maintained through changes in marriage rates and not primarily by changes in marital fertility per se.

5. Indeed, the rates reported in Table 4-1 suggest that death rates are forecasted to be higher among high-income than low-income countries. This may reflect substantive differences in the mortality experiences between high- and low-income countries. More likely, the discrepancy reflects differences in the age composition of the two populations—the percentage of the aged in the populations of high-income countries is higher than that of other countries.

6. The Human Development Index was proposed by UNDP (1990). The index is a linear combination of life expectancy, literacy, and real per capita Gross Domestic Product.

7. Montgomery and Casterline (1993:458) state, "As regards fertility control, we define the essence of diffusion by the following: Diffusion exists when the adoption of innovative ideas (and corresponding behavior) by some individuals influences the likelihood of adoption by others." Chung (1994:6) states, "Diffusion exists when the reproductive behavior of one individual or the information available to that individual has an influence on the reproductive behavior of another, by a private means." Bongaarts and Watkins (1996:657) provide the broadest definition, "It is possible to distinguish analytically at least three aspects of social interaction that are likely to be relevant for fertility change: the exchange of information and ideas, the joint evaluation of their meaning in a particular context, and social influence that constrains or encourages action."

8. The term social multipliers is due to Cooper and John (1988). The multiplier concept is traditionally associated with Keynesian models of economic fluctuations. Keynes argued that a dollar allocated to investment increases national income by more than a dollar as the original investment expenditure works its way through the economy.

9. We employ notions from noncooperative game theory because we envision these models providing insights into societies of many individuals in which binding agreements on behavior cannot be achieved due to the absence of any way to enforce them.

10. Recall that

$$tanh(x) = \frac{e^x - e^{-x}}{e^x + e^{-x}}.$$

REFERENCES

Anderson, S., A. de Palma, and J.F. Thisse
   1992   *Discrete Choice Theory of Product Differentiation.* Cambridge: MIT Press.

Bongaarts, J., and S. Watkins
   1996   Social interactions and contemporary fertility transitions. *Population and Development Review* 22:639–682.

Brock, W., and S. Durlauf
   1999a   Discrete Choice with Social Interactions. Unpublished internal document, University of Wisconsin at Madison.
   1999b   Interactions-based models. In *Handbook of Econometrics, Volume 5*, J. Heckman and E. Leamer, eds. Amsterdam: North-Holland.

Bryk, A., and S. Raudenbusch
   1992   *Hierarchical Linear Models.* Newbury Park: Sage Publications.

Chung, W.
   1994   *Effects of Social Leadership on the Diffusion of Fertility Control: An Analysis of Social Network Data.* Working Paper no. 94-03, University of North Carolina at Chapel Hill.

Coale, A.
   1986   The decline of fertility in Europe since the eighteenth century as a chapter in demographic history. In *The Decline of Fertility in Europe.* A. Coale and S. Watkins, eds. Princeton: Princeton University Press.

Coale, A., and S. Watkins, eds.
   1986   *The Decline of Fertility in Europe.* Princeton: Princeton University Press.

Cooper, R., and A. John
   1988   Coordinating coordination failures in Keynesian models. *Quarterly Journal of Economics* CIII:441–464.

Dasgupta, P.
   1993   *An Inquiry into Well-Being and Destitution.* Oxford: Clarendon Press.

1995   The population problem: Theory and evidence. *Journal of Economic Literature* 33: 1879–1902.

Demeny, P.
1986   Population and the invisible hand. *Demography* 23:473–487.

Durlauf, S.
1997   Statistical mechanics approaches to socioeconomic behavior. In *The Economy as an Evolving Complex System II*. W. B. Arthur, S. Durlauf, and D. Lane, eds. Menlo Park, CA: Addison-Wesley.

Entwisle, B., J. Casterline, and H. Sayed
1989   Villages as contexts for contraceptive behavior in rural Egypt. *American Sociological Review* 54:1019–1034.

Entwisle, B.J., and W. Mason
1985   Multilevel effects of socioeconomic development and family planning programs on children ever born. *American Journal of Sociology* 91:3, 616–649.

Entwisle, B.J., W. Mason, and A. Hermalin
1986   The multilevel dependence of contraceptive use on socioeconomic development and family planning program strength. *Demography* 23:2, 199–216.

Feller, W.
1971   *An Introduction to Probability Theory and Its Applications, Volume I*. New York: John Wiley.

Föllmer H.
1974   Random economies with many interacting agents. *Journal of Mathematical Economics* 1:51–62.

Horowitz, J.
1998   *Semiparametric Methods in Econometrics*. New York: Springer-Verlag.

Kohler, H.P.
1997   Fertility and Social Interaction: An Economic Approach. Unpublished P.h.D dissertation, University of California at Berkeley.

Manski, C.
1988   Identification of binary response models. *Journal of the American Statistical Association* 83:729–738.
1993   Identification of endogenous social effects: The reflection problem. *Review of Economic Studies* 60:531–542.

Mason, K.
1997   Explaining fertility transitions. *Demography* 34:443–454.

Montgomery, M., and J. Casterline
1993   The diffusion of fertility control in Taiwan: Evidence from pooled cross-section time-series models. *Population Studies* 47:457–479.

Pollak, R.
1976   Interdependent preferences. *American Economic Review* 66:309–320.

Pollak, R., and S. Watkins
1993   Cultural and economic approaches to fertility: Proper marriage or *Mésalliance? Population and Development Review* 19:3, 467–496.

Schelling, T.
1971   Dynamic models of segregation. *Journal of Mathematical Sociology* 1:143–186.

Schultz, T.P.
1997   Demand for children in low-income countries. In *Handbook of Population Economics*, Volume 1A, M. Rosenzweig and O. Stark, eds. New York: North-Holland.

United Nations Development Programme (UNDP)
1990   *Human Development Report*. New York: Oxford University Press.

Watkins, S.
1986   Conclusions. In *The Decline of Fertility in Europe*, A. Coale and S. Watkins, eds. Princeton: Princeton University Press.

5

Social Processes and Fertility Change: Anthropological Perspectives

ANTHONY T. CARTER

At the core of recent studies of social processes and fertility change is the proposition that fertility declines are the result, in whole or in part, of the diffusion of new knowledge and ideas "from one locale, social group, or individual to another" (Retherford and Palmore, 1983:296; see also Cleland and Wilson, 1987, Rosero-Bixby and Casterline, 1993; Montgomery and Casterline, 1993). From the perspective of contemporary anthropology, this work has several salient features. Diffusion is thought to be at work in producing a fertility decline when two criteria are met. First, knowledge of parity-dependent birth control and ideas sanctioning its use must, in fact, be new. Second, their spread in space and time must match diagnostic patterns; "birth control and resulting marital fertility decline" spread to all parts of "culturally homogeneous populations" very rapidly (Cleland and Wilson, 1987:24), "date is a better predictor of the onset of decline than socio-economic indicators" (van de Kaa, 1996:421). Implicit in such theories is the assumption that ideas and items of knowledge remain unchanged as they spread from one population to another and from one person to another within a population. Diffusion, therefore, tends to move a population from one homogeneous state to another.

Accounts of fertility change emphasizing the role of social processes have been constructed against a background of microeconomic models of fertility determinants (e.g., Easterlin, 1978, 1983). Cleland and Wilson

---

Anthony Carter is professor of anthropology at the University of Rochester.

138

(1987) see theories of diffusion and of economic demand as mutually exclusive, while Montgomery and Casterline (1996) see them as empirically indistinguishable and mutually reinforcing, but the two approaches always are opposed conceptually.[1] Microeconomic theories attend to the choices of representative individuals or couples abstracted from their social settings. Diffusion theories attend to communities in which people interact. Observing, discussing, criticizing, and evaluating, people pass information from one to another and from public sources to groups. Communication along interpersonal channels and through impersonal media provides information about "the existence of new behavioral options," narrows "the range of uncertainty regarding the consequences of new choices," and "reduce[s] the costs of innovation" by modifying social norms (Montgomery and Chung, 1999:181). Learning is social as well as individual.

Attention to the role of social processes in fertility change has led to renewed interest in community-level effects.[2] In microeconomic accounts of fertility change, structural characteristics of communities such as the level of nonagricultural employment, literacy, and accessibility are conceived of as determining the costs and benefits of children and the costs of fertility regulation. In accounts of fertility change based on diffusion, social learning may produce a process of endogenous feedback that causes changes in fertility to outpace changes in socioeconomic determinants. Influenced by one another, the members of a community also may develop distinctive patterns of contraceptive use. The boundaries between communities, whether ethnic, linguistic, or cultural, are seen as impeding the flow of communication, thus setting communities on divergent paths of fertility change.

All of this points us toward a socially informed theory of fertility change, but it remains dependent on outdated concepts of culture. Paralleling Hammel's (1990:456) "agenda . . . for a culturally smart microeconomics,"[3] this paper sketches an approach to research on diffusion informed by contemporary developments in the theory of culture.[4] The first section of the paper briefly reviews the place of diffusion in three moments of twentieth-century anthropology: early studies of the history and geographical distribution of cultural traits, mid-century studies of the structure and function of sociocultural systems, and the more recent turn from structural functionalism to practice. The second section argues that key anthropological studies, largely in the classic structural functional mold, undercut or sharply qualify two key assumptions of theories of diffusion based on imitation or contagion: that knowledge and ideas concerning birth control are likely to be novel and that they remain unchanged as they spread from one culture to another. The third and fourth sections, based on contemporary developments in practice theory, outline an alternative view of the social processes through which diffusion takes place and suggest some elements of a program of ethnographic research.

DIFFUSION IN ANTHROPOLOGY: A BRIEF HISTORY

Contemporary sociocultural anthropologists are likely to respond to ideas about diffusion with considerable suspicion (e.g., Kreager, 1998). Nevertheless, there is considerable anthropological interest in theories that comprehend human agency as embedded in or spread over culture and social organization. The key to these diverse responses to research on social processes and fertility change is the history of anthropological theory.

Diffusion theories played important roles in several anthropological debates in the nineteenth and early twentieth centuries. For a clear and sympathetic account of this work, we may turn to the distinguished American anthropologist, Alfred Kroeber. As Levi-Strauss (1953:533) noted, Kroeber was a "highly structure-minded scholar" who nevertheless devoted "most of his time to distribution studies." In Kroeber's (1931:139) words

> [d]iffusion is the process, usually but not necessarily gradual, by which elements or systems of culture are spread; by which an invention or a new institution adopted in one place is adopted in neighboring areas and in some cases continues to be adopted in adjacent ones until it may be spread over the whole earth.

It was recognized that diffusion takes place from one individual to another, within as well as between cultures. However, the focus of anthropology was "cultures rather than . . . the persons carrying them, so that attention has been centered on the relations between cultures or between the several parts of one culture" (Kroeber, 1931:140). Kroeber observed that the "psychological basis" of all forms of cultural transmission, diffusion as well as tradition, is imitation.[5] Diffusion occurs when persons belonging to different populations and carrying different cultural units are brought into proximity by "migration and colonization, that is, ethnic movements; conquest; missionization; commerce; revolution; and gradual infiltration" (Kroeber, 1931: 140). Diffusion produces and may be recognized by patterns of distribution in time and space (Rouse, 1953:71).

In the later years of the nineteenth century and the first years of the twentieth, there were two principal schools of anthropological diffusionism. The German-Austrian school was polygenetic, conceiving of the history of human culture in terms of "seven or eight original" culture complexes (*Kulturkreise*) that originated at different times and places and subsequently spread over the whole world, mixing in different places in varying ways. The rather more colorful English school was monogenetic. What were termed "primitive cultures" were regarded as stagnant. The history of human culture prior to the invention of civilization by the Greeks was held to be a consequence of the fact

> at one time and place . . . namely in Egypt around 3000, B.C., an unusual constellation of events produced a cultural spurt leading to the rapid development of agriculture, metallurgy, political organization and kingship, priesthood, concern with the after life and mummification, writing and other cultural institutions. From this center of origination this great cultural complex was carried in whole or in part, with secondary embellishments and degenerations, to Mesopotamia and the Mediterranean world, to India, Oceania, Mexico and Peru and in fragmentary form even to remote peoples who remained otherwise primitive (Kroeber, 1931:141).

Elements of the German-Austrian school were introduced into American anthropology by its founding figure, the German immigrant Franz Boas, and his students. Recognizing that the partisans of the German-Austrian and British schools "very early took a long a priori leap" from a "modest empirical beginning" (Kroeber, 1931:142), American anthropologists eschewed historicist cultural archetypes and universal patterns in cultural history. Instead, they used careful historical accounts of the independent invention and diffusion of cultural elements as diagnostic devices to discern the ways in which the different components of a culture are connected.

Diffusionist arguments went out of fashion in anthropology between the two world wars. They lost their appeal when anthropology ceased to regard cultures as collections of distinct traits for which historical explanations were appropriate and began to conceive of cultures and societies as systems of mutually defining elements for which functionalist and structuralist explanations were appropriate.

Two arguments were decisive. One was Malinowski's argument from functionalism. On the one hand, Malinowski strenuously objected to the idea that inventions could ever be independent. Beyond calling attention to the fact that particular inventions are made repeatedly by different persons in the same culture and in different cultures, he insisted that they are what would now be called socially distributed achievements.

> Each invention is arrived at piece-meal, by infinitely many, infinitely small steps, a process in which it is impossible to assign a precise share to any one worker or still less to connect a definite object and a definite idea with a single contribution (Malinowski, 1927:29).

On the other hand, Malinowski argued that all cultures are independently driven by the demand to meet the functional requirements of human exis-

tence. Because the elements of each culture fit together to meet such requirements as the "biological need for propagation and the cultural need
for educating each generation," any custom or artifact borrowed by one
culture from another has to be "reinvented" to fit into—to function in—its
new setting (Malinowski, 1927:37, 42). The borrowed element thus becomes something new. The result is that diffusion as it was conventionally
defined

> never takes place; it is always a readaptation, a truly creative process, in
> which external influence is remoulded by inventive genius. . . . Civiliza-
> tion is fortunately not a disease—not always at least—and the immunity
> of most people to culture is notorious: *culture is not contagious!* (Mali-
> nowski, 1927:46).

The notion that a borrowed element became something different in a
new environment was driven home by structuralism. First, preeminently,
in the linguistics of Saussure (1986) and then in the anthropology of, for
example, Radcliffe-Brown (1922), structuralism insisted that the meaning
of an element of language or culture inhered not in its isolated essence but
rather in its relationships to other elements of the system of linguistic or
cultural signs in which it occurred. Together with attacks on "pseudo-
history" (e.g., Radcliffe-Brown, 1950:1–2), these arguments resulted in a
new emphasis on synchronic explanations. No longer were institutions
and customs to be explained in terms of their origins. Rather, as Fortes
(1953:25) put it in his inaugural lecture as William Wyse Professor of
Social Anthropology at Cambridge,

> Functional research investigates either the part played by institutions
> and customs in operating and maintaining the total structure of a soci-
> ety or of a type of society; or conversely, it seeks to analyse the action
> upon one set of institutions of the other parts of the social system.

In the past several decades, the mid-century structural-functionalist
consensus has broken up, and not a few anthropologists have turned to
one or another version of practice theory.[6] Practice theorists reject structural functionalism's sharp separation of culture and human agency, the
former conceived of as a set of rules or meanings and the latter as universal, abstract rationality. From the perspective of practice theory, culture
no longer exists outside of and prior to action but instead takes shape as it
enters into activity. Conversely, human agency is shaped by and spread
over its social contexts. As Hammel put it in his 1990 essay "A Theory of
Culture for Demography," culture is a "negotiated symbolic understanding" or an "evaluative conversation," a "constantly modified and elaborated system of moral symbols" produced and reproduced by "the evaluative behavior of actors." These evaluative behaviors or

symbolic expressions . . . become part of culture as guidance mechanism by entering into the social discourse. Actors respond to this discourse; their actions are guided by it, whether it is spoken in their presence, recalled from their socialization, or anticipated for their repute or their salvation.

Social action takes place in, is shaped by, and at the same times shapes "an intensely evaluative cloud of commentary" (Hammel, 1990:467). Nor is history secondary to synchronic analysis. The activities of human subjects are shaped by structured contexts that are the products of past human activity. At the same time, human activities, as structured products, become structured contexts that shape future activity. The formation of the populations/societies studied by demographers and anthropologists occurs "at the *intersection of global and local histories*. . . . local groups . . . [are seen] as the products of centuries of social, economic, political, and cultural processes, some indigenous, other originating at regional, national, and global levels" (Greenhalgh, 1990:90).[7] If structural functionalism decisively refuted theories of diffusion based on imitation or diffusion, these features of practice theory together point to a view of social processes in which a different form of diffusion is ubiquitous.

THE LIMITS OF DIFFUSION

Clearly, diffusionism in anthropology and in studies of fertility change are distinctly different beasts. Where diffusionism in anthropology was concerned with changes that take place over centuries, diffusionism in studies of fertility change is concerned with changes that take place over decades or even years. Where diffusionism in anthropology was concerned almost exclusively with the spread of cultural elements from one society to another, diffusionism in studies of fertility change gives at least equal attention to the spread of knowledge and ideas concerning contraception from one person to another within populations.[8] In its heyday, diffusionism in anthropology was embedded in arguments about the meaning of human cultural diversity, the psychic unity of mankind, and the mechanisms of human progress. Until the advent of structural functionalism, the principal alternatives were various theories of universal stages of cultural evolution. Drawing on studies of the diffusion of new technologies, diffusionism in demography is embedded in much more focused arguments concerning the causes of fertility transition. In these debates, it has a close affinity to theories of ideational change and an ambiguous relation to microeconomic theories of the demand for children (van de Kaa, 1996:420–422).

Nevertheless, the two diffusionisms share some core ideas. Both are in their origins theories of "social imitation"[9] modeled on contagion (Rosero-Bixby and Casterline, 1993:163–164; Montgomery and Chung,

1999:167). Both are historicogeographical as well. The operation of diffusion leaves behind, and can be studied through, characteristic patterns of distribution in time and space. It seems not unlikely, therefore, that "the limits of diffusionism" (Kreager, 1998) in demography are related to the limits of diffusionism in anthropology. These limits turn on arguments that birth control is not and cannot be new and that the meanings of birth control technologies change as they move from one culture to another.

On the Novelty of Birth Control

Cleland and Wilson offer the strongest claims for the novelty of contraception within marriage in pretransition societies. To begin with, they argue that "[t]he conscious exercise of birth control within marriage in its modern parity-specific form is probably absent in most traditional societies" (Cleland and Wilson, 1987:27). The evidence for this claim is diverse. In some cases, "natural fertility may be inferred with confidence from the age pattern of fertility." In other cases, surveys find "[v]ery low levels of knowledge of any method of contraception" (1987:13). That the practice of parity-specific birth control within marriage was genuinely absent is supported by the fact that the level of fertility is not adjusted to the economic value of children for their parents. The absence of birth control within marriage can therefore be regarded as a real absence rather than as a consequence of "a universally high demand for children" (1987:11).

Anthropologists have expressed serious reservations about the novelty of parity-specific birth control for some little time. These reservations rest not on scattered ethnographic observations, but rather on fundamental theoretical principles. Ethnographers do not deny that Western contraceptive devices are new. Nor do they deny that it would be useful to trace their spread in societies into which they are introduced.[10] However, like Cleland and Wilson, they recognize that parity-specific contraception can be achieved in the absence of modern contraceptives. And they argue that modern contraceptive technologies can be used for purposes other than the control of completed family size (see below). If family planning goals are separated from the means employed, two critical issues remain. One is the occurrence of parity-specific contraception. The other is the relation between family size goals and other family planning concerns.

In the conventional view of family formation (e.g., Easterlin, 1978, 1983; Bulatao et al., 1983), deliberate control of family size occurs in populations in which the supply of children exceeds the demand and the costs of fertility regulation are not prohibitively high. The supply of children is a group characteristic, the product of exogenous mortality and the biology of reproduction as modified by cultural norms. The gender of children usually is ignored. These propositions combine to support the preconception that the conscious control of fertility within marriage takes only one form, the control of family size through parity-dependent contraception (Bongaarts, 1978).

Only if conscious control of family formation is limited in this way to parity-specific contraception does it make sense to think of it as either present or absent (see Polgar, 1972). However, though the presumption that effective control of fertility requires modern contraceptive technologies has a degree of plausibility,[11] the claim that the supply of children is the product of "natural fertility" and exogenous mortality is clearly false. With it goes the presumption that fertility in pretransition populations is universally natural (see Carter, 1998:256ff).

The anthropologist Susan Scrimshaw (1978, 1983) argued in general terms that high infant mortality might be taken as a response to high fertility rather than the other way around. In effect, various forms of infanticide may be used to control family composition as well as family size ex post facto.[12]

More detailed analyses build on comparative studies of family systems and household management.[13] The historian Thomas Smith's (1977) work on farm families in Nakahara, an eighteenth-century Japanese village, was one of the first studies of this kind. Seen through the lens of the age pattern of marital fertility, eighteenth-century Japan appears to conform to the criteria for natural fertility (Smith, 1977:61–62; see also Hanley and Yamamura, 1977). However, analyses of the distribution of completed family size, the age at which couples stop child bearing, the gender of next surviving children in relation to the gender of previous children, and the length of particular birth intervals, all within the framework of the movement of persons and resources into and out of stem family households, demonstrate that parents in Nakahara actively attempted to control the composition and timing of formation as well as the size of their families. They did this in part through sex-selective infanticide. "[C]ouples had a marked tendency to have [that is, to permit to live and then to register] a next child of the sex underrepresented in their present [registered] family" (Smith, 1977:65).

A recent paper by the anthropologist G. William Skinner (1997) incisively synthesizes a broad range of work along these lines. As Skinner observes, "a given family system virtually specifies the relative desirability of differently configured offspring sets, thereby setting effective goals for family planning within the society" (1997:84). Again, there is considerable evidence of infanticide. The results of Skinner's own studies of three villages in Mino Province, Japan, from 1717 to 1868 mirror Smith's work in Nakahara. A different pattern of immediate or deferred infanticide is found in India. Much, though by no means all, of the subcontinent is characterized by virilocal joint family systems together with patrilineal kinship groups, both systems with a pronounced gender bias in favor of males. In 1961–1962, when the Indian crude birth rate was in the neighborhood of 41 or 42 (Cassen, 1978:116) and the Khanna study was observing the convex age-specific fertility curves characteristic of natural fertility (Wyon and Gordon, 1977:141), data from the National Sample Survey on the incidence of surviving offspring sets with different gender compositions indicate a marked bias in favor of male children (Skinner, 1997:69–72).

Skinner also details evidence of the influence of family gender composition goals on stopping behavior. In samples collected in Taiwan in 1973 and Korea in 1974, both countries with patrilineal joint family systems, parity-specific stopping ratios vary sharply with the sex composition of the surviving offspring set. In both populations, at parity four the percentage of couples who have no further children is lowest among couples who have only female children, higher for couples who have only male children, and highest for couples who have one or two daughters.[14]

Skinner does not address the distribution of different kinds of contraceptive practices. Indeed, he suggests that "[f]amily systems per se are silent concerning means; the overall objectives of family planning may be deduced from family system norms, but not the mechanisms for achieving them" (1997:66). Nevertheless, his concern with the gender biases inherent in different kinds of family systems provides a useful link to the volume edited by Newman (1985) on *Women's Medicine: A Cross-Cultural Study of Indigenous Fertility Regulation.* Skinner appears to assume that men and women share the family planning goals specified by the family system in which they participate. The gender bias that characterizes such systems thus would consist of nothing more than the fact that men are likely, in different ways, to benefit from the system more than women. Against this perspective, feminist scholarship on the household has suggested that gender biases in fact specify different goals and strategies for men and women (Dwyer and Bruce, 1988). Cutting through considerable ethnographic diversity, many of the studies collected in *Women's Medicine* describe societies with patriarchal family systems in which men do not wish their wives to control their fertility. Concerned with their own health and that of their children and with their own family strategies, women in such societies commonly see things rather differently. Constrained to manage their reproductive health covertly, they often turn to traditional substances and practices that are at once emmenagogues and abortifacients. These substances and practices allow a degree of fertility control that shelters in a space defined as menstrual regulation and regarded as the exclusive concern of women. Such fertility control may not show up in studies of the age pattern of fertility or in conventional surveys of knowledge of contraceptive methods, but it is likely to be quite widespread, nevertheless (see also van de walle and Renne, 2001).

On the Conservation of Meaning

The mid-twentieth-century structural-functionalist theories of socio-cultural systems that played a key role in the demise of diffusionism in anthropology do not imply that birth control technologies cannot spread across the boundaries of societies or social groups. But they do cast doubt on the idea that the meanings of birth control technologies are conserved as they move from one sociocultural system to another.

Looking at the use of Western contraceptives—especially birth control pills and Depo-Provera—"through the local Gambian cultural lens," the Bledsoe et al. (1994:86; 1998) study of contraceptive practices in a West African population is an unusually well-documented example of the ways in which the meanings of contraceptive technologies change as they are translated from one cultural setting to another. In general, contraceptive pills and Depo-Provera are not identical phenomena in the Western and Gambian contexts; "different attributes" of these technologies are salient in the two settings (Bledsoe et al., 1994:105).

Rural Gambia appears to be a classic natural fertility population with high fertility and long, highly regular birth intervals. Paradoxically, it also is a population in which the Gambian Ministry of Health, Save the Children (U.S.), the Gambian Family Planning Association (an affiliate of the International Planned Parenthood Federation), and a variety of private pharmacies and personal connections have managed to make Western contraceptives surprisingly widely understood and available. The 1990 Gambian contraceptive prevalence survey found "only 6 percent of all women and 7 percent of married women were using Western contraceptives," but these levels were "quite high in view of the area's negligible levels of female education" (Bledsoe et al., 1994:84–85).

The key observation of Bledsoe et al. is that rural Gambian women use Western contraceptives in ways that confound the expectations of the agencies that distribute them. Rather than using birth control pills and Depo-Provera to stop child bearing and reduce fertility, they employ them to manage birth intervals and enhance the ability to bear large numbers of children. Three elements of the Gambian cultural logic are crucial. First, men and women value large families. However, large families are not attained automatically if only nothing is done to prevent them. On the contrary, if they are to achieve their goals both men and women must nurture women's reproductive capacities in the face of poor nutrition, frequent illness, and reproductive mishaps. Second, Gambians continue to value long birth intervals, seeking to avoid a subsequent pregnancy until the preceding child is weaned. But, third, postpartum abstinence, the means through which this traditionally was achieved, is coming under increasing pressure, perhaps as the result of "increases in female schooling, declines in polygyny, women's growing needs to maintain a sexual link to a supportive male, or nonpolygynous men's growing insistence on resuming sexual relations earlier" (Bledsoe et al., 1994:88–90).

In this environment, Western contraceptives are used alongside traditional contraceptives in ways that were not anticipated by outside family planning agencies and Western social scientists. They are used in part to achieve the otherwise unreconcilable goals of resuming sexual relations while continuing to maintain long birth intervals. Thus the use of all forms of contraception, traditional as well as Western, rises steadily in the months following a delivery only to drop off sharply after the 29th month (Bledsoe et al., 1994:96). It also rises as women who have been fully breastfeeding their last-born child switch to partial breastfeeding but, again, drops off sharply when the last-born child is weaned (Bledsoe et al., 1994:99). Overall, "some 55 percent of the use of Western contraception . . . is found within 18 months following a birth" (Bledsoe et al., 1994:97). The use of Western contraception is especially concentrated among women who have experienced a reproductive mishap—a miscarriage or stillbirth—and, still intent on a larger family, feel that they must rest from child bearing in order to restore their reproductive capacities (Bledsoe et al., 1998).

Rural Gambian contraceptive users are not the opinion leaders of diffusion theories, "a discrete group whose background characteristics set them apart" as especially educated or modern. Instead, they comprise "the tip of a moving wave of numerous *temporary* users who were simply using contraceptives for small slices of time to space their births. . . . Most 'acceptors' rapidly and predictably became 'non-acceptors' (and vice versa) over the sequence of pregnancy, lactation and weaning" (Bledsoe et al., 1998:21). Within this wave, the use of Western contraceptives was particularly concentrated among older women, while "most users of 'traditional' contraceptives" were younger women who were more likely to have some schooling. The younger women are concerned that the Western contraceptives are such powerful substances that they will put their capacity to bear subsequent children at risk, while the older women are more likely to be concerned about the "dangers of high-parity pregnancy and childbearing" (Bledsoe et al., 1994:100–102).

THE REACH OF SOCIAL PROCESSES

The arguments of mid-century structural functionalism established to the satisfaction of most anthropologists that simple imitation diffusion is at best a severely limited social process. But developments in practice theory suggest that a different form of diffusion is a ubiquitous feature of social life. These developments also suggest new ways to conceive of the social processes through which diffusion is accomplished.

The Ubiquity of "Diffusion"

The connection between conceptions of culture informed by practice theory and the ubiquity of a more complex variety of diffusion can be made through the work of the Swedish sociocultural anthropologist Ulf Hannerz. Hannerz's work on "the global ecumene" has attracted the attention of scholars interested in the role of social processes in fertility change at the regional and global levels, but has been taken to reinforce the interest in spreading cultural uniformity. At the core of his work, however, is the very different idea that the normal state of culture is "the organization of diversity" rather than "the replication of homogeneity." Hannerz relates this characteristic of culture to what he calls "cultural flow." In common with many others, Hannerz (1992:3) defines culture as "the meanings which people create, and which create people, as members of society." It is located "in a set of public meaningful forms, which can most often be seen or heard, or are somewhat less frequently known through touch, smell, or taste, if not through some combination of senses" (1992:2-3). It is produced and reproduced through human activities that interpret previous meaningful forms and make available new ones. "The cultural flow thus consists of the externalizations of meaning which individuals produce through arrangements of overt forms, and the interpretations which individuals make of such displays—those of others as well as their own" (Hannerz, 1992:4).

The ubiquity of diffusion follows from the idea that culture exists in practices or processes of communication rather than as bodies of knowledge. On the one hand, communication does not require nor does it necessarily produce a uniformly shared language code. People who share a great deal of linguistic knowledge still may fail to understand one another if they disagree about what is happening in their interaction. Conversely, people who speak different languages may succeed in communicating if they are able to negotiate some degree of agreement concerning the nature of their engagement (see Hanks, 1996b:229). On the other hand, if culture exists in practices of communication rather than as bodies of knowledge, then "the collective cultural inventory of meanings and meaningful external forms ... is [differentially and impermanently] spread over a population and its social relationships" (Hannerz, 1992:7). People are differently exposed to the flow of culture because of their different location in everyday forms of life, states, markets, and social movements (Hannerz, 1992:41-61). They possess their own perspectives on that flow as the result of their differentiated role repertoires and life histories.

> As a social organization of meaning, culture can be seen as made up of ... a network of perspectives, with a continuous production of overt cultural forms between them. In this manner, the perspectivation of meaning is a powerful engine in creating a diversity of culture within the complex society. Call the network a polyphony, as the perspectives are at the same time voices; term it a conversation, if it appears fairly low-key and consensual; refer to it all as a debate, if you wish to emphasize contestation; or describe it as a cacophony, if you find mostly disorder. (Hannerz, 1992:68)

Cultural anthropology's emerging awareness of the polyphony of meanings and perspectives has strong parallels in contemporary linguistic anthropology where Hannerz's "public meaningful forms" are conceived of as signs. "A sign," in Peirce's formulation, "is something which stands to somebody for something in some respect or capacity." Communication takes place, culture flows, when a sign is produced and there is created in the mind(s) of the persons to whom they are addressed corresponding sign(s) that are the *"interpretant[s]* of the first sign" (Peirce, 1955:99). In the Saussurian view of language that underlies the ideas that cultures are homogeneous and that meaning is conserved as it is communicated from one person to another, a sign and its interpretant are taken to be identical. Following Peirce, however, linguistic anthropologists now recognize that signs and their interpretants can, and routinely do, differ from one another in an indefinitely large number of ways.

Social Learning

The linked concepts of social learning and social influence are key elements of work on diffusion and fertility change. A recent essay by Montgomery and Casterline (1996) outlines these concepts with particular care. In their view, "[s]ocial learning takes place interpersonally" when the information that a person takes into account "[i]n weighing alternatives and making decisions" comes from other individuals. Social learning takes place "impersonally" when some of the information taken into account by a given decision maker is formed "by communications emanating from impersonal sources, such as the mass media, markets, and other aggregate social structures." Social influence has to do with "the effects of interpersonal interactions . . . that are expressed in individuals' preferences as well as in their information sets." It includes "the pressure to be similar to peers" and to obey or defer to the wishes of those with authority or power (Montgomery and Casterline, 1996:153–157).

These notions separate diffusion theories in which individuals are seen as "embedded in various networks and other structures of social relationships" from economic theories in which "rational and autonomous individuals . . . act against a background of impersonal markets" (Montgomery and Casterline, 1996:152), but they remain tied to a conventional view of learning as intramental, "a process by which a learner internalizes knowledge, whether 'discovered,' 'transmitted from others,' or 'experienced in interaction' with others" (Lave and Wenger, 1991:47).

Contemporary anthropology offers a still more social conception of learning. In fact, there are hints of this in the pioneering study by Coleman et al. (1966) of the diffusion of a new drug among physicians in three small Midwestern cities. A key feature of this study is the authors' careful distinction between approaches that take individuals as the unit of analysis and those that focus on the community. In the former, relationships among individuals are treated as external influences on any particular individual's choices. Personal relationships with colleagues are thus equivalent to contacts with commercial representatives, the use of professional journals and commercial periodicals, participation in professional meetings, and visits to medical institutions in other cities. In analyses that focus on communities, the status of personal relationships among individuals is sharply altered, becoming itself the "target of outside stimuli." Defined as "a set of personal relationships" or, alternatively, as a "structure of social and professional relations," the community mediates the effects of outside stimuli on individuals. It is "a network of communication through which information, influence, and innovation flow" (Coleman et al., 1966:69–71).

Coleman et al. further argue that social processes involving community mediation are manifested in distinctive outcomes. One is the "snowball" effect in which the probability that an individual who has not yet done so will adopt the innovation during a given month increases over time. Community mediation also is manifested in the degree to which pairs of interacting persons employ similar practices at a given moment or adopt new practices simultaneously. Especially during the early phases of a diffusion process, when potential adopters are feeling their way with an unknown novel practice, pairs of individuals bound together by some variety of face-to-face relationship are likely to adopt new practices simultaneously (Coleman et al., 1966:114–120). In situations involving no novelty but in which individuals are faced with similar ambiguity, the consequences of community mediation are such that pairs of interacting individuals are likely to employ the same or very similar practices from the community's existing repetoire (Coleman et al., 1966:120–123).

Though it is not such an explicit part of their analysis, Coleman et al. also suggest that channels of influence or outside stimuli have different sorts of effects when they are viewed from the perspectives of individual or interaction diffusion. Viewed from both perspectives, channels of influence provide information concerning the existence and defining features of a novel practice and legitimate its adoption. Impersonal mass media and face-to-face contacts with commercial representatives are especially connected with information. Participation in local organizations and personal contacts with other potential adopters are sources of legitimation (Coleman et al., 1966:60). Viewed from the perspective of community mediation or interaction diffusion, the community-level personal channels of influence that mediate the other outside stimuli also provide "share[d] . . . definition[s] of the situation," in novel as well as other ambiguous circumstances (Coleman et al., 1966:123).

> Confronted with the need to make a decision in an ambiguous situation—in a situation that does not speak for itself—people turn to each other for cues as to the structure of the situation. When a new drug appears, doctors who are in close interaction with their colleagues will similarly interpret for one another the new stimulus that has presented itself, and will arrive at some shared way of looking at it. (1966:117–119)

This appears to be a very social view of learning indeed. Rather unexpectedly, it intersects with much more recent research in anthropology and psychology on cognition in everyday contexts and on teaching and learning in formal and informal settings.[15] In the terms of this research, learning is no longer confined to the heads of individuals. Nor does it become social merely because other individuals or organizations are the source of information or influence. On the contrary, learning is located in or distributed over relationships of coparticipation and the settings in which they occur. It is ineluctably social.

Channels of Communication

Social learning and social influence are accomplished through channels of communication among individuals and between individuals and impersonal sources. Though the diffusion literature contains many references to different, culturally specific kinds of communication—visits from drug company detail men, medical journals, hospital grand rounds, and consultations with other physicians in the American Midwest (Coleman et al., 1966); the famous Korean Mother's Clubs (Park et al., 1976); and women's voluntary associations (*tontines*) in Cameroon (Valente et al.,

1997)—in analysis these typically are reduced to standardized links that, as regards any two persons, are either present or absent. In the network models reviewed and elaborated on by Valente (1995), they are reduced to the lines that connect the points representing persons in a sociogram. In the simulation model of Rosero-Bixby and Casterline (1993), they are reduced to generic interpersonal contacts.

Moreover, where the channels of communication are reduced to generic interpersonal contacts, the content of communication tends to be treated as a set of propositions unambiguously and completing attached to sentences or other utterances independently of context. Against this, linguistic anthropologists and others have observed that the vast majority of utterances are elliptical and that few, if any, are unambiguous. Instead of being transparently attached to sentences, meaning is negotiated through processes of interaction inextricably bound up with their context.[16] It follows that the forms of communication are extraordinarily diverse, that the differences between consulting a senior physician in Midwestern city and participating in a meeting of a Cameroonian *tontine*, for example, are differences that make a difference.

Among the tools developed by linguistic anthropologists to understand how meaning is produced, Levinson's (1992) work on activity types and inference promises to be particularly useful for work on social processes and fertility change. Building on Wittgenstein's (1958) concept of "language games"—a "form of use of language against a background context of a form of life" (Kenny, 1973:166)

> take[s] the notion of an activity type to refer to a fuzzy category whose focal members are goal-defined, socially constituted, bounded, events with constraints on participants, setting, and so on, but above all on the kinds of allowable contributions. Paradigm examples would be teaching, a job interview, a jural interrogation, a football game, a task in a workshop, a dinner party, and so on.[17]—Levinson (1992:69)

In relation to fertility change, we might add the "little universities" and convivial Monday evening gatherings of the artisans who, with their wives, produced the first fertility transition in Sicily (Schneider and Schneider, 1996:222–225); family planning counseling (Candlin and Lucas, 1986; Carter, 2001a, 2001b; Kim et al., 1998; Maternowska, 2000); and doctor-patient consultations concerning contraception (Todd, 1983, 1984; Fisher and Todd, 1986).

The meaning of utterances is inextricably bound up with and contingent on such activity types. On the one hand, the indexical functions of linguistic signs, those that point to or invoke the "copresence of [their] object[s] in the same place and time as [they] occur" (Hanks, 1996b:46), anchor utterances in an ever-shifting play of activity types. "To speak is to take up a position in a social field in which all positions are moving and defined relative to one another" (Hanks, 1996b:201). On the other hand, "to each and every clearly demarcated activity there is a corresponding set of inferential schemata" (Levinson, 1992:72). Participants in communicative events draw on their culturally specific knowledge of these schemata to ascribe meaning to otherwise elliptical and ambiguous utterances.

It should be noted that from this point of view, gossip, which often is treated as a generic term for interpersonal communication, is a highly specific form of talk. Beyond the fact that it is framed or cued in particular ways, two features of gossip are relevant here. First, the parties to gossip—the person who produces it, the recipient, and the absent subject of gossip—must be acquainted with one another. Second, the information communicated in gossip is news for a particular social unit, some relatively small network of persons who are acquainted in some way (Bergmann, 1993:45–70). New information is unlikely to travel widely as a result of gossip.

Community and Social Structure

Sliding away from microeconomic accounts of fertility change along the continuum from *gesellschaft* to *gemeinschaft*, the new line of demographic research appears to assume that villages, provinces, nation-states, and regions are, in fact, more or less inclusive communities, collectivities of persons whose interactions are marked by communion and mutuality. It appears to assume, too, that as far as diffusion is concerned, the one critical characteristic of such communities is communication networks. Other aspects of social organization that might affect the flow of communication are given minimal attention. Anthropologists are prone to see rather less community and a great deal more variation in social structure.[18] The dimensions of this variation include systems of kinship and marriage, social stratification, and relationships to state institutions.

One way to bring this into perspective and to sketch its implications is to contrast recent research on Thailand with studies of other developing peasant societies. Consider, for example, the descriptions of village structure in the fascinating recent study by Entwisle et al. (1996) of contraceptive choice in 51 villages in Nang Rong district, some 250 kilometers northeast of Bangkok. Armed with an unusual and valuable household survey that provided contraceptive choice data for all the women in the sample villages, Entwisle et al. (1996:1) are able to show that "[t]ypically one method predominated among users within a village but villages varied greatly as to which method was most popular." To explain this remarkable finding, the investigators collected data on four groups of conventional village "structural characteristics": agriculture, migration patterns, social development, and accessibility. Interested in "social communit[ies], bound together by social interaction," they also asked focus groups about conversational networks.

The paper makes excellent use of limited resources, but it entirely lacks any picture of the internal organization of Thai villages and its consequences for village talk.[19] This is all the more remarkable from the perspective of anthropology, for anthropologists have long regarded the social structure of Thailand as distinctly unusual. As Potter (1976:149) observes, "Thai villages are extremely variable and no two are exactly alike. But they are recognizably Thai instead of Balinese or Indian or Chinese villages because they all are constructed from a limited number of structural principles."

Thai villages do, in fact, appear to be unusually communal. Potter describes Chiangmai village, a village in the far north of Thailand with 875 inhabitants in 1972, as

> a corporate group with a common identity; the temple committee and the school committee form quasi-governing boards which make decisions on behalf of the villagers as a whole and resolve disputes between community members. Village society includes cooperative groups and voluntary associations, ranging from the funeral society and neighborhood groups which send food to the temple, to labor exchange groups. Cooperation is the dominant ideology of village social relations. (1976:147)

One may doubt that one village is representative of the whole of Thai rural society and suspect that a dominant ideology is just that, but there are structural supports for the communal character of Thai villages. Though there is significant internal variation, much of rural Thailand has a "matrilineal stem family system." When sons marry they leave their natal families and, for a time, live with the families of their wives. Daughters are expected to marry in order of age. "Each daughter and her husband lives in her parents' house for a period which varies from a few months to several years," forming a stem family consisting of two conjugal units. When the next older daughter marries and is joined by her husband, her elder sister's family moves out of the parental household and establishes a new household nearby, preferably in the same compound, where they remain under the control of the wife's parents until they can acquire their own land. The youngest daughter and her husband are expected to reside permanently in her parents' household and succeed to their positions (Potter, 1976:121–123).

One of the consequences of this system is that Thai villages are populated by matrilineages of short genealogical depth (Potter, 1976:141–146). Thai women are thus placed in an unusual position. In the patrilineal joint family systems that predominate in South Asia and China, for example, women are isolated from natal kin in their marital villages and must struggle over a period of years to construct networks of peers with whom they may gossip and who will support them in conflicts.[20] Rural Thai women remain near their mothers and are surrounded by their sisters and other close female matrilineal kin.

The communal character of Thai villages also may be fostered by relatively moderate social stratification. The population of Chiangmai fell into five classes—landlords, rich peasants, middle peasants, poor peasants, and landless laborers—but, according to Potter (1976:58–59), landlords were landlords on "a Lilliputian stage" and were "not hated figures, as they are in many societies." A consequence of the family system is that many landless and poor peasant households are linked by ties of matrilateral kinship to landed households and will, when inheritance is complete, become better off themselves.

Again, this picture of relative equality contrasts sharply with the situation in South Asia. Most villages in India are divided into a number of castes with enormous differences in economic and ritual status. Class status and ritual are conceptually distinct, but the two not infrequently overlap and mutually reinforce each other. Indian landlords often are hated figures. Because castes generally are endogamous, the numerous social strata of a stereotypical Indian village are not bound together by ties of kinship. Instead, the members of a caste in any one village are linked by horizontal ties[21] of caste identity, affinity, and kinship with members of their caste in other villages. Fellow villagers do not entirely lack mutual interests, but in many respects Indian villages are the arenas in which caste differences are experienced and competition for ritual status is played out.[22]

The preceding paragraphs have been concerned with features of what Potter calls "the 'natural' village community." In Thailand, this is a "spatially defined rural village, which receives the allegiance of its members, furnishes an important part of their social identity, manages its own affairs and its common property, and has its own temple and school" (Potter, 1976:203). I have also rather downplayed variation among Thai villages. One of the things Thai village communities share with village communities in other state systems is a complicated relation with changing administrative villages. In Thailand, administrative villages consist of territories delimited by the state, each with a headman elected according to procedures laid down by the state. Because

> state bureaucrats drew uniform grids across the country-side, paying little attention to how the resulting administrative units corresponded to preexisting social, economic, and religious networks of the peasantry, about which the state functionaries knew little and cared less . . . administrative villages . . . often are different from nonadministrative commu-

nities, temple affiliations, market ties, and irrigation system membership. (Potter, 1976:215)

This is one of the factors that produces variation among villages.[23] Virtually all the possible geographical relationships between natural and administrative villages, temples, and schools are represented in the Thai countryside.[24] Some natural villages are divided among two or more administrative villages. Some administrative villages contain more than one natural village.

The very interesting findings reported by Entwisle et al. (1996) cannot be fully understood without considering these features of village social structure. Nor can they be generalized without qualification to other parts of Thailand, let alone other agrarian societies, unless it is assumed that none of this affects the shape of communication networks and the ways in which their members communicate. This is patently not the case. The overwhelming weight of ethnographic research decisively demonstrates that people playing particular kinds of social roles talk or do not talk to people playing other kinds of social roles in particular kinds of ways about particular kinds of things. In some cases, certain sorts of persons may communicate about some topics in front of certain other sorts of persons, but not to them or with them. As communication takes place, the exchange of knowledge or ideas is saturated with and qualified by information concerning the social identities of the participants.

RESEARCH STRATEGIES

All of this underlines the Caldwells' (Caldwell et al., 1988:263–273; Caldwell et al., 1987) call for ethnographic research in the study of population processes. Revolving around a commitment to being with the people one is studying while they are doing what one is studying, ethnographic research is designed to learn what activities mean from the actor's point of view and how they fit into their cultural and social context. At its best, it aspires to shift analysis and interpretation from "experience distant" concepts derived from the theories of observers to "experience near" concepts used "naturally and effortlessly" by informants to make sense of their experience (Geertz, 1983:57). In order to track the political economy of fertility, i.e., the ways in which it is embedded in and responds to "historically developed local, regional, national, and global processes" (Greenhalgh, 1995:13; see also Greenhalgh, 1990), including initiatives of the international population movement, efforts should be made to carry out coordinated ethnographic studies in "multiple sites of observation and participation that cross-cut dichotomies such as the 'local' and the 'global,' the 'lifeworld' and the 'system' " (Marcus, 1994).[25]

Ethnographic research on the diffusion or flow of knowledge involved in fertility change in some selected society might focus on local social structure or, as Valente (1995:1) puts it, "who communicates with whom." What is the community's stock of communicative activity types (see above)? How are these distributed over the network of groups and relationships around which the community is organized? In which kinds of communicative activity types is it appropriate to talk about which aspects of family formation, household management, sexuality, contraception, etc.? How is such talk managed? And what are its consequences?

Toward an Ethnography of Family Planning Counseling

The following reflections on the Kenya Provider and Client Information, Education and Communication Project, a study of family planning counseling in Kenya by Young-Mi Kim and others at the Johns Hopkins Center for Communications Programs (Kim et al., 1998; and Kim, Kols, and Mucheke, 1998), indicate some of the things that might be learned from ethnographic research on key communicative activity types thought to be involved in fertility change.

Much of the policy-related literature on family planning and reproductive health services and fertility change is prescriptive. In this literature, counseling is conceived of as "any face-to-face communication between providers and clients that helps clients make free and informed choices about family planning and to act on those choices" (Gallen, Lettenmaier, and Green, 1987:2). Service providers—"doctors, nurses, midwives, community-based health workers, and trained retailers selling contraceptives" as well as counselors—who use counseling skills appropriately are said to be able to adopt the "user" or "client perspective," "finding out about and respecting clients' values, attitudes, needs, and preferences." Clients as well as providers participate actively, "exchang[ing] information and discuss[ing] the client's feelings and attitudes about family planning and about specific contraceptive methods" (Gallen and Lettenmaier, 1987:3, 15; see also Bruce, 1987, 1990).

So defined, counseling is widely regarded as a key channel of communication through which the knowledge and recommendations of the international population movement are diffused to target populations and an essential component of effective family planning and reproductive health services in low- as well as high-fertility populations (Alwando-Edyegu and Marum, 1999; Baker, 1985; Bruce, 1987, 1990; Centers for Disease Control and Prevention, 1998; Gallen, Lettenmaier, and Green, 1987; Grimely et al., 1993; Kim, Kols, and Mucheke, 1998; Namerow et al., 1989; Nathanson, 1991:167–177; Nathanson and Becker, 1985; Strader and Beaman, 1992).

The Kenya Provider and Client Information, Education and Communication Project is arguably the best available study of family planning counseling. Unlike the studies of client-provider interactions in family planning agencies reviewed by Simmons and Elias (1994), the work of Kim and her colleagues is based on direct observation. The project staff observed, audiotaped, "translated . . . from the local language into English and made written transcript[s]" of 176 counseling sessions involving new and continuing "female family planning clients and clinic- and community-based providers at 25 service delivery sites in Kenya" in 1993 (Kim, Kols, and Mucheke, 1998:4, 6).

For an analysis of interaction between counselor and client, each turn taken by a participant in a transcribed interaction was coded using techniques borrowed from Roter and Hall's (1987) studies of medical interaction. A client's entire speech during a turn was coded as "asks question," for example, if it was judged to fit the description "asks provider for information." A provider's speech was coded as "counseling" if it fit the description "advises clients based on their personal situation" (Kim et al., 1998:11–12). For an analysis of informed choice and decision making, Kim and her colleagues identified stretches of transcribed interaction that matched behavioral elements of a four-step model of decision-making thought to incorporate the criteria of informed choice: "[d]iscuss client's reproductive goals," "[o]ffer sufficient information," "[e]xplore client's reasons for choice," "schedule future visits or further counseling," etc. (Kim, Kols, and Mucheke, 1998:5–6).

Nevertheless, like the several "mystery client" studies of family planning counseling (e.g., Huntington et al., 1990; Huntington and Schuler, 1993; León et al., 1994), Kim and her colleagues appear to assume that the claims of the prescriptive literature are both accurate and complete. They attempt to measure the degree to which counselors conform to the GATHER guidelines of Gallen, Lettenmaier, and Green (1987) or the fit between the behaviors of counselors and clients and an idealized model of informed choice, but describe no other features of the content or context of counseling sessions. And, even though it is based on direct observation, the linked decisions to base all of the analyses on English translations of the original Kenyan-language transcriptions and to use observers' categories to code the transcripts effectively erase the cultural content and social setting of the material. Indeed, one cannot be confident that an utterance in an English translation of a Kenyan counseling session that is coded as, say, a question without regard to what was said before and after it actually functioned as a question in the language of the original exchange.[26]

An ethnographic approach to the audiotapes collected by the Kenya Provider and Client Information, Education and Communication Project would attempt to provide a richer picture of the social processes involved in counseling sessions by retaining their cultural and social specificity. Rather than using exclusively "experience distant" analytical categories, it would attend to the "experience near," local "meanings that people create, and that create people, as members of society" (Geertz, 1983:57; Hannerz, 1992:2).

Family planning and reproductive health counseling sessions may be regarded as a culturally variable type of communicative activity (Levinson, 1992, see above) or, more generally, as a species of evaluative conversation (Hammel, 1990). They may be analyzed using the tools of linguistic anthropology. This focuses on the ways in which participants in counseling sessions use culturally specific language to represent their experience and concerns to their interlocutors and to themselves and the manner in which they "use such representations for constitutive social acts" (Duranti, 1997:3; see also Bakhtin and Medvedev, 1985; Bourdieu, 1991; Hanks, 1996b; Voloshinov, 1986). The ways in which the uses of language are anchored in and dependent on their contexts through the indexical character of linguistic signs, —their capacity, that is, to achieve meaning by invoking links between selected aspects of an ongoing activity and aspects of other activities (Duranti, 1997; Hanks, 1987, 1989, 2000a, 2000b)— is particularly important. Conversation analysis, with its focus on sequences of utterances in conversations and conversational activity and on positioned turns within sequences, offers additional insights.[27]

Studies in linguistic anthropology and conversation analysis of provider/client interactions in a variety of other settings and my own preliminary investigations of family planning counseling in the United States (Carter, 2001a, 2001b) suggest that the uses of language in family planning and reproductive health counseling sessions are very much more complicated than the analyses of the Kenya Provider and Client Information, Education and Communication Project would suggest. To begin, counseling is affected by a range of factors associated with setting. Provider-client interactions in office settings differ from those in the street or field (Rowe, 1999:89–105). Medical consultations in public hospitals differ from those in private clinics (Ainsworth-Vaughn, 1998:6). The shape of service encounters also is affected by status differences between providers and clients (e.g., Erickson and Shultz, 1982), by providers' ideas about what they are doing and how (Peräkylä, 1995), and by the use of writing along with spoken interaction (Frankel, 1989). An ethnographic treatment of the Kenya Project material would pay attention to ethnic and other differences between providers and clients and to the differences between clinic- and community-based encounters.

If one of the aims of counselors is to create "an interpersonal context that enables [a client] to profit from" new information (Frank and Frank,

1991:45),[28] then more is involved than "[e]xpressing positive feelings and praising clients," "[a]sking open-ended questions or asking for the client's opinion," and so on (Kim et al., 1998:11). In general, the interpersonal relationship of counseling, that is, the positioning and repositioning of the counselor and client in relation to each other, is accomplished through the performance, or socially situated and framed enactment, of cultural symbols and by indexical features of the spoken and written language of counseling. Performance and indexicality also anchor counseling to its contexts (Hanks, 1984, 1996a, 2000a, 2000b).

Turning to sequences of utterances in provider/client interactions, Ainsworth-Vaughn shows that both doctors and patients in American medical consultations use repetition "to show participation and agreement" and "formulations . . . of shared cultural knowledge" (1998:136).[29] Peräkylä (1995:57) demonstrates that AIDS counselors in a London hemophilia clinic induce their patients to talk about sensitive, private concerns and to address "dreaded issues"—severe illness, disability, and death—they might prefer to avoid in part through the recurrent use of a common asymmetric pattern of interaction in which counselors produce questions and statements and clients produce answers. The counselor asks a question, the patient answers, the counselor then has an option to comment on the patient's answer and the right to ask another question (1995). Explicitly using a theory of family interaction, the counselors also constrain their patients to speak about sensitive matters by formulating questions in a way that takes advantage of culturally specific notions of relationships and knowledge. Clients are understood to be the "owners" of their experience, but their relatives and partners should also have some knowledge of what the clients are experiencing. The latter notion constrains family members who accompany clients to respond to questions about the clients' private concerns. The former notion constrains clients to confirm or disconfirm and to elaborate on the family members' responses. Finally, the counselor may properly close discussion of a topic and/or the counseling session as a whole when the patient's future has been "portrayed as *manageable.*" The patient's face is protected "by constructing the future world in such a way where the client is an active, successful agent. After this restoration of the client's 'agency,' the participants are free to exit from the world they thus have completed" (1995:327).

In his work on American doctor-patient consultations and related discussions among physicians, Cicourel (1985, 1986) demonstrates that people use different kinds of language to invoke and put into circulation different kinds of knowledge. Everyday, localized knowledge is talked and written about in informal language marked by the use of anaphora and deictic pronouns. Schematized, professional knowledge is indexed by displays of formal spoken and written language.

The work of Ochs et al. (1997) suggests that the transfer of knowledge from one person to another may be seen in instances of co-narration. Narratives recapitulate and evaluate "past experience by matching a verbal sequence of clauses to the sequence of events which (it is inferred) actually occurred" (Labov, 1972:359). A co-constructed narrative is one in which the components of the verbal sequence are shared among two or more speakers. In their study of the stories told by "20 white, English-speaking, American families" at dinner, Ochs et al. (1997:95) stress the cognitive consequences of verbal interaction (see also Wertsch and Hickman, 1987). The sharing of the rights to tell a story "makes participants' perceptions of the world vulnerable to coauthored change" (Ochs et al., 1997:109). This happens especially when a co-narrator feels that information vital to understanding the problem that motivates the actions and reactions of protagonists and others in the storytelling situation is missing. "Co-narrators [then] return, sometimes again and again, like Lieutenant Columbo, to pieces of the narrative problem in an effort to find 'truth' through cross-examination of the details, sometimes struggling for an illuminating shift in perspective" (Ochs et al., 1997:98). The occurrence of such cognitive changes on the part of a person whose story is co-narrated is signaled by the emergence of new information and its incorporation into the story's meaning.

Clearly, the patterns of interaction in counseling sessions are dauntingly complex. Nevertheless, there appear to be a variety of quantitative approaches to the assessment of counseling sessions that are simpler and easier to execute than the coding strategies used by Kim and her colleagues in the Kenya Provider and Client Information, Education and Communication Project. For example, Erickson and Shultz (1982) show that guidance counseling sessions in an American junior college, which participants subsequently characterize after reviewing audiotapes as having gone well, also have relatively few awkward pauses and other arrhythmias.[30] This finding could be tested cross-culturally by measuring the association between participants, assessments of counseling sessions and the occurrence of "uh huh," "umm," and other speech particles or monitoring devices on the one hand, and pauses on the other. Conversational analysts have demonstrated that across a range of cultures, people use monitoring devices to show that they are interested in and paying attention to what is being said. They use long pauses to signal a lack of interest in continuing a conversation (Schegloff, 1982; Jefferson, 1989).[31]

Another approach focuses on what Silverman calls "disposal statements," the utterances in which doctors indicate how they propose to deal with the results of a consultation. Silverman suggests that such utterances can be divided into three groups: those in which the doctor seeks to impose a decision himself ["Passive voice ('Management would be')"], those in which he seeks to persuade the patient or the patient's parent(s) ["Voices of I and We ('*I* think *we* should')"], and those in which he elicits the patient's and/or the patient's parent(s) participation in a shared decision ["Voices of I, We and You ('*I* think . . . but *we* would . . . if *you* thought')"] (Silverman, 1987:57 and passim). In the English pediatric consultations studied by Silverman, the form of disposal statement the doctor uses in any particular consultation depends on prior sequences of verbal and nonverbal actions as well as overarching "medical" and "social" discursive environments. Given the concerns addressed in family planning counseling (contraceptive choice, abortion, etc., versus the management of severe heart defects) and the ideology of choice and empowerment that informs family planning and reproductive health counseling, one would expect that in "successful" or "proper" counseling sessions, disposal statements generally would be uttered by clients or, if the counselor utters a disposal statement, that it would be framed in a way that invites the client's participation in a shared decision.

Finally, the talk that occurs in family planning and reproductive health service encounters (see Goffman, 1961:321ff) opens a window on other channels of communication and social processes involved in flows of knowledge concerning fertility. Talk about fertility and contraception in other settings is likely to be intermittent and difficult to observe ethnographically. But men as well as women not infrequently bring these concerns to counselors at family planning clinics, crisis pregnancy centers, and STD clinics; genetic counselors; the staff of school-based clinics; nurses, midwives, gynecologists, pediatricians, internists, and family medicine physicians; other kinds of healers; and clergy. Such consultations are themselves part of one's sexual and reproductive life. In these settings, men as well as women provide accounts of their conduct that are endogenous to their ongoing projects rather than responses to exogenous research interventions. Here, as Hammel (1990:475) puts it, informants "speak to one another and can be overheard."

For example, one of the counseling sessions I observed opens with an extended co-narrative (Ochs et al., 1997, see above) that includes the following references to a woman's connections with friends, sister, and boyfriend:

1	Counselor	You came in for a pregnancy test today.
2	Client	Mm, mm.
3	Counselor	Tell me a little bit about why you decided to come in.
4	Client	Well I really already know I'm pregnant. I don't really know what I want to do. It's like I'm between two decisions—I don't know if I want to have an abortion or if I want to keep it.

5	Counselor	Okay.
6	Client	And it's like, you know a couple of my friends, well my sister's had an abortion before and a couple of my friends have had kids and they are like just go to Planned Parenthood and then make up your own mind.
7	Counselor	Yeah.
8	Client	It's like most of my friends, you know, they're like "oh have it." It's like well you guys aren't going to be there, you know, all the time to help me with everything and it's not just an easy decision. (nervous chuckle) [Several utterances deleted.]
21	Counselor	Okay. And tell me where, who you have talked to and what the conversations have been like.
22	Client	Well, I talked to my boyfriend, of course. I have talked to a couple of my friends. Oh my boyfriend is like, you know he is like a very important part for the—like he's going to help me, I don't know—he's not very "there." He's like it's your decision, but then again I don't want you to have it. You know what I mean—he's kind of like contradicting himself?
23	Counselor	Mm, mm.
24	Client	Like, I appreciate that he is being honest. That he's not ready for one cause really I'm not either but there's a part of me that really doesn't want to have an abortion.
25	Counselor	Tell me why, tell me about that part of you that really doesn't want to have an abortion, what is it that, that makes you feel that way?
26	Client	I'm pro-choice but I always—like I believe it's the woman's right to decide but for me I've always kind of been just for my personal, I guess, morals I never wanted to have an abortion like my sister. (Inaudible) But she's had, she has three kids and she's had a lot of abortions, a lot. And I've been there a couple of times when she was having an abortion and I just never wanted to be like that. I mean I don't want to go through that. And I don't think it's the child's fault that I'm not responsible. You know what I mean? I mean it's somebody's right to decide but I just think it's wrong, well for me personally.

Here the client and the counselor together construct an account, albeit one that is selective and interpreted, of a "sequence of events which (it is inferred) actually occurred" (Labov, 1972:359). The presuppositions in terms of which narratives make sense are constituents of the knowledge schemas—"expectations about people, objects, events and settings in the world" (Tannen and Wallat, 1993:60)—that participants use in everyday life (Giddens, 1979:57). As the Caldwells note, a body of such ethnographic material would help investigators using quantitative methods to develop culturally appropriate questions and hypotheses concerning the social processes and flows of knowledge that shape fertility conduct (Caldwell, Reddy, and Caldwell, 1988:263–273; Caldwell, Caldwell, and Caldwell, 1987).

Survey Research

The following reflections on the network questions used by Valente et al. (1997) in their research in Yaoundé, Cameroon, on the associations between contraceptive use and communication among members of women's voluntary associations (*tontines*) indicate some of the ways in which quantitative research might be informed by ethnography.

In the first of this set of questions, informants are asked to name the five women in their group with whom they had talked most often in the past six months. A follow-up question confirmed that the person named was a member of the informant's group. Women who were not members of the informant's group were dropped from the analysis (Valente et al., 1997:679). Subsequent network questions ask how often the informant talked to each of the women she named, how long the informant and each of her interlocutors had known each other and how they were related, and what kinds of help and advice the informant received from each of her interlocutors. The remaining questions concerned the informant's beliefs concerning her interlocutors' use of and approval of contraception and whether or not the informant had been encouraged by her interlocutors to use contraception herself. The responses to the question concerning the way in which an informant and her interlocutors were related were coded as follows: "family member," "tribal member," "coworker," "friend or neighbor," and "other" (Valente et al., 1997:686–687).

From an ethnographic perspective, this set of questions features several notable absences. The positions in the social structure available to informants and their interlocutors—family, "tribe," work, friendship, and neighborhood—are very restricted. Though it is probable that many social relationships in urban Cameroon are multidimensional, only one dimension is coded and that according to rules that are not specified. There is nothing on Cameroonian communicative activity types, the manner in which they are situated in the local social organization, or the kinds of topics appropriate in each.

An alternative approach would break the question concerning the relationship between informants and their interlocutors ("How are you related to _____?") into two more detailed sets. In the West African context, particular attention should be paid to kinship groups more inclusive than families or domestic groups and to the effects of polygyny and relationships among co-wives. In all but a few societies, attention also should be paid to the difference between natal family (i.e., family of origin) and marital family. Relationships formed in school also might be important. One set of questions would be aimed at the informant's position in society: minimally natal lineage affiliation, natal tribal affiliation, marital history and current marital status, husband's lineage affiliation and tribal affiliation, educational history, employment history and current employment, place of residence, and membership in voluntary associations. One imagines that many of these questions were included in Valente et al.'s larger questionnaire. If informants were asked to describe their interlocutors in parallel terms, it would then be possible to code more dimensions of the relationships between informants and their interlocutors. Where an interlocutor is a member of the informant's "family," it would be possible to code this relationship more precisely as mother, wife of male member of natal lineage, co-wife, husband's mother, husband's mother's co-wife, wife of male member of husband's lineage, etc. This would provide a richer view of an informant's knowledge of her interlocutors and a fuller picture of the composition of voluntary associations.

An additional set of questions is required to identify the ways in which any two Cameroonian women discuss family planning. When (on what date and at what time of day) did you or do you and _____ discuss family planning? Where did or do these discussions take place? At the market, in your home or _____'s home, during or on the margins of a voluntary association meeting, etc.? Who else was or is present? What do people call this kind of talk?

It goes without saying that the language of the survey and the procedures used to administer it should be consistent with the discoursive practices of the community in which it is carried out (see Briggs, 1986; Duranti, 1997:102–110).

SUMMARY

Classic structural-functional anthropology decisively rejected its own diffusionist past and with it all versions of diffusion based on simple imitation or contagion. Elements of one culture routinely are adopted by others but they are systematically reinvented in the process. Birth control is new only if various forms of "child control" (Greenhalgh, 1988:639)are set aside by definition.

However, the contemporary turn to practice theory in which culture is produced and reproduced through processes of interaction suggests that a very much more complicated version of diffusion is a pervasive feature of social life. The ubiquity of diffusion conceived of as cultural flow is not simply a reflex of the rapidity with which new knowledge is generated by the scientific establishment of the rich nations at the core of the global economy and transmitted to all the nooks and crannies of the periphery by global institutions devoted to development and technological transfer. Novelty is generated continuously throughout the global system, including its more or less peripheral nooks and crannies. Learning is inherently social, spread over the projects of interacting persons and the contexts of their interactions. The communicative resources through which new ideas concerning family planning are spread, translated, and continuously modified, and the social structures in which those resources are situated, are culturally defined and immensely variable. Variations in communicative resources and social structure are intimately connected to the outcome of diffusion processes.

Research on the spread, translation, and continuous alteration of new ideas concerning family planning requires detailed knowledge of a social system's communicative resources and the social structure in which they are situated. Ethnographic research is a key tool for obtaining such knowledge.

It should be noted that if learning is social in this sense, that is, located in processes of co-participation and the contexts in which they occur, so are the decisions of economic men and women (Hammel, 1990; Carter, 1988, 1995, 1998). A culturally smart diffusion and culturally smart microeconomics are virtually indistinguishable.

NOTES

1. See also Rosero-Bixby and Casterline (1993) and Montgomery and Casterline (1993).
2. The Princeton European Fertility Project's early work on communities as units of fertility change focused on the administratively established provinces of modern nation-states (Coale and Watkins, 1986; Watkins, 1991). More recent work has extended this concept of community to villages in developing countries (e.g., Entwisle et al., 1996, 1997; Kohler, 1997; Valente et al., 1997) and to regions composed of a number of culturally similar nation-states (Bongaarts and Watkins, 1996).
3. See also Carter (1988, 1995, 1998).
4. For a cognate approach to the role of education in fertility change, see Carter (1999).
5. Here Kroeber cites Tarde's (1903) *The Laws of Imitation*.
6. The turn to practice theory in anthropology was announced, somewhat after the fact, by Ortner (1984). Key contemporary theoretical sources are Bourdieu (e.g., 1977) and Giddens (e.g., 1979, 1984).
7. See also Greenhalgh (1995) and Carter (1988, 1995, 1998, 1999).
8. Bongaarts and Watkins (1996) are unusual in extending studies of social interaction within national populations to the analysis of regions consisting of several such populations. There is, of course, a long-standing interest in the operation of agencies designed to transfer contraceptive technologies and ideas concerning their use from the societies in which they originated to societies that do not possess them (see, for example, Retherford and Palmore,

1983:312–319). This has been given renewed impetus in the work of Watkins and her colleagues (e.g., Hodgson and Watkins, 1997; Watkins and Hodgson, 1998).

9. Like Kroeber, Rosero-Bixby and Casterline (1993:165, n47) cite Tarde (1903).

10. Curiously, there appear to be very few studies of this kind. The only one I have found is the geographer Blaikie's (1975) locational analysis of the family planning program in Purnea District, Bihar, India.

11. But see Schneider and Schneider (1992) and Santow (1993, 1995) on withdrawal.

12. On infanticide in South Asia, see also Chen et al., (1981), Das Gupta (1987), Levine (1987), and Miller (1981). Scheper-Hughes' (1992) study of an impoverished and economically marginalized community in northeastern Brazil provides ethnographic support for Scrimshaw's argument. European historical studies include Fuchs (1984, 1992), Kertzer (1991, 1993), and Ransel (1988).

13. There is an enormous anthropological literature on family or household systems, full of technical disputes. Early versions of the "developmental cycle in domestic groups" (e.g., Goody, 1958) are apparent in Lesthaeghe's (1980) theory of "the social control of human reproduction." For more recent work on the household, see Netting et al. (1984). For a discussion of the utility of distinguishing between families and households, see Carter (1984).

14. For Taiwan, Skinner cites Coombs and Sun (1978). His source for Korea is Park (1983). For an elegant analysis of "deliberate birth control in [rural] China before 1970," see Zhao (1997).

15. For brief reviews of this work, see Carter (1999) or Pelissier (1991). Among the key texts are Lave (1988, 1989, 1991), Lave and Wenger (1991), Rogoff and Lave (1984), and Scribner (1997).

16. For a concrete example with important implications for health communications, see Nations and Monte's (1997) analysis of the 1994 cholera control campaign in northeastern Brazil. In this radically stratified setting, the residents of urban slums denied the existence of cholera and actively resisted the efforts of public health workers. They understood posters with the caption "Cholera, Don't Close your Eyes to Life: Help Combat Cholera" as signaling a campaign to exterminate not the disease, but "we the cholera poor" (Nations and Monte, 1997:458–459).

17. See also the discussions of genres of communication in Hymes (1974), Bergmann (1993: 26–32), and Hanks (1996b:242–249 and passim).

18. See also McNicoll (1985, 1988), Cain (1985), and Greenhalgh (1990).

19. Also missing is any indication of village size.

20. See, for example, Wolf (1972:32–43).

21. Where marriage is hypergamous, "horizontal" should be read as "less vertical."

22. This is a major theme of Mayer's (1966) classic ethnography of "a village and its region." For a general review of the literature, see Dumont (1980).

23. Other sources include the processes through which villages grow and produce new natural villages and the links between natural villages and agrarian ecology.

24. Since the data used by Entwisle et al. come from a census and concern units that have headmen, it would appear that the unit of analysis in this paper is the administrative village. However, the paper does not specify this. Nor does it say anything about the relationship between the administrative village and the natural village in Nang Rong district.

25. Much of the recent work of Watkins approximates this approach. See, for example, Kaler and Watkins (1999) and Watkins and Hodgson (1998).

26. Linguists commonly observe that there is no one-to-one correspondence between the form of an utterance and its meaning and force. On the contrary, the sense of an utterance is spread over and inseparable from its context (see Levinson, 1983:286ff; Hanks, 1996b; Duranti, 1997; Ainsworth-Vaughn, 1998). These difficulties are compounded by changes introduced by translation.

27. On conversation analysis, see Sacks (1984), Sacks et al. (1974), Schegloff et al. (1977), and Levinson (1983:284–370).

28. As Kaler and Watkins (1999) demonstrate, this is very much an empirical question. The aims of counselors and of clients no doubt vary from one setting to another and in any case are unlikely to correspond perfectly.

29. See also Ferrara (1994:108–127) on "echoing" in psychotherapeutic interactions.

30. Felicitous sessions also have relatively few occasions on which the counselor takes over the conversation with protracted explanations, and more instances in which the counselor offers extra assistance.

31. On the cross-cultural robustness of some of the more straightforward findings of conversation analysis, see Boden (1994) and Lerner and Takagi (1999).

REFERENCES

Ainsworth-Vaughn, N.
1998   *Claiming Power in Doctor-Patient Talk.* Oxford: Oxford University Press.
Alwando-Edyegu, M.G., and E. Marum
1999   *Knowledge Is Power: Voluntary HIV Counseling and Testing in Uganda.* Geneva: UNAIDS.
Baker, A.
1985   *The Complete Book of Problem Pregnancy Counseling.* Granite City, IL: The Hope Clinic for Women, Ltd.
Bakhtin, M.M., and P.M. Medvedev
1985   *The Formal Method in Literary Scholarship: A Critical Introduction to Sociological Poetics.* Translated by A.J. Wehrle. Cambridge, MA: Harvard University Press.
Bergmann, J.R.
1993   *Discreet Indiscretions: The Social Organization of Gossip.* Translated by J. Bednarz. New York: Aldine de Gruyter.
Blaikie, P.M.
1975   *Family Planning in India.* London: Edward Arnold.
Bledsoe, C.H., F. Banja, and A.G. Hill
1998   Reproductive mishaps and Western contraception: An African challenge to fertility theory. *Population and Development Review* 24(1):15–57.
Bledsoe, C.H., A.G. Hill, U. D'Alessandro, and P. Langerock
1994   Constructing natural fertility: The use of Western contraceptive technologies in rural Gambia. *Population and Development Review* 20(1):81–113.
Boden, D.
1994   *The Business of Talk: Organizations in Action.* Cambridge, MA: Polity Press.
Bongaarts, J.
1978   A framework for analyzing the proximate determinants of fertility. *Population and Development Review* 20(1):81–113.
Bongaarts, J., and S.C. Watkins
1996   Social interactions and contemporary fertility transitions. *Population and Development Review* 22(4):639–682.
Bourdieu, P.
1977   *Outline of a Theory of Practice.* Translated by Richard Nice. Cambridge, Eng.: Cambridge University Press.
1991   *Language and Symbolic Power*, John B. Thompson, ed. Cambridge, MA: Harvard University Press.

Briggs, C.
    1986   *Learning How to Ask: A Sociolinguistic Appraisal of the Role of the Interview in Social Science Research.* Cambridge, Eng.: Cambridge University Press.
Bruce, J.
    1987   Users' perspectives on contraceptive technology and delivery systems. *Technology in Society* 9:359–383.
    1990   Fundamental elements of the quality of care: A simple framework. *Studies in Family Planning* 21(2):61–91.
Bulatao, R.A. et al.
    1983   A framework for the study of fertility determinants. In *Determinants of Fertility in Developing Countries*, R. A. Bulatao and R.D. Lee, eds. New York: Academic Press.
Cain, M.
    1985   Intensive community studies. In *The Collection and Analysis of Community Data*, John B. Casterline, ed. Voorburg, Neth.: International Statistical Institute.
Caldwell, J.C., B. Caldwell, and P. Caldwell
    1987   Anthropology and demography: The mutual reinforcement of speculation and research. *Current Anthropology* 28:25–34.
Caldwell, J.C., P.H. Reddy, and P. Caldwell
    1988   *The Causes of Demographic Change: Experimental Research in South India.* Madison: University of Wisconsin Press.
Candlin, C.N., and J. Lucas
    1986   Interpretations and explanations in discourse: Modes of "advising" in family planning. In *Discourse Analysis and Public Life*, T. Ensink, A. van Essen, and T. van der Geest, eds. Dordrecht, Neth.: Foris Publications.
Carter, A.T.
    1984   Household histories. In *Households: Comparative and Historical Studies of the Domestic Group*, Robert McC. Netting, Richard R. Wilk, and Eric J. Arnould, eds. Berkeley: University of California Press.
    1988   Does culture matter? The case of the demographic transition. *Historical Methods* 21(4): 164–169.
    1995   Agency and fertility: For an ethnography of practice. In *Rethinking Reproduction*, Susan Greenhalgh, ed. Cambridge, Eng.: Cambridge University Press.
    1998   Cultural models and reproductive behavior. In *New Approaches to Anthropological Demography*, Alaka Basu, ed. Oxford: Oxford University Press.
    1999   What is meant, and measured, by "education"? Pp. 49–79 in *Critical Perspectives on Schooling and Fertility in the Developing World.* Committee on Population. C.H. Bledsoe, J.B. Casterline, J.A. Johnson-Kuhn, and J.G. Haaga, eds. Commission on Behavioral and Social Sciences and Education. Washington, DC: National Academy Press.
    2001a   Legitimate Tangential Participation: Toward an Ethnography of Family Planning Counseling. Paper presented at the IUSSP Seminar on the Production and Circulation of Population Knowledge, March 20-24. Providence, RI.
    2001b   Time and Temporalization in Pregnancy Test Counseling. Paper presented at the XXIV IUSSP General Conference, August 18-24. Salvador, Brazil.
Cassen, R.H.
    1978   *India: Population, Economy, Society.* London: Macmillan.
Centers for Disease Control and Prevention
    1998   *Fundamentals of HIV Prevention Counseling: Participant's Manual.* November 1998. Available: http://hivinsite.ucsf.edu/InSite.jsp?page=pr-02-02&doc=2098.445e [June 18, 2001].

Chen, L., E. Huq, and S. D'Souza
1981   Sex bias in the family allocation of food and health care in rural Bangladesh. *Population and Development Review* 13(1):77–100.
Cicourel, A.V.
1985   Text and discourse. *Annual Review of Anthropology* 14:159–185.
1986   The reproduction of objective knowledge: Common sense reasoning in medical decision making. In *The Knowledge Society*, G. Böhme and N. Stehr, eds. Dordrecht, Neth.: D. Reidel Publishing Co.
Cleland, J., and C. Wilson
1987   Demand theories of the fertility transition: An iconoclastic view. *Population Studies* 41:5–30.
Coale, A.J., and S.C. Watkins, eds.
1986   *The Decline of Fertility in Europe*. Princeton: Princeton University Press.
Coleman, J.S., E.Katz, and H. Menzel
1966   *Medical Innovation: A Diffusion Study*. Indianapolis: Bobbs-Merrill.
Coombs, L.C., and T.-h. Sun
1978   Family composition preferences in a developing culture: The case of Taiwan 1973. *Population Studies* 32:43–64.
Das Gupta, M.
1987   Selective discrimination against female children in India. *Population and Development Review* 13(1):77–100.
Dumont, L.
1980   *Homo Hierarchicus*. 2d ed. Translated by M. Saisbury, L. Dumont, and B. Gulati. Chicago: University of Chicago Press.
Duranti, A.
1997   *Linguistic Anthropology*. Cambridge, Eng.: Cambridge University Press.
Dwyer, D., and J.Bruce, eds.
1988   *A Home Divided: Women and Income in the Third World*. Stanford: Stanford University Press.
Easterlin, R.A.
1978   The economics and sociology of fertility: A synthesis. In *Historical Studies of Changing Fertility*, Charles Tilly, ed. Princeton: Princeton University Press.
1983   Modernization and fertility: A critical essay. In *Determinants of Fertility in Developing Countries*, Vol. 2, Rodolfo A. Bulatao and Ronald D. Lee, eds. New York: Academic Press.
Entwisle, B., R.R. Rindfuss, D.K. Guilkey, A. Chamratrithirong, S.R. Curran, and Y. Sawangdee
1996   Community and contraceptive choice in rural Thailand: A case study of Nang Rong. *Demography* 33(1):1–11.
Entwisle, B., R.R. Rindfuss, S.J. Walsh, and S.R Curran
1997   Geographic information systems, spatial network analysis, and contraceptive choice. *Demography* 34(2):171–187.
Erickson, F., and J. Shultz
1982   *The Counselor as Gatekeeper*. New York: Academic Press.
Ferrara, K.W.
1994   *Therapeutic Ways with Words*. Oxford: Oxford University Press.
Fisher, S. and A.D. Todd
1986   Friendly persuasions: The negotiation of decisions to use oral contraception. In *Discourse Analysis and Public Life*, T. Ensink, A. van Essen and T. Van der Geest, eds. Dordrecht, Hol.: Foris Publications.

Fortes, M.
    1953   *Social Anthropology at Cambridge since 1900.* Cambridge, Eng.: Cambridge University Press.
Frank, J.D., and J.B. Frank
    1991   *Persuasion and Healing: A Comparative Study of Psychotherapy.* 3d ed. Baltimore: The Johns Hopkins University Press.
Frankel, R.M.
    1989   "I wz wondering—uhm could *Raid* uhm effect the brain permantently d'y know?": Some observations on the intersection of speaking and writing in calls to a poison control center. *Western Journal of Speech Communication* 53:195–226.
Fuchs, R.
    1984   *Abandoned Children: Foundlings and Child Welfare in Nineteenth Century France.* Albany: State University of New York Press.
    1992   *Poor and Pregnant in Paris: Strategies for Survival in the Nineteenth Century.* New Brunswick: Rutgers University Press.
Gallen, M., C. Lettenmaier, and C. Green
    1987   *Counseling Makes a Difference.* Population Reports, Series J, No. 35. Baltimore, MD: Johns Hopkins University, Population Information Program.
Geertz, C.
    1983   *Local Knowledge: Further Essays in Interpretive Anthropology.* New York: Basic Books.
Giddens, A.
    1979   *Central Problems in Social Theory.* Berkeley: University of California Press.
    1984   *The Constitution of Society.* Berkeley: University of California Press.
Goffman, E.
    1961   *Asylums: Essays on the Social Situation of Mental Patients and Other Inmates.* Garden City, NY: Anchor Books.
Good, B.
    1994   *Medicine, Rationality and Experience.* Cambridge, Eng.: Cambridge University Press.
Goody, J., ed.
    1958   *The Developmental Cycle in Domestic Groups.* Cambridge Papers in Social Anthropology, No. 1. Cambridge, Eng.: Cambridge University Press.
Greenhalgh, S.
    1988   Fertility as mobility: Sinic transitions. *Population and Development Review* 14(4):629–674.
    1990   Toward a political economy of fertility: Anthropological contributions. *Population and Development Review* 16(10):85–106.
    1995   Anthropology theories reproduction: Integrating practice, political economic, and feminist perspectives. In *Situating Fertility: Anthropology and Demographic Inquiry,* S. Greenhalgh, ed. Cambridge, Eng.: Cambridge University Press.
Grimely, D.M., G.E. Riley, J.M. Bellis, and J.O. Prochaska
    1993   Assessing the stages of change and decision-making for contraceptive use for the prevention of pregnancy, sexually transmitted diseases and acquired immunodeficiency syndrome. *Health Education Quarterly* 20(4):455–470.
Hammel, E.
    1990   A theory of culture for demography. *Population and Development Review* 16(3):455–485.
Hanks, W.F.
    1984   Santification, structure, and experience in a Yucatec ritual event. *Journal of American Folklore* 97:131–166.
    1987   Discourse genres in a theory of practice. *American Ethnologist* 14(4):668–692.

1989 Text and textuality. *Annual Review of Anthropology* 18:95–127.

1996a Exorcism and the description of participant roles. In *The Natural History of Discourse*, M. Silverstein and G. Urban, eds. Chicago: University of Chicago Press.

1996b *Language and Communicative Practices*. Boulder, CO: Westview Press.

2000a Copresence and alterity in Maya ritual practice. In *Intertexts: Writings on Language, Utterance, and Context*. Lanham, MD: Rowman and Littlefield.

2000b Indexicality. *Journal of Linguistic Anthropology* 9(1-2):124–126.

Hanley, S.B., and K. Yamamura
1977 *Economic and Demographic Change in Preindustrial Japan, 1600–1868*. Princeton: Princeton University Press.

Hannerz, U.
1992 *Cultural Complexity: Studies in the Social Organization of Meaning*. New York: Columbia University Press.

Hodgson, D., and S. Watkins
1997 Feminists and neo-Malthusians: Past and present alliances. *Population and Development Review* 23(3):469–523.

Huntington, D., C. Lettenmaier, and I. Obeng-Quaidoo
1990 User's perspective of counseling training in Ghana: The "mystery client" trial. *Studies in Family Planning* 21(3):171–177.

Huntington, D., and S.R. Schuler
1993 The simulated client method: Evaluating client-provider interactions in family planning clinics. *Studies in Family Planning* 24(3):187–193.

Hymes, D.
1974 Ways of speaking. In *Explorations in the Ethnography of Speaking*, R. Baumann and J. Scherzer, eds. Cambridge, Eng.: Cambridge University Press.

Jefferson, G.
1989 Notes on a possible metric which provides for a "standard maximum silence" of approximately one second in conversation. In *Conversation: An Interdisciplinary Perspective*, C. Roger and P. Bull, eds. Clevedon, Eng.: Multilingual Matters.

Kaler, A., and S. Watkins
1999 Disobedient Distributors: Pills, Parity and Clashing Agendas in Rural Kenya. Unpublished paper presented at the Annual Meeting of the Population Association of America, March 25–27, New York.

Kenny, A.
1973 *Wittgenstein*. Harmondsworth, Eng.: Penguin Books.

Kertzer, D.I.
1991 Gender ideology and infant abandonment in nineteenth-century Italy. *Journal of Interdisciplinary History* 22:1–25.

1993 *Sacrificed for Honor: Italian Infant Abandonment and the Politics of Reproductive Control*. Boston: Beacon Press.

Kim, Y.-M., A. Kols, and S. Mucheke
1998 Informed choice and decision-making in family planning counseling in Kenya. *International Family Planning Perspectives* 24(1):4–11.

Kim, Y.-M., A. Kols, M. Thuo, S. Mucheke, and D. Odallo
1998 *Client-Provider Communication in Family Planning: Assessing Audiotaped Consultations from Kenya*. Working Paper 5. Baltimore: Johns Hopkins University Center for Communication Programs.

Kohler, H.-P.
1997 Learning in social networks and contraceptive choice. *Demography* 34(3):369–383.

Kreager, P.
    1998   The limits of diffusionism. In *New Approaches to Anthropological Demography*, A. Basu, ed. Oxford: Oxford University Press.
Kroeber, A.L.
    1931   Diffusionism. In *Encyclopaedia of the Social Sciences*, E.R.A. Seligman, ed. New York: Macmillan.
Labov, W.
    1972   The transformation of experience in narrative syntax. *Language in the Inner City*. Philadelphia: University of Pennsylvania Press.
Lave, J.
    1988   *Cognition in Practice*. Cambridge, Eng.: Cambridge University Press.
    1989   The acquisition of culture and the practice of understanding. In *The Chicago Symposia on Human Development*, J. Stigler, R. Shweder, and G. Herdt, eds. Cambridge, Eng.: Cambridge University Press.
    1991   Situated learning in communities of practice. In *Perspectives on Socially Shared Cognition*, L.B. Resnick, J.M. Levine, and S.D. Teasley, eds. Washington, DC: American Psychological Association.
Lave, J., and E. Wenger
    1991   *Situated Learning: Legitimate Peripheral Participation*. Cambridge, Eng.: Cambridge University Press.
León, F.R., G. Quiroz, and A. Brazzoduro
    1994   The reliability of simulated clients' quality-of-care ratings. *Studies of Family Planning* 25(4):184–190.
Lerner, G., and T. Takagi
    1999   On the place of linguistic resources in the organization of talk-in-interaction: A co-investigation of English and Japanese grammatical practice. *Journal of Pragmatics* 31(1):49–75.
Lesthaeghe, R.
    1980   On the social control of human reproduction. *Population and Development Review* 6(4):527–548.
Levine, N.
    1987   Differential child care in three Tibetan communities. *Population and Development Review* 13(2):281–304.
Levinson, S.C.
    1983   *Pragmatics*. Cambridge, Eng.: Cambridge University Press.
    1992   Activity types and language. In *Talk at Work*, P. Drew and J. Heritage, eds. Cambridge, Eng.: Cambridge University Press.
Levi-Strauss, C.
    1953   Social structure. In *Anthropology Today*, A. L. Kroeber, ed. Chicago: University of Chicago Press.
Malinowski, B.
    1927   The life of culture. In *Culture: The Diffusion Controversy*, G.E. Smith, B. Malinowski, H.J. Spinden, and A. Goldenweiser, eds. New York: W.W. Norton and Company, Inc.
Marcus, G.A.
    1994   Ethnography in/of the world system: The emergence of multi-sited ethnography. *Annual Review of Anthropology* 24:95–117.
Maternowska, M. C.
    2000   A clinic in conflict: A political economy case study of family planning in Haiti. In *Contraception Across Cultures*, A. Russell, E.J. Sobo and M.S. Thompson, eds. New York: Berg.

Mayer, A.C.
  1966   *Caste and Kinship in Central India: A Village and its Region.* Berkeley: University of California Press.
McNicoll, G.
  1985   The nature of institutional and community effects on demographic behavior. In *The Collection and Analysis of Community Data*, J.B. Casterline, ed. Voorburg, Neth.: International Statistical Institute.
  1988   On the local context of demographic change. In *Micro-Approaches to Demographic Research*, J. Caldwell, A. Hill, and V. Hull, eds. London: Kegan Paul.
Miller, B.D.
  1981   *The Endangered Sex.* Ithaca: Cornell University Press.
Montgomery, M.R., and J.B. Casterline
  1993   The diffusion of fertility control in Taiwan: Evidence from pooled cross-section time-series models. *Population Studies* 47:457–479.
  1996   Social learning, social influence and new models of fertility. *Population and Development Review* 22(supplement):151–175.
Montgomery, M.R., and W. Chung
  1999   Social networks and the diffusion of fertility control in the Republic of Korea. In *Dynamics of Values in Fertility Change*, R. Leete, ed. Oxford, Eng.: Clarendon Press.
Namerow, P.B., N. Weatherby, and J. Williams-Kaye
  1989   The effectiveness of contingency-planning counseling. *Family Planning Perspectives* 21(3):115–119.
Nathanson, C.A.
  1991   *Dangerous Passage: The Social Control of Sexuality in Women's Adolescence.* Philadelphia: Temple University Press.
Nathanson, C.A., and M.H. Becker
  1985   The influence of client-provider relationships on teenage women's subsequent use of contraception. *American Journal of Public Health* 75(1):33–38.
Nations, M., and C.G. Monte
  1997   "I'm not dog, no!": Cries of resistance against cholera control campaigns in Brazil. In *The Anthropology of Infectious Disease*, M.C. Inhorn and P.J. Brown, eds. Amsterdam: Gordon and Breach Publishers.
Netting, R.M., R.R. Wilk, and E.J. Arnould, eds.
  1984   *Households: Comparative and Historical Studies of the Domestic Group.* Berkeley: University of California Press.
Newman, L.F., ed.
  1985   *Women's Medicine: A Cross-Cultural Study of Indigenous Fertility Regulation.* New Brunswick, NJ: Rutgers University Press.
Ochs, E., R.C. Smith, and C.E. Taylor
  1997   Detective stories at dinnertime: Problem solving through co-narration. In *Disorderly Discourse: Narrative, Conflict, and Inequality*, C.L. Briggs, ed. Oxford: Oxford University Press.
Ortner, S.
  1984   Theory in anthropology since the sixties. *Comparative Studies in Society and History* 26(1):126–166.
Park, C.B.
  1983   Preference for sons, family size, and sex ratio: An empirical study in Korea. *Demography* 20:333–352.
Park, H.J., D.L. Kincaid, K.K. Chung, D.S. Han, and S.B. Lee
  1976   The Korean Mothers' Club Program. *Studies in Family Planning* 7(10):275–283.

Peirce, C.S.
  1955   *Philosophical Writings of Peirce,* Edited by J. Buchler. New York: Dover Publications.
Pelissier, C.
  1991   The anthropology of teaching and learning. *Annual Review of Anthropology* 20:75–
          95.
Peräkylä, A.
  1995   *AIDS Counselling: Institutional Interaction and Clinical Practice.* Cambridge, Eng.:
          Cambridge University Press.
Polgar, S.
  1972   Population history and population policies from an anthropological perspective.
          Current Anthropology 13(2):203–211.
Potter, J.M.
  1976   *Thai Peasant Social Structure.* Chicago: University of Chicago Press.
Radcliffe-Brown, A.R.
  1922   *The Andaman Islanders.* Cambridge, Eng.: Cambridge University Press.
  1950   Introduction. In *African Systems of Kinship and Marriage,* A.R. Radcliffe-Brown and
          D. Forde, eds. London: Oxford University Press.
Ransel, D.L.
  1988   *Mothers of Misery: Child Abandonment in Russia.* Princeton: Princeton University
          Press.
Retherford, R.D., and J.A. Palmore
  1983   Diffusion processes affecting fertility regulation. In *Determinants of Fertility in
          Developing Countries,* Vol. 2, R.A. Bulatao and R.D. Lee, eds. New York: Academic
          Press.
Rogoff, B., and J. Lave, eds.
  1984   *Everyday Cognition: Its Development in Social Context.* Cambridge, MA: Harvard
          University Press.
Rosero-Bixby, L., and J.B. Casterline
  1993   Modeling diffusion effects in fertility transition. *Population Studies* 47:147–167.
Roter, D., and J.A. Hall
  1987   Physicians' interviewing styles and medical information obtained from patients.
          Journal of General Internal Medicine 2(5):325–329.
Rouse, I.
  1953   The strategy of culture history. In *Anthropology Today,* A.L. Kroeber, ed. Chicago:
          University of Chicago Press.
Rowe, M.
  1999   *Crossing the Border: Encounters between Homeless People and Outreach Workers.* Berke-
          ley: University of California Press.
Sacks, H.
  1984   Notes of methodology. In *Structures of Social Action,* J.M. Atkinson and J. Heri-
          tage, eds. Cambridge, Eng.: Cambridge University Press.
Sacks, H., E. Schegloff, and G. Jefferson
  1974   A simplest systematics for the organization of turn-taking for conversation. *Lan-
          guage* 50:676–735.
Santow, G.
  1993   Coitus interruptus in the twentieth century. *Population and Development Review*
          19(4):767–792.
  1995   Coitus interruptus and the control of natural fertility. *Population Studies* 49(1):19–43.
Saussure, F. de
  1986   *Course in General Linguistics.* Translated by Roy Harris. La Salle, IL: Open Court.

Schegloff, E.
  1982 Discourse as an interactional achievement: Some uses of "uh huh" and other things that come between sentences. In *Analyzing Discourse: Text and Talk*, D. Tannen, ed. Washington, DC: Georgetown University Press, Round Table in Languages and Linguistics.
Schegloff, E., G. Jefferson, and H. Sacks
  1977 The preference for self-correction in the organization of repair in conversation. *Language* 53:361–382.
Scheper-Hughes, N.
  1992 *Death without Weeping: The Violence of Everyday Life in Brazil*. Berkeley: University of California Press.
Schneider, J., and P. Schneider
  1992 Going forward in reverse gear: Culture, economy, and political economy in the demographic transitions of a rural Sicilian town. In *The European Experience of Declining Fertility*, J.R. Gillis, L.A. Tilly, and D. Levine, eds. Cambridge, MA: Blackwell.
  1996 *Festival of the Poor*. Tucson: University of Arizona Press.
Scribner, S.
  1997 *Mind and Social Practice*. Cambridge, Eng.: Cambridge University Press.
Scrimshaw, S.C.M.
  1978 Infant mortality and behavior in the regulation of family size. *Population and Development Review* 4:385–403.
  1983 Infanticide as deliberate fertility regulation. Pp. 245–266 in *Determinants of Fertility in Developing Countries*, Vol. 2, R. Bulatao and R. Lee, eds. New York: Academic Press.
Silverman, D.
  1987 *Communication and Medical Practice*. London: Sage Publications.
Simmons, R., and C. Elias
  1994 The study of client-provider interactions: A review of methodological issues. *Studies in Family Planning* 25(1):1–17.
Skinner, G.W.
  1997 Family systems and demographic regimes. In *Anthropological Demography*, D.I. Kertzer and T. Fricke, eds. Chicago: Unversity of Chicago Press.
Smith, T.C.
  1977 *Nakahara: Family Farming and Population in a Japanese Village, 1717–1830*. Stanford: Stanford University Press.
Strader, M.K., and M.L. Beaman
  1992 Theoretical components of STD counselors' messages to promote clients' use of condoms. *Public Health Nursing* 9(2):109–117.
Tarde, G.
  1903 *The Laws of Imitation*. Translated by E.C. Parsons. New York: Henry Holt and Company.
Todd, A.D.
  1983 A diagnosis of doctor-patient discourse in the prescription of contraception. In *The Social Organization of Doctor-Patient Communication*, S. Fisher and A.D. Todd, eds. Washington, DC: The Center for Applied Linguistics.
  1984 The prescription of contraception: Negotiations between doctors and patients. *Discourse Processes* 7:171–200.
Valente, T.W.
  1995 *Network Models of the Diffusion of Innovations*. Creskill, NJ: Hampton Press.

Valente, T.W., S. Watkins, M.N. Jato, A. van der Straten, and L.-P.M. Tsitsol
    1997   Social network associations with contraceptive use among Cameroonian women
            in voluntary associations. *Social Science and Medicine* 45(5):677–687.
van de Kaa, D.J.
    1996   Anchored narratives: The story and findings of half a century of research into the
            determinants of fertility. *Population Studies* 50:389–432.
van de Walle, E., and E. P. Renne, eds.
    2001   *Regulating Menstruation.* Chicago: University of Chicago Press.
Voloshinov, V.N.
    1986   *Marxism and the Philosophy of Language.* Translated by L. Metejka and I.R. Titunik.
            Cambridge, MA: Harvard University Press.
Watkins, S., and D. Hodgson
    1998   From mercantilists to neo-Malthusians: The international population movement
            and the transformation of population ideology in Kenya. Unpublished paper
            prepared for discussion at the National Academy of Sciences Workshop on Social
            Dynamics of Fertility Change in Developing Countries, January 29–30, Washing-
            ton, DC.
Watkins, S.C.
    1991   *From Provinces into Nations: The Demographic Integration of Western Europe, 1870–
            1960.* Princeton: Princeton University Press.
Wertsch, J.V., and M. Hickman
    1987   Problem solving in social interaction: A microgenetic analysis. In *Social and Func-
            tional Approaches to Language and Thought*, M. Hickman, ed. Orlando, FL: Aca-
            demic Press.
Wittgenstein, L.
    1958   *Philosophical Investigations.* Oxford: Blackwell.
Wolf, M.
    1972   *Women and the Family in Rural Taiwan.* Stanford: Stanford University Press.
Wyon, J.B., and J.E. Gordon
    1977   *The Khanna Study.* Cambridge, MA: Harvard University Press.
Zhao, Z.
    1997   Deliberate birth control in China before 1970. *Population and Development Review*
            23(4):729–767.

6

Learning and Using New Ideas:
A Sociocognitive Perspective

KATHLEEN M. CARLEY

One of the key ways in which individuals garner new information is through their interaction with others. Sometimes, individuals act as passive receptors and like a sponge soaking up new ideas, while at others times they actively seek new information. How individuals acquire and use such information is a function of both cognition and structure, the way they think and their position in the social world. Recent research in psychology, sociology, cognitive science, and communication theory has increased our understanding of the way in which individuals acquire and use information and the cognitive and social constraints on these processes.

It is useful to think about the acquisition and use of information as occurring within an interaction-knowledge network. From an individual's perspective, the nodes in the network can be the various sources of information, such as other individuals, organizations, books, or news shows. Most empirical studies, however, focus on networks with only one type of node—individuals. In this network, the ties between the nodes can be any type of linkage; examples include economic, advice, friendship, or social support. Again most empirical studies focus on only a small set of these linkages. However, the reality is that individuals acquire and use information within networks composed of multiple types of nodes and organized through a multiplex of relations. At the node level, cognitive constraints on the way individuals process information

Kathleen Carley is professor of sociology at Carnegie Mellon University.

affects behavior such as their ability to acquire and communicate information. At the tie level, structural constraints on the pattern of relations affect behavior. Most research focuses at either the node or the tie level. Recently, however, there has been some progress in understanding information diffusion from a combined cognitive and structural perspective.

COGNITION AND INFORMATION

It has become fairly commonplace for researchers in the behavioral and cognitive sciences to argue that human decision making is not rational. One form of this argument states that individuals are at least boundedly rational (Simon, 1976, 1979; Cyert and March, 1956, 1963; Carley and Newell, 1994; Carley and Prietula, 1994). The second form of this argument states that humans deviate in fairly systematic ways from the prescriptions of expected utility theory (Tversky and Kahneman, 1974; Ross et al., 1977; Kahneman et al., 1982). Research following both of these paradigmatic arguments is informing our understanding of how individuals acquire and use information.

Humans as Boundedly Rational

To say that humans are boundedly rational implies both that they are cognitively limited in their ability to process information and that they are structurally limited in their ability to acquire and disseminate information. A great deal of research in cognitive psychology, social psychology, and organization science points to the fact that in making decisions, individuals do not have full information and do not use all of the information they do have. For example, Feldman and March (1981) note that in organizations, most information that is collected is never used. They argue that information is often collected, particularly within organizations, simply to give others the appearance that one is acting rationally. Because the control of and access to information are instruments of power (Branscomb, 1994), information collection and dissemination become a means of maintaining and exercising power. Consequently, issues of individual response to power and status differentials play a role in understanding whether people will acquire and use information from particular sources.

A wide range of findings exists about the specific way in which humans process information. A classic cognitive limitation has to do with memory: the primacy and recency effect. The basic idea is that individuals have a tendency to remember information they heard first and last and to forget the material in between. Other cognitive limitations have to do with the complexity of the information (the classic 7 + -2 rule) and the fact that if individuals chunk information (e.g., by using memory tricks and mnemonics), they can remember more. Cognitive limitations essentially slow the rate of information diffusion.

One of the most interesting cognitive limitations is the way in which individuals assess causality; specifically, individuals use a "covariation principle" to assess causality (Heider, 1958; Kelley, 1967). The covariation principle states that if event A accompanies outcome B, and if event A is absent when outcome B is absent, then people tend to attribute A as the cause of B. There is ample evidence that individuals see causality and correlation as going together. In particular, individuals seem to construct correlations to confirm their prior expectations about what causes what (Chapman and Chapman, 1967, 1969). Individuals look for salient cues in suggesting causal links, rather than calculating them from the statistical occurrences (Fiske and Taylor, 1991). In other words, individuals seek out obvious indicators of what they think should be causing some outcome and use such cues to make predictions about others. From an information diffusion perspective, this means that individuals may incorrectly assume that the diffusion of a new birth control technique may have various beneficial or deleterious effects simply because of accidental temporal correlations.

Today, cognitive scientists are in the process of developing sophisticated models of cognition that are consistent with these and other known limitations. These models often take the form of computational models, such as ACT-R and Soar (for a more detailed review, see National Research Council, 1998). A key element of each of these models is that for an individual, future action (including learning and use of new information) is a function of what the individual already knows. In these models, as individuals learn they alter their mental models and typically cannot reconstruct how they thought about a problem prior to getting the new information. This effect, referred to as hindsight bias, has been shown in empirical studies to cause individuals to be unable to reproduce the decision that they would have made prior to knowing the true outcome (Wasserman et al., 1991). Or in other words, it is difficult for people to judge ahead of time how likely they are to accept new information and to judge, after the information has diffused, whether they were originally predisposed to accepting that information.

Much of the recent work in cognitive science focuses on the relation between information, language, and cognition (Hanson, 1990). Some of this work lies in the area of belief formation. In fact, there is a substantial literature on the role of messages in affecting individuals' attitudes and beliefs: for example, the work on reinforcement theory (Fishbein and Ajzen, 1975; Ajzen and Fishbein, 1980; Hunter et al., 1984) and information processing theory (Hovland and Pritzker, 1957; Anderson and Hovland, 1957;

Anderson, 1959, 1971; Hunter et al., 1984; for a more complete review, see National Research Council, 1998). This work often focuses on how attributes of the message, message content, and the sender affect the receiver's beliefs. Numerous empirical studies provide empirical evidence linking belief change to message content. Some studies suggest that more established beliefs are more difficult to change (Cantril, 1946; Anderson and Hovland, 1957; Hovland, 1972; Danes et al., 1984). Additional studies demonstrate the following (Whittaker, 1967, and Insko, 1967, contain reviews): unless extreme beliefs are associated with more information, they are generally more affected by contradictory information; when neutral messages lead to a belief change, the change is typically that predicted by a discrepancy model; and belief shifts are in the direction of the message for non-neutral messages. Information, unlike a disease, is not simply learned through contact. Information diffusion is not a contagion process but a complex sociocognitive process. The likelihood of the diffusing information affecting behavior is a function of whether those others one comes into contact with know the information (contagion), the extent to which those others have social influence on the receiver, and whether the message about the information is couched to support or disconfirm existing related beliefs.

Overall, much of the work that takes this approach to rationality is directed at specifying cognition at both a process and a knowledge level. Thus, issues of representation are as important as issues of process. The recent work on mental models is in this representational vein (Fauconnier, 1985). Additional process questions include: the role of emotions, speed and accuracy of response, and utilization of analogies (such as those used to comprehend time and distance). Much of this work has the potential to impact our understanding of communication and information seeking and usage behavior. However, further research is needed to illuminate this connection.

Humans as Deviates from Expected Utility Theory

Research in this area has focused on the way in which humans deviate from expected utility theory. Research in the past two decades has resulted in a number of findings about decision making in very context-specific domains. For example, work in this area suggests that individuals view losses and gains differently (Kahneman and Tversky, 1979); that how the information is presented creates a framing effect that then influences the ultimate decision (Tverksy and Kahneman, 1981); that decisions are often made on the basis of regret (i.e., what could have been) instead of the expected benefit (i.e., utility) of an outcome (Bell, 1982; Loomes and Sugden, 1982); that even minimal interaction leads to altruistic behavior (Orbell et al., 1988; Orbell and Dawes, 1993); and so on.

These deviations from expected utility theory are often referred to as biases or fallacies. Let us consider four of these: false consensus, representativeness, availability, and false uniqueness. The false consensus bias refers to the fact that most individuals tend to believe that others are like themselves (Dawes and Mulford, 1996; Dawes, 1989, 1990; Orbell and Dawes, 1993). Thus, people tend to overestimate the degree to which their own past behavior, as well as their expected future behavior, is truly diagnostic of other individuals' future behavior. Consequently, people will often assume agreement even when it does not exist, and so will fail to critically assess new information.

The representativeness bias refers to the fact that individuals often make decisions based on the similarity of the current situation (its characteristics and attributes) to a previous situation, rather than objective data (Tversky and Kahneman, 1974). This heuristic can cause individuals to believe in "the law of small numbers." Thus, people generally believe that random samples will resemble each other and the population more closely than statistical sampling theory would predict (Plous, 1993). When people use this heuristic, they will typically ignore base rate information. A base rate is the relative frequency with which some event is seen in the general population. A consequence is that individuals will make decisions based on what the situation reminds them of, rather than on statistical likelihoods.

The availability bias refers to the fact that individuals often make decisions based on what information is most salient. People often assess the "frequency of a class or the probability of an event by the ease with which instances or occurrences can be brought to mind" (Tversky and Kahneman, 1974:1127). This mental shortcut does not necessarily result in a biased judgment. However, it can when the information that is the most available is not the information that is most accurate due, for example, to recency or primacy effects.

The false uniqueness effect refers to the fact that individuals often rate themselves as better than others (Fiske and Taylor, 1991). For example, when asked to rate themselves on some task, such as driving ability, most people tend to see themselves as better than average. Most people, when asked to rate their contribution to a group, tend to view themselves as one of the strongest contributors, if not the strongest. This possible overrating of self is seen as related to a need by individuals to think of their abilities as relatively unique (Marks, 1984; Kernis, 1984). An interesting point is that while most individuals see their abilities as unique (and better than average), they see their opinions as shared by others (false consensus). Consequently, for matters of opinion individuals may be less likely to seek information from others simply because they assume they will not learn anything new.

Uncertainty and Stress

Human beings are not only not rational but most classical models of individual decision making provide little guidance for how people actually use information and make decisions in most settings (Connolly, 1993). The work on individual decision making under stress and uncertainty comes out of both approaches to rationality, and draws on work on decision making in naturalistic settings. Collectively, this work suggests that individual differences and the context are both important determinants of how individuals acquire and use information when faced with uncertainty. Cognitive biases, personal characteristics, and various sources of uncertainty combine to affect the way in which individuals use the information they acquire (Fischoff et al., 1981; MacCrimmon and Wehrung, 1986). Fischoff et al. (1981) suggest that when individuals must make a decision in an uncertain situation, their decision will be affected by: (1) uncertainty about the nature of the problem; (2) difficulties in assessing the facts; (3) difficulties in assessing the values; (4) uncertainty about what other people will do, think, or believe; and (5) difficulties in assessing the quality of the decision.

In general, people differ in the way in which they cope with new information and events, particularly those that induce stress (Thoits, 1991). Differences in coping styles cause people to want, and possibly to need, different information when confronted with stressful events (Miller, 1995). Emotional states, such as depression, can alter individuals' information seeking and giving behavior (Alloy, 1988). An individual's affective state can impact the extent to which an individual sees a situation as stressful, and stress can alter an individual's affective state. This complex interaction between stress and affective state in turn impacts how an individual searches and uses information. Moreover, people respond to others, at least in part, at an affective level (Heise, 1979; Heise and McKinnon, 1987; Smith-Lovin, 1987a, 1987b). Thus information is interpreted differently, is likely to be remembered differently, and will be sought differently depending on the affective basis of the interaction. For example, some researchers argue that individuals hold attitudes or beliefs because they meet particular psychological or affective needs (Katz, 1960; Herek, 1987); hence, erroneous beliefs might be held regardless of the amount of information learned because they reduce stress or increase feelings of self-esteem.

One of the current theoretical perspectives, naturalistic decision making, argues that individuals make decisions on the fly, often employing analogies with earlier events. Klein (1993), a leading proponent of this theoretical approach, has suggested a model of decision making in which the individual's first action is to recognize the linkage between the current event and something previous. This recognition primes the decision process and influences the subsequent outcome. Klein suggests that particularly under time stress, this is the key to the way in which people make decisions. From a naturalistic perspective, reasoning from argument and from case examples are the dominant ways in which individuals use information.

From the communication side, research has shown that not attending to the needs of the target audience can reduce the likelihood that they will retain the information provided and decreases the likelihood that they will pass it on. For example, Mita and Simmons (1995), after examining the diffusion of family planning information to young unmarried women in Bangladesh, argued that to be effective the communications needed to pay greater attention to the contraceptive needs of young women. The principle underlying this is that of immediate comprehension (Carley, 1986). The likelihood of a message being comprehended and remembered increases if the message is directly related to information already known by the receiver. Essentially, for most information receivers, to be really effective the information provider needs to make the link for the receiver between the new information and what the consumer already knows and wants to know. This decreases processing time on the part of the receiver and allows them to focus in on the new information.

Groups and Cognition

Researchers interested in cognition have also examined how being in a group or team affects cognition. Both theoretical and empirical work suggests the existence of information processing effects at the group level (Cannon-Bowers and Salas, 1990; Salas et al., 1994; Innami, 1992; Walsh and Fahey, 1986). This work has had a wide range. Three different issues that have been addressed are particularly important from a diffusion perspective: group think, distributed cognition, and transactive memory.

It is often argued that collections of individuals engage in group think (Janis, 1982). Group think is the tendency of groups to converge on ideas and to sanction aberrant ideas in such a fashion that important information may be ignored and erroneous decisions may be made. Groups also tend to polarize; that is, their decisions are more extreme than the average decision of the group members (Pruitt, 1971a, 1971b). Thus, groups tend to make decisions that are much more or much less risky than would the individuals in isolation (Pruitt, 1971a, 1971b). From a diffusion perspective, this means that learning new information in a group setting can cause the individuals to misestimate its importance and either overattend or underattend to the new information. Recent work in this area suggests that these group behaviors may be a function of both the initial distribution of information, beliefs, attitudes, and decisions as well as the underlying network connecting group members (Friedkin and Johnsen, 1990; Friedkin, 1991; Rice, 1993).

From a distributed standpoint, groups have an intelligence that is outside of the cognition of the individual members. Accordingly, group intelligence lies, in part, in the way in which information is distributed across group members and the linkages among group members. The work on distributed cognition suggests that groups and organizations as computational units are able to collectively represent and solve problems in ways that go beyond the cognitive abilities, knowledge, and possibly even awareness of the individuals in the group (Hutchins, 1995). The communication structure in the group is seen to influence the computational approach of the group to problems and the resultant decision (Carley and Svoboda, 1996).

Transactive memory refers to the ability of groups to have a memory system that exceeds that of the individuals in the group (Wegner, 1987; Wegner et al., 1991; Moreland, in press). Related ideas are joint remembering (Edwards and Middleton, 1986) and group remembering. Research on transactive memory, like that on distributed cognition, relies on the idea that knowledge is stored as much in the connections among individuals as in the individuals. Wegner developed the theory (Wegner, 1987) and an associated computational model (Wegner, 1995) at the dyadic level by drawing on work in computer science. He argues that processing factors that are relevant when linking together computers (such as directory updating, information allocation, and coordination of retrieval) are also relevant when linking together the memories of humans into a group memory. Empirical research suggests that the memory of natural groups is better than the memory of assigned groups even when all individuals involved know the same things (even for groups larger than dyads, Moreland, in press). Further, Moreland et al. (1996, in press) have shown that transactive memory tends to improve group performance. And groups of individuals who train together tend to have better recall of how to approach problems than do groups where the individuals train separately (Liang et al., 1995). Collectively, this body of research suggests that for individuals and especially for the group, knowledge of who knows what may be as important a determinant of group performance as task knowledge.

SOCIAL STRUCTURE AND INFORMATION

Individual cognition is an important determinant of the way in which individuals acquire and use information. However, as hinted at by the work on transactive memory, cognition is not the sole determinant of information-based behavior. One reason for this is that there is a difference between "reality" and reality as perceived by the individual (Cooley, 1902; Mead, 1962; Festinger, 1954, 1957). Reality as perceived by the individual is often a function of his or her position in the underlying social network. This point is eloquently made by the decades of research on social structure that has repeatedly demonstrated that an individual's beliefs, attitudes, knowledge, and actions are as much a function of who is known as it is of what is known and that the underlying social structure is critical to the diffusion process (Rapoport, 1953; Katz, 1961; Rogers, 1995). This research has led to a more thorough understanding of the way in which the underlying social network influences individual, group, organizational, and community behavior (Wellman and Berkowitz, 1988; Wellman, 1997). Collectively this work has repeatedly shown the influence of who you know, and the position of the individual in the network, on the individual's consequent actions.

Studies of information diffusion have demonstrated the utility of the social network approach and the value of many of the network-based measures for understanding diffusion (Coleman et al., 1966; Burt, 1973, 1980; Valente, 1995; Morris, 1994; Carley with Wendt, 1991; Friedkin, 1993). These studies suggest that what information the individual has, what decisions the individual makes, what beliefs the individual holds, and how strongly the individual holds a belief are all affected by the individual's social network. A variety of network effects, such as whether or not the individual is peripheral or central in the network, the number of other individuals communicated with, the strength of the relationship with those other individuals, whether the tie is embedded in a triad, and the symmetry of the relationship, play a role in the way in which individuals acquire and use information. For example, central individuals (those connected to a large number of other individuals) are in a better position to acquire new information (Freeman, 1979; Weenig and Midden, 1991) and are more likely to have access to novel information (Valente, 1995). The higher the level of network cohesion, the higher the level of communication about the issue of concern (Friedkin, 1993). More peripheral individuals may be more likely to act on novel information or to generate innovations (Burt, 1973, 1980; Lin and Burt, 1975). Individuals who are more central may be overconstrained and so unable to act on novel information, particularly if they are embedded in a large number of triadic (Simelian) relations (Krackhardt, 1999a, 1999b). Such individuals are so constrained by being involved in a large number of triadic relations that owing allegiance to all can act for none.

From an information diffusion perspective, the literature clearly shows that different factors influence the diffusion of ideas and technologies. For example, institutional constraints (Strang and Meyer, 1993), cost, and network externalities such as how many people use a technology are important determinants of technology adoption (Kraut et al., 1997). However, cost in particular has less to do with the diffusion of information. Herein, the focus is primarily on the diffusion of ideas. Research in this area has a long tradition (Festinger et al., 1948; Allen, 1977; Cole and Cole, 1973; Valente, 1995). Researchers have examined the diffusion of many different types of information, including rumors (Festinger et al., 1948, Festinger et al., 1950), job openings (Granovetter, 1974), scientific information (Price, 1965a, 1965b; Carley, 1990), technological information (Allen, 1977), and information about family planning (Valente et al., 1997). Collectively, this research has led to a number of findings. For example, information flows more quickly in integrated groups (Coleman et al., 1966), but only if the groups are relatively small and have relatively simple cultures (Carley, 1991; Kaufer and Carley, 1994). Individuals are often more willing to seek group-threatening information (such as information about new jobs) from individuals with whom they have little regular contact (weak ties) (Granovetter, 1973, 1974). Altering the communication technology can alter the flow of information and thus the overall performance of the group (Rice, 1994). Whether information flows from one group to another depends on both the degree of interaction within the two groups and the degree of interaction between the two groups (Kaufer and Carley, 1994). Although information diffuses through networks, the likelihood that the information will actually diffuse to a specific individual depends on the number of network ties (Weenig and Midden, 1991). The likelihood that the information will actually diffuse from one group to another, and the speed with which it will diffuse, depends on the heterogeneity of each group and the number of ties or boundary spanners between the two groups (Kaufer and Carley, 1993).

The underlying social network influences what information the individual acquires, how that information is used, and the way that information is filtered into terms affecting individual choice. In other words, social networks have both a social learning and a social influence effect (Montgomery and Casterline, 1996). Social learning involves the acquisition of information from others. In this case, the individual's position in his or her social network, the "who talks to whom," influences diffusion. The information that is learned might have to do with what new technologies are available, with who uses what technology, or with the health, social, political and economic consequences of various choices. The information need not be accurate and may encompass beliefs. Social influence is the weight of authority, deference, reciprocity, and social conformity pressures that individuals place on each other. The individual's position in his or her social network and the opinions held by those in that network collectively influence the individual's opinion (Friedkin and Johnsen, 1990).

Recent work on contraceptive use demonstrates the myriad of ways in which the underlying social network affects choice (Entwisle and Godley, 1998). In a study of Cameroonian women, Valente et al. (1997) demonstrated that individuals who were advised to engage in a behavior by their network were more likely to engage in that behavior. Further, an individual's perception of how his or her network will respond to a situation is an important determinant of the individual's behavior regardless of whether the individual's perceptions are accurate (Valente et al., 1997). Nevertheless, although an individual's network position may affect whether or not the individual hears about an innovation, the position itself may not determine adoption of the innovation. In fact, research on diffusion networks has found mixed support for the claim that network exposure increases adoption (Valente, 1995). A person's network exposure is the proportion of others in the individual's personal network that are themselves adopters. Consequently, although network position is perhaps the primary determinant of what information the individual acquires, it is only one of the determinants of how the individual uses that information and what actions are subsequently taken. In terms of information usage, a variety of factors are critical, including personal characteristics, cognitive processing abilities and biases, the individual's network position, the individual's perception of his or her network, and the consequent influence of others on one's actions.

In most societies there are multiple types of ties that link individuals (e.g., see Sampson, 1969; Roethlisberger and Dickson, 1939). This is referred to as multiplexity (White et al., 1976). Ties include socioemotional ties such as friendship, and instrumental ties such as advice giving and money lending. Different types of ties are often used to access different types of information. Moreover, individuals receive not just different information, but different types of social support through different ties (Wellman, 1992; Wellman and Wortley, 1990). Such ties have both a direct effect on the individual's information-gathering ability (changing what information is accessible) and an indirect effect by influencing the degree of social support, which influences the individual's mental health and affective state. This in turn affects the individual's propensity to seek information and the way in which information is interpreted once it has been found.

One question is whether such multiplexity enhances or constrains the flow of new ideas. The stronger the multiplex of relations that connect two individuals, the more likely they are to find it easy to communicate and to have a host of shared experiences on which to base their communication, and the less likely they are to know information not known by the other. For example, if the individual is seeking out sensitive information, or information not commonly known by the group, then weak ties may be key. This is known as the weak tie hypotheses (Granovetter, 1973). Further, different types of information flow through different ties. As a trivial example, work-related information rarely flows through kinship ties. Thus, highly multiplexed relations may actually inhibit the flow of new ideas, particularly for ideas originating outside of the group. For getting new information, nonsymmetric relationships may be key. In particular, individuals are more likely to seek out and try to acquire information from those with whom they are relatively more similar even if those others do not seek them out (Carley and Krackhardt, 1996).

An important factor in information diffusion may have to do with whether individuals are information seekers or passive receptors of information, although it may be difficult to disentangle the two (Leenders, 1997). In the seeking model, individuals are information processors who actively seek information. According to the seeking model, the resultant distribution of information is dependent on the goal orientation of the individuals. Information-seeking behavior is not viewed as random, but subject to constraints and the topology of the social space. Because of time and resource constraints, individuals seek information-using channels with which they are familiar. Moreover, channel characteristics (weak or strong ties) appear to affect what information is sought, and the success of that search (Granovetter, 1973, 1974). Motivation then affects the way in which the channels are used, but not whether the social structure bears a relation on diffusion. A type of variant on the information-seeking models is the utility maximization model. Here individuals interact because doing so is expected to increase their utility (Durlauf, 1996).

Social networks are not static but change over time, often dramatically (Weesie and Flap, 1990; Doreian and Stokman, 1997). However, only a few models exist for predicting this change (Holland and Leinhardt, 1977; Sanil et al., 1995; Banks and Carley, 1996). Much of the work on network evolution has focused on change in friendship networks (Johnson, 1986; Carley and Krackhardt, 1996; Zeggelink, 1993, 1995, 1996). This work shows that networks are incredibly homogeneous (that is, most people in an individual's network are, for example, of the same gender, race, or educational level). Further, as networks of friends evolve, the overall network of individuals becomes organized into a set of self-reinforcing groups (Zeggelink et al., 1996; Stokman and Zeggelink, 1996). Individuals who are under stress tend to drop from their social network individuals with whom they have less in common and are more weakly tied (Behrens, 1997). An important source of change in underlying social networks is change in the distribution of information. Such cultural-level changes can be a function of technology.

Technology and Information Diffusion

Communication technologies play an important role in getting information to people (Valente et al., 1994). Gantz et al. (1986), in discussing a local news event, noted that 80 percent of the subjects first heard of the event through interpersonal sources. However, in terms of follow-up details, the mass media quickly assumed a dominant role as the primary diffuser of information. Print media, and indeed any communication media that encapsulate the views of the author, increase the author's reach and so make possible the wider and more rapid spread of information (Kaufer and Carley, 1993, 1994, 1996). The mass media often become the primary source of details on new information because of their one-to-many capabilities and ability to transmit an encapsulated message with less change in that message. Nevertheless, at an individual level, different types of people will choose to communicate their ideas by different media (Haythornthwaite et al., 1995).

Communication technologies are not guaranteed to increase the extent to which individuals are informed. Telecommunication technologies often have been touted as the mechanism by which the knowledge gap across people will be reduced. However, recent research suggests that it is possible that such technologies will simply create an information elite and that under such technologies the knowledge gap will widen (Alstyne and Brynjolfsson, 1995, 1996; Carley, 1995, 1996). Moreover, such technology can increase competition among ideas, leading to overload rather than clarification (Carley, 1995, 1996). Changing access to technology can alter the underlying network structure and so alter who is likely to have access to what information (Alstyne and Brynjolfsson, 1996; Carley, 1995, 1996) and thus change the distribution of power (Barley, 1990; Butler and Gibbons, 1997).

Perhaps the most important feature of the new telecommunication technologies is that they are a source of both information and social support (Hiltz and Wellman, 1997). New communication technologies can have substantial social, and even psychological, consequences as they alter the way in which individuals acquire and use new information (see, for example, Price, 1965b; Rice, 1984; Sproull and Kiesler, 1991). For example, technologies such as e-mail can reduce social status cues and increase anonymity, thus facilitating the acquisition of novel and "stressful" information (Sproull and Kiesler, 1991). Communication technologies that enable some of an individual's ideas to remain intact and unchanged over time, and to be communicated without the individual being present, facilitate communication at great geographical and temporal distances (Kaufer and Carley, 1993). In fact, one of the reasons that technology is expected to have such a profound effect on the redistribution of knowledge, networks, and power is because the technology is expected to overcome the profound influence of physical space.

Physical Space and Information Diffusion

One of the most prevalent findings in the communication of information and the consequent impact of that information is that distance matters. Physical distance impacts information diffusion both at a micro level (diffusion within the same organization or living complex) and at a macro or societal level (diffusion across a country or between countries). At the micro level, people tend to interact more with those to whom they are proximate (Allen, 1977; Latane et al., 1995). People are also more likely to be influenced by the attitudes of those to whom they are proximate (Rice and Aydin, 1991). In fact, communication bridges that increase the physical proximity among people are thought to be critical to successful innovation (Allen, 1977). Entwisle et al. (1996) found that village location and placement of family planning services had a critical impact on patterns of contraceptive choice.

Latane et al. (1995) found that the physically closer in space two individuals are to each other, the more frequent are the interactions they recall. Results suggest that the relationship between distance and interaction frequency may be describable by an inverse power law with a slope of −1. At the societal level, spatial factors also affect the flow of information between nations and organizations (Strang and Tuma, 1993). Geographers have worked on the problem of diffusion and spatial models for a long time (for a review of this work, see Abler et al., 1971). Modern GIS systems and new statistical techniques for taking location into account are providing a better understanding of the spatial determinants of position. Computational multiagent models using spatial positioning now can be used to develop veridical theories of the impact of location on information diffusion and choice. Further, the new Geographic Information Systems may ultimately enable analyses such as that conducted by Entwisle et al. (1996) to become more economically feasible.

Recent work in this area is suggesting that it is not physical space per se that may be important, but rather perceived distance. In particular, low-cost telecommunication options are providing individuals with the opportunity to create physically distant socioemotional support networks. In other words, electronic groups are beginning to look like virtual social networks and provide information and support needs (Wellman, 1997). This can be an important source of information for individuals, particularly for information about rare events and new technology. The presence of computers and access to the Internet could become a key determinant of the patterns of contraceptive choice in countries with otherwise low access to telecommunication technology.

Recent Advances Linking Structure and Cognition

An information processing perspective links much of the work on both cognition (Reitman, 1965) and information diffusion (Rogers, 1995). However, there are few theories, let alone formal models, that consider the joint role of cognition and structure on information diffusion. The work in this area tends to focus on diffusion in one of two ways: linking individuals' differences and social position or linking culture and social structure.

Individual Difference Perspectives

Numerous empirical studies demonstrate that social pressure influences individuals' attitudes. In particular, an individual's attitude is influenced by what he or she thinks others believe and social norms (Molm, 1978; Humphrey et al., 1988; Fulk, 1993, for example). The plethora of research on these social processes and pressures has led to a number of different theories about the way in which individuals process and use social information, including social comparison theory (Festinger, 1954), social learning (Bandura, 1977), social information processing (Salancik and Pfeffer, 1978; Rice and Aydin, 1991), and social influence theory (Friedkin and Johnsen, 1990). Most theories posit a simple process by which individuals interact with a small group of others, learn their attitudes or beliefs, weight this information by their network ties to these others, and then alter their beliefs (e.g., Rice and Aydin, 1991; Fulk, 1993; Rice, 1993). In the demographic research, individual perceptions and beliefs are conspicuously absent (Montgomery, 1997, 1999). New models of individuals' perceptions of fertility and the risk of conception are needed that offer a social learning perspective that accounts for differences (Montgomery and Casterline, 1996).

Valente's (1996) threshold model of diffusion posits a role for both cognition (in the form of individual differences) and structure (in terms of relational influences) in determining the acquisition and use of information. In this model, each individual has an internal threshold for accepting or acting on new information that depends on the type of information and possibly individual psychological traits such as the need for acceptance (Valente, 1995). This threshold can be interpreted as the number of surrounding others who need to accept or act on a piece of information before the individual in question does. There are two unique features to this model. First, it enables researchers to compare relational versus structural influences by varying parameters of social influence (near versus distal others, relational versus structural weighting). Second, this model demonstrates that individuals, or other adopting units, vary in the amount of social influence needed for them to adopt.

Interestingly, this literature has also shown some support for the idea that individuals' personal characteristics influence the likelihood that they will discover new information (Allen, 1977). However, the overall context may affect what self-image is evoked and so how the individual responds to information (Ridgeway and Smith-Lovin, 1996). In particular, as was previously discussed, the individual's emotional state affects the access to and use of information.

Cultural Perspectives

Cognition and culture are inextricably woven together (Carley, 1991; Hutchins, 1995). The pattern of communication among individuals creates a joint cognition and serves to alter culture (Kaufer and Carley, 1993; Hutchins and Hazlehurst, 1991). Current work in this area is being carried out through computational analysis. Computer simulations of groups jointly working, exchanging information, and communicating are used to explore how individualized cognition and connections among individuals can work together to lead to the emergence of social change, new social structures, and social cognition. As individuals interact and exchange ideas, beliefs, and attitudes, the underlying sociocultural environment changes. Subgroups (Carley, 1991) and subcultures form (Latane and Bourgeois, 1996). Certain beliefs come to dominate (Krackhardt, 1997; Boorman and Levitt, 1980). Three basic approaches are being examined: spatial basis, cultural connections, and sociobiological approach. All three approaches draw on the fact that empirical evidence demonstrates that, over time through interaction, group members become more alike and their attitudes and beliefs become correlated (Latane and Bourgeois, 1996). All three approaches assume some form of dynamics.

The first approach examines the interaction between structure and cognition by focusing on interaction exchange among actors who are structurally constrained by their physical position in a space. A key feature of this approach is that individuals tend to be more influenced by those who are physically nearby. Thus spatial factors that influence who interacts with whom can give rise to locally consistent patterns of shared attitudes, meanings, and beliefs. An example of this approach is Latane's dynamic social impact theory (DSIT), which suggests that individuals who interact with and influence each other can produce organized patterns at the group or unit level that serve as a communicable representation which can be identified by others (Latane, 1996; Huguet and Latane, 1996). Latane (1996) uses an evolutionary approach to suggest ways in which communication can lead to change in attitudes as individuals develop cognitive bundles of information that then become distributed through the social space. A similar approach to Latane's is taken in the work on A-Life by Epstein and Axtell (1996). A simplified version of such theories can be modeled as a game of artificial life. Actors are laid out spatially on a grid. Actors can interact with those nearest (e.g., those to the north, south, west, and east). Individuals begin with one of two competing messages or attitudes or beliefs. These diffuse simultaneously. Generally, these two beliefs are treated as being in opposition, and an individual cannot hold both simultaneously. Initially beliefs may be distributed randomly; however, over time, actors come to hold beliefs similar to those near them.

The second approach assumes that actors structure their own space by forming and reforming connections among themselves as they interact and exchange information while doing some tasks. A key feature of this approach is that part of the intelligence of the society is thought to reside in the pattern of connections among actors and not just within the minds of the actors. An example of this approach is constructural theory (Carley, 1990, 1991, 1995; Kaufer and Carley, 1993). Constructural theory posits that both the individual cognition and the sociocultural environment are continuously constructed and reconstructed as individuals concurrently go through a cycle of interaction, adaptation, and motivation that moves them through an interaction-knowledge space (Carley, 1991). According to the basic formulation, individuals engage in a fundamental interaction-shared knowledge cycle in which individuals provide information to and receive information from those with whom they interact, thereby irrevocably altering their future interaction and communication behavior. According to this theory, the concurrent actions by individuals necessarily lead to the coevolution of social structure and culture. Concurrent actions lead to the redistribution of information and interaction partners across the actors (Carley, 1999). The innovator's position in the sociocultural environment determines how fast new ideas diffuse, consensus forms, and cliques form. However, as ideas diffuse, consensus forms, and cliques evolve, the innovator's position changes. A consequence is that very minute initial differences in the underlying sociocultural configurations may facilitate or hinder information diffusion and consensus formation. Communication technologies affect which sociocultural configurations best facilitate information diffusion and consensus formation, because they affect the properties of the actor and the way in which the actor can engage others in the exchange of information. A second consequence is that what norms or social biases the group, organization, or society form may well be the result of the relative rate of change in information diffusion, consensus formation, and clique formation (Carley and Hill, 2001).

According to the constructural perspective, beliefs and attitudes mediate one's interpersonal relationships through a process of "social adjustment" (Smith et al., 1956; Smith, 1973), and social structure affects what attitudes and beliefs the individual holds (Heider, 1946) as well as other behavior (White et al., 1976; Burt, 1982). It follows that if those with whom the individual interacts hold an erroneous belief, then the individual can become convinced of the erroneous belief despite factual evidence, and will in turn persuade others. For controversial information, such as beliefs, what belief dominates is a function of the size of the population and the extent of the underlying information. Consequently, large information-poor groups can become dominated by erroneous beliefs. For example, in an information-poor group, such as members of a third-world country, an erroneous belief may persist, such as a belief that there is high infant mortality even after the mortality rate has declined. Because the perceptions of mortality declines are related to fertility declines (Montgomery and Casterline, 1998), an underlying constructural process that results in lagged mortality perceptions may be at the root of delayed changes in fertility-related behavior.

The third approach draws on the work in sociobiology to argue for a joint structural and behavioral basis for information transfer (Krackhardt, 1997; Boorman and Levitt, 1980). The basic idea is that the diffusion of controversial information, like beliefs, is a socially determined phenomenon. Thus, when there are competing beliefs, whether individuals hold a belief depends not just on what they know, but also on whether or not those surrounding them also hold that belief. Social change and the dominance of particular beliefs is a function of the social structure (number of groups, size of groups, pattern of connection among groups, mobility between groups, and initial distribution of beliefs) and individual differences (likelihood of an individual changing a belief as he or she encounters others). There are three main findings from this research. First, in a large undifferentiated society, no controversial innovation can survive unless it begins with a large proportion of believers in the innovation. Second, there are structured conditions under which even a very small minority of innovators can take over a large society. And finally, once the innovation has taken hold across the society, it is virtually impossible for the preinnovation state to recover dominance in the organization, even if it begins with the same structural conditions that the innovators enjoyed.

TOWARD A SOCIOCOGNITIVE APPROACH
TO INFORMATION DIFFUSION

Communication theorists typically argue that the individual who receives a message changes his or her attitude toward both the subject of the message and the individual from whom he or she receives the message as a function of the message (Hunter et al., 1984). Empirical evidence supports this contention. Thus, information diffusion is both affected by and affects what individuals know and whom they know. Cognition and social structure become linked in a dynamic cycle in which the communication of information alters the underlying cognitive and social structures. Thus policies seeking to aid or inhibit the diffusion of particular information need to consider not just the foibles of human cognition, not just the underlying social networks of the relevant individuals, but also the basic dynamic processes through which the social networks and knowledge coevolves.

Some theories of the fertility transition take diffusion effects into account. Following Montgomery and Casterline (1996) in the most sophisticated of the diffusion models, both social learning and social influence are considered. When this is done, the models fit the empirical data better and enable an explanation for why fertility choices lag mortality decline. In particular, simple simulation models demonstrate that as the size of individuals' networks and the extent to which they are influenced by others increases, information converges faster and there is consequent greater homogeneity in choice (Montgomery and Casterline, 1998). However, even in these models the social network is decoupled from learning; that is, the network is treated as static.

The brief summary provided in this paper suggests that choice is a function of both the social network and human cognition. At a minimum, this means that the diffusion process can be better characterized by taking into account both what the individual knows and who the individual knows. More than this, however, recent work, both empirical and theoretical, indicates that the social and the cognitive are linked. To make clear the relations, it is worth thinking in terms of four constructs: people, knowledge, location, and choice. This defines a set of networks (see Table 6-1). What this summary has indicated is that each of these networks plays a role in affecting fertility-related behavior. Most studies, however, have considered only a couple of cells in the metamatrix at a time, and kept the others fixed. For example, Montgomery and Casterline (1998) model diffusion

TABLE 6-1 Metamatrix of Networks and Choice

	People	Knowledge	Location	Choice
People	Social network	Knowledge network	Physical network	Choice network
Knowledge		Information network	Community network	Decision network
Location			Geographic network	Voting network
Choice				Tradeoffs network

and choice (thus the knowledge network and choice network) by keeping the social network fixed and ignoring all other networks.

The diffusion models that have been used in social and organizational studies have two key advantages over those currently used in fertility studies. First, in some of these models the social network and knowledge network coevolve; neither is taken as fixed. This enables the long-run consequence of policy interventions to be evaluated more completely. Second, in these models the agents are heterogeneous; that is, they vary in terms of their social, knowledge, physical, and choice networks. Human networks are quite heterogeneous. For example, some people cite less than five people they talk to about health matters while others cite dozens. The impact of influence will vary based on the size of their individual networks. Thus, multiagent models that capture this heterogeneity may afford better predictions and more accurate estimates of the impact of policies.

Multiagent models where the agents' interactions are constrained by where they are physically located in space, their social networks, what they already know, the choices they need to make, and the available telecommunication technology hold out a promise for improved theoretical understanding of the diffusion process.

REFERENCES

Abler, R., J.S. Adams, and R.F.P. Gould
　　1971　*Spatial Organization*. Englewood Cliffs, NJ: Prentice-Hall.
Ajzen, I., and M. Fishbein
　　1980　*Understanding Attitudes and Predicting Social Behavior*. Englewood Cliffs, NJ: Prentice-Hall.
Allen, T.J.
　　1977　*Managing the Flow of Technology: Technology Transfer and the Dissemination of Technological Information Within the R and D Organization*. Cambridge, MA: MIT Press.
Alloy, L.B., ed.
　　1988　*Cognitive Processes in Depression*. New York: Guilford Press.
Alstyne, M.v., and E. Brynjolfsson
　　1995　Communication Networks and the Rise of an Information Elite—Does Communication Help the Rich Get Richer? Unpublished paper presented at the International Conference on Information Systems, December 14–17, Amsterdam.
　　1996　Wider access and narrower focus: Could the Internet Balkanize science? *Science* 274(5292):1479–1480.
Anderson, N.H.
　　1959　Test of a model for opinion change. *Journal of Abnormal and Social Psychology* 59:371–381.
　　1971　Integration theory and attitude change. *Psychological Review* 78:171–206.
Anderson, N.H., and C. Hovland
　　1957　The representation of order effects in communication research. In *The Order of Presentation in Persuasion*, C. Hovland, ed. New Haven: Yale University Press.

Bandura, A.
  1977   *Social Learning Theory*. Englewood Cliffs, NJ: Prentice-Hall.
Banks, D., and K.M. Carley
  1996   Models of social network evolution. *Journal of Mathematical Sociology* 21(1-2):173–196.
Barley, S.
  1990   The alignment of technology and structure through roles and networks. *Administrative Science Quarterly* 61–101.
Behrens, D.M.
  1997   Self-Isolation and The Structuring of Support: The Relationship Between Stress and Network Evolution. Unpublished Ph.D. dissertation, Carnegie Mellon University.
Bell, D.E.
  1982   Regret in decision making under uncertainty. *Operations Research* 30:961–981.
Boorman, S.A., and P.R. Levitt
  1980   *The Genetics of Altruism*. New York: Academic Press.
Branscomb, A.W.
  1994   *Who Owns Information? From Privacy to Public Access*. New York: Basic Books.
Burt, R.S.
  1973   The differential impact of social integration on participation in the diffusion of innovations. *Social Science Research* 2:125–144.
  1980   Innovation as a structural interest: Rethinking the impact of network position innovation adoption. *Social Networks* 4:337–355.
  1982   *Toward a Structural Theory of Action*. New York: Academic Press.
Butler, B.S., and D.E. Gibbons
  1997   Power distribution as a catalyst and consequence of decentralized technology diffusion. In *Information Systems and Technology: Innovation and Diffusion*, T. Larsen and G. McGuire, eds. Hershey, PA: Idea Group.
Cannon-Bowers, J.A., and E. Salas
  1990   Cognitive Psychology and Team Training: Shared Mental Models in Complex Systems. Unpublished paper presented at the annual meeting of the Society for Industrial and Organizational Psychology, Miami, FL.
Cantril, H.
  1946   The intensity of an attitude. *Journal of Abnormal and Social Psychology* 41:129–135.
Carley, K.M.
  1986   An approach for relating social structure to cognitive structure. *Journal of Mathematical Sociology* 12(2):137–189.
  1990   Structural constraints on communication: The diffusion of the homomorphic signal analysis technique through scientific fields. *Journal of Mathematical Sociology* 15(3-4):207–246.
  1991   A theory of group stability. *American Sociological Review* 56(3):331–354.
  1995   Communication technologies and their effect on cultural homogeneity, consensus, and the diffusion of new ideas. *Sociological Perspectives* 38(4):547–571.
  1996   Communicating new ideas: The potential impact of information and telecommunication technology. *Technology in Society* 18(2):219–230.
  1999   On the evolution of social and organizational networks. Pp. 3–30 in Vol. 16 (special issue), Research in the Sociology of Organizations in *Networks In and Around Organizations*, Steven B. Andrews and David Knoke, eds. Stamford, CT: JAI Press, Inc.
Carley, K.M., and V. Hill
  2001   Structural change and learning within organizations. In *Dynamics of Organizational Societies: Models, Theories and Methods*, Alessandro Lomi, ed. Cambridge, MA: MIT Press/AAAI Press/Live Oak.

Carley, K.M., and D. Krackhardt
1996 Cognitive inconsistencies and non-symmetric friendship. *Social Networks* 18:1–27.
Carley, K.M., and A. Newell
1994 The nature of the social agent. *Journal of Mathematical Sociology* 19(4):221–262.
Carley, K.M., and M.J. Prietula
1994 ACTS Theory: Extending the model of bounded rationality. Pp. 55–88 in *Computational Organization Theory*, K.M. Carley and M.J. Prietula, eds. Hillsdale, NJ: Lawrence Erlbaum Associates.
Carley, K.M., and D.M. Svoboda
1996 Modeling organizational adaptation as a simulated annealing process. *Sociological Methods and Research* 25(1):138–168.
Carley, K.M., with K. Wendt
1991 Electronic mail and scientific communication: A study of the soar extended research group. *Knowledge: Creation, Diffusion, Utilization* 12(4):406–440.
Chapman, L.J., and J.P. Chapman
1967 Genesis of popular but erroneous psychodiagnostic observations. *Journal of Abnormal Psychology* 72(3):193–204.
1969 Illusory correlation as an obstacle to the use of valid psychodiagnostic signs. *Journal of Abnormal Psychology* 74(3): 271–280.
Cole, J.R., and S. Cole
1973 *Social Stratification in Science*. Chicago: University of Chicago Press.
Coleman, J.S., E. Katz, and H. Menzel
1966 *Medical Innovation: A Diffusion Study*. New York: Bobbs-Merrill Company, Inc.
Connolly, T.
1993 Why classical decision theory is an inappropriate standard for evaluating and aiding most human decision making. Chap. 2 in *Decision Making in Action: Models and Methods*, Gary A. Klein, ed. Norwood, NJ: Ablex.
Cooley, C.
1902 *Human Nature and Social Order*. New York: Scribner.
Cyert, R., and J.G. March
1956 Organizational factors in the theory of oligopoly. *Quarterly Journal of Economics* 70:44–64.
1963 *A Behavioral Theory of the Firm*. Englewood Cliffs, NJ: Prentice-Hall.
Danes, J.E., J.E. Hunter, and J. Woelfel
1984 Belief change and accumulated information. In *Mathematical Models of Attitude Change: Change in Single Attitudes and Cognitive Structure*, J. Hunter, J. Danes, and S. Cohen, eds. Orlando, FL: Academic Press.
Dawes, R.M.
1989 Statistical criteria for establishing a truly false consensus effect. *Journal of Experimental Social Psychology* 25:1–17.
1990 The potential non-falsity of the false consensus effect. Pp. 179–199 in *Insights in Decision Making: A Tribute to Hillel J. Einhorn*, R.M. Hogarth, ed. Chicago: University of Chicago Press.
Dawes, R.M., and M. Mulford
1996 The false consensus effect and overconfidence: Flaws in judgment or flaws in how we study judgment? *Organizational Behavior and Human Decision Processes* 65(3):201–211.
Doreian, P., and F.N. Stokman, eds.
1997 *Evolution of Social Networks*. Amsterdam: Gordon and Breach Publishers.
Durlauf, S.N.
1996 Statistical Mechanics Approaches to Socioeconomic Behavior. Working Paper, Santa Fe Institute, Santa Fe, NM.

Entwisle, B., R.R. Rindfuss, D. Guilkey, A. Chamratrithirong, S.R. Curran, and Y. Sawangdee
  1996   Community and contraceptive choice in rural Thailand: A case study of Nan Rong. *Demography* 33(1):1–11.
Entwisle, B., and J. Godley
  1998   Village Networks and Patterns of Contraceptive Choice. Unpublished paper presented at the Workshop on The Social Processes on Underlying Fertility Change in Developing Countries, January 29–30, Washington, DC.
Epstein, J., and R. Axtell
  1996   *Growing Artificial Societies*. Boston: MIT Press.
Fauconnier, G.
  1985   *Mental Spaces: Aspects of Meaning Construction in Natural Language*. Cambridge, MA: MIT Press.
Feldman, M.S., and J.G. March
  1981   Information in organizations as signal and symbol. *Administrative Science Quarterly* 26:171–186.
Festinger, L.
  1954   A theory of social comparison processes. *Human Relations* 7:114–140.
  1957   *A Theory of Cognitive Dissonance*. Evanston, IL: Row Peterson.
Festinger, L., D. Cartwright, K. Barber, J. Fleishl, J. Gottdanker, A. Keysen, and G. Leavitt
  1948   The study of a rumor: Its origin and spread. *Human Relations* 1:464–486.
Festinger, L., S. Schachter, and K. Back
  1950   *Social pressures in informal groups: A study of human factors in housing*. Palo Alto, CA: Stanford University Press.
Fischoff, B., S. Lichtenstein, P. Slovic, S. Derby, and R. Keeney
  1981   *Acceptable Risk*. New York: Cambridge University Press.
Fishbein, M., and I. Ajzen
  1975   *Belief, Attitude, Intention and Behavior*. Reading, MA: Addison-Wesley.
Fiske, S., and S. Taylor
  1991   *Social Cognition*. New York: McGraw-Hill.
Freeman, L.C.
  1979   Centrality in social networks: Conceptual clarification. *Social Networks* 1:215–239.
Friedkin, N.E.
  1991   Theoretical foundations for centrality measures. *American Journal of Sociology* 96(6):1478–1504.
  1993   Structural bases on interpersonal influence in groups: A longitudinal case study. *American Sociological Review* 56(6):861–872.
Friedkin, N.E., and E.C. Johnsen
  1990   Social influence and opinions. *Journal of Mathematical Sociology* 15:193–205.
Fulk, J.
  1993   Social construction of communication technology. *Academy of Management Journal* 36(5):921–950.
Gantz, W., K.A. Krendl, and S.R. Robertson
  1986   Diffusion of a proximate news event. *Journalism Quarterly* 63(2):282–287.
Granovetter, M.S.
  1973   The strength of weak ties. *American Journal of Sociology* 78(6):1360–1380.
  1974   *Getting a Job: A Study of Contacts and Careers*. Cambridge, MA: Harvard University Press.
Hanson, P.P., ed.
  1990   *Information, Language, and Cognition*. Vancouver: University of British Columbia Press.
Haythornthwaite, C., B. Wellman, and M. Mantei
  1995   Work relationships and media use: A social network analysis. *Group Decision and Negotiation* 4:193–211.

Heider, F.
1946   Attitudes and cognitive organization. *Journal of Psychology* 21:107–112.
Heider, F.
1958   *The Psychology of Interpersonal Relations.* New York: Wiley.
Heise, D.R.
1979   *Understanding Events: Affect and the Construction of Social Action.* Cambridge, Eng.: Cambridge University Press.
Heise, D.R., and N.J. McKinnon
1987   Affective bases of likelihood judgments. *Journal of Mathematical Sociology* 13:133–151.
Herek, G.
1987   Can functions be measured? A new perspective on the functional approach to attitudes. *Social Psychology Quarterly* 50:285–303.
Hiltz, S.R., and B. Wellman
1997   Asynchronous learning networks as a virtual classroom. *Communications of the ACM* 40(9):44–49.
Holland, P.W., and S. Leinhardt
1977   A dynamic model for social networks. *Journal of Mathematical Sociology* 3:85–111.
Hovland, C.
1972   Reconciling conflicting results derived from experimental and survey studies of attitude change. In *The Handbook of Social Psychology*, G. Lindzey, ed. Reading, MA: Addison-Wesley.
Hovland, C., and H. Pritzker
1957   Extent of opinion change as a function of amount of change advocated. *Journal of Abnormal and Social Psychology* 54:257–261.
Huguet, P., and B. Latane
1996   Social representations as dynamic social impact. *Journal of Communication* 46(4):57–63.
Humphrey, R.H., P.M. O'Malley, L.D. Johnston, and J.G. Bachman
1988   Bases of power, facilitation effects, and attitudes and behavior: Direct, indirect, and interactive determinants of drug use. *Social Psychology Quarterly* 51:329–345.
Hunter, J.E., J.E. Danes, and S.H. Cohen
1984   *Mathematical Models of Attitude Change.* New York: Academic Press.
Hutchins, E.
1995   *Cognition in the Wild.* Cambridge, MA: MIT Press.
Hutchins, E., and B. Hazlehurst
1991   Learning in the cultural process. In *Artificial Life II*, C. Langton, C. Taylor, J.D. Farmer, and S. Rasmussen, eds. Reading, MA: Addison-Wesley.
Innami, I.
1992   Determinants of the quality of group decisions and the effect of consensual conflict resolution. *Academy of Management Best Papers Proceedings* 217–221.
Insko, C.
1967   *Theories of Attitude Change.* New York: Appleton-Century-Crofts.
Janis, I.
1982   *Groupthink.* 2d ed. Boston: Houghton Mifflin Company.
Johnson, E.C.
1985   Structure and process: Agreement models for friendship formation. *Social Networks* 8:257–306.
Kahneman, D., P. Slovic, and A. Tversky
1982   *Judgment Under Uncertainty: Heuristics and Biases.* London: Cambridge University Press.

Kahneman, D., and A. Tversky
    1979   Prospect theory: An analysis of decision under risk. *Econometrica* 47:263–291.
Katz, D.
    1960   The functional approach to the study of attitudes. *Public Opinion Quarterly* 24:163–
            204.
Katz, E.
    1961   The social itinerary of technical change: Two studies on the diffusion of innova-
            tion. In *Studies of Innovation and of Communication to the Public*, W. Schramm, ed.
            Stanford: Stanford University, Institute for Communication Research.
Kaufer, D.S., and K.M. Carley
    1993   *Communication at a Distance: The Effect of Print on Socio-Cultural Organization and
            Change.* Hillsdale, NJ: Lawrence Erlbaum Associates.
    1994   Some concepts and axioms about communication: Proximate and at a distance.
            Written Communication 11(1):8–42.
    1996   The influence of print on social and cultural change. *Annual Review of Applied
            Linguistics* 16:14–25.
Kelley, H.H.
    1967   Attribution theory in social psychology. In *Nebraska Symposium on Motivation*,
            D.L. Vine, ed. Lincoln: University of Nebraska Press.
Kernis, M.H.
    1984   Need for uniqueness, self-schemas, and thought as moderators of the false–con-
            sensus effect. *Journal of Experimental Social Psychology* 20:350–362.
Klein, G.A., ed.
    1993   *Decision Making in Action: Models and Methods.* Norwood, NJ: Ablex.
Krackhardt, D.
    1997   Organizational viscosity and the diffusion of controversial innovations. *Journal of
            Mathematical Sociology* 22:177–199.
    1999a   The ties that torture: Simmelian tie analysis of organizations. *Research in the Soci-
            ology of Organizations* 16:183–210.
    1999b   Simmelian tie: Super strong and sticky. Pp. 21–38 in *Power and Influence in Organi-
            zations*, Roderick Kramer and Margaret Neale, eds. Thousand Oaks, CA: Sage.
Kraut, R., R.E. Rice, C. Cool, and R. Fish
    1997   Varieties of social influence: The role of utility and norms in the success of a new
            communication medium. *Organization Science* 9(4):437–453.
Latane, B.
    1996   Dynamic social impact: The creation of culture by communication. *Journal of Com-
            munication* 46(4):13–25.
Latane, B., and M.J. Bourgeois
    1996   Experimental evidence for dynamic social impact: The emergence of subcultures
            in electronic groups. *Journal of Communication* 46(4):35–47.
Latane, B., J.H. Liu, A. Nowak, M. Bonevento, and Zheng Long
    1995   Distance matters: Physical space and social impact. *Personality and Social Psychol-
            ogy Bulletin* 21(8):795–805.
Leenders, R.T.A.J.
    1997   Longitudinal behavior of network structure and actor attributes: Modeling inter-
            dependence of contagion and selection. Pp. 165–184 in *Evolution of Social Net-
            works*, Patrick Doreian and Frans N. Stokman, eds. Amsterdam: Gordon and
            Breach.
Liang, D.W., R. Moreland, and L. Argote
    1995   Group versus individual training and group performance: The mediating role of
            transactive memory. *Personality and Social Psychology Bulletin* 21(4):384–393.

Lin, N., and R.S. Burt
   1975   Differential effects of information channels in the process of innovation diffusion. *Social Forces* 54:256–274.
Loomes, G., and R. Sugden
   1982   Regret theory: An alternative theory of rational choice under uncertainty. *Economic Journal* 92:805–824.
MacCrimmon, K.R., and D.A. Wehrung
   1986   *Taking Risks: The Management of Uncertainty.* New York: Free Press.
Marks, G.
   1984   Thinking one's abilities are unique and one's opinions are common. *Personality and Social Psychology Bulletin* 10:203–208.
Mead, G.H.
   1962   *Mind, Self, and Society.* Chicago: University of Chicago Press.
Miller, S.M.
   1995   Monitoring versus blunting styles of coping with cancer influence the information patients want and need about their disease: Implications for cancer screening and management. *Cancer* 76(1):177–197.
Mita, R., and R. Simmons
   1995   Diffusion of the culture of contraception: Program effects on young women in rural Bangladesh. *Studies in Family Planning* 26(1):1–13.
Molm, L.D.
   1978   Sex–role attitudes and the employment of married women: The direction of causality. *Sociological Quarterly* 19:522–533.
Montgomery, M.R.
   1997   Learning and lags in mortality perceptions. Pp. 112–127 in *From Death to Birth: Mortality Decline and Reproductive Change,* Barney Cohen and Mark Montgomery, eds. Committee on Population, Commission on Behavioral and Social Sciences and Education. Washington, DC: National Academy Press.
   1999   Mortality Decline and the Demographic Response: Toward a New Agenda. PRD Working Paper 122, Population Council.
Montgomery, M.R., and J.B. Casterline
   1996   Social learning, social influence, and new models of fertility. *Population and Development Review* (Supplement) 22:151–175.
   1998   Social Networks and the Diffusion of Fertility Control. PRD Working Paper 119, Population Council.
Moreland, R.L.
   in   Transactive memory in work groups and organizations. In *Shared Knowledge in*
   press   *Organizations,* L. Thompson, D. Messick, and J. Levine, eds. Mahwah, NJ: Lawrence Erlbaum Associates.
Moreland, R.L., L. Argote, and R. Krishnan
   1996   Socially shared cognition at work: Transactive memory and group performance. Pp. 57–84 in *What's Social About Social Cognition? Research on Socially Shared Cognition in Small Groups,* J.L. Nye and A.M. Brower, eds. Newbury Park, CA: Sage Publications.
   in   Training people to work in groups. In *Applications of Theory and Research on Groups*
   press   *to Social Issues,* R.S. Tindale, J. Edwards, and E.J. Posvac, eds. New York: Plenum Press.
Morris, M.
   1994   Epidemiology and social networks: Modeling structured diffusion. Pp. 26–52 in *Advances in Social Network Analysis,* S. Wasserman and J. Galskiewicz, eds. Thousand Oaks, CA: Sage.

National Research Council
  1998 *Modeling Human and Organizational Behavior: Application to Military Simulations.* Panel on Modeling Human Behavior and Command Decision Making: Representations for Military Simulations. Richard W. Pew and Anne S. Mavor, eds. Commission on Behavioral and Social Sciences and Education. Washington, DC: National Academy Press.

Orbell, J.M., and R.M. Dawes
  1993 Social welfare, cooperators' advantage, and the option of not playing the game. *The American Sociological Review* 58(6):787–800.

Orbell, J.M., A.J.C. van de Kragt, and R.M. Dawes
  1988 Explaining discussion-induced cooperation. *Journal of Personality and Social Psychology* 54(5):811–819.

Plous, S.
  1993 *The Psychology of Judgment and Decision Making.* New York: McGraw-Hill.

Price, D.J.
  1965a Networks of scientific papers. *Science* 149:510–515.
  1965b Is technology independent of science? *Technology and Culture* 6:553–568.

Pruitt, D.
  1971a Choice shifts in group discussion: An introductory review. *Journal of Personality and Social Psychology* 20:339–360.
  1971b Conclusions: Toward an understanding of choice shifts in group discussion. *Journal of Personality and Social Psychology* 20:495–510.

Rapoport, A.
  1953 Spread of information through a population with socio-structural bias: II. Various models of partial transitivity. *Bulletin of Mathematical Biophysics* 15:535–546.

Reitman, W.R.
  1965 *Cognition and Thought; An Information-Processing Approach.* New York: Wiley.

Rice, R.E.
  1984 *The New Media: Communication, Research, and Technology.* Beverly Hills, CA: Sage.
  1993 Using network concepts to clarify sources and mechanisms of social influence. Pp. 43–52 in *Advances in Communication Network Analysis,* W. Richards, Jr., and G. Barnett, eds. Norwood, NJ: Ablex.
  1994 Relating electronic mail use and network structure to R&D work networks and performance. *Journal of Management Information Systems* 11(1):9–20.

Rice, R.E., and C. Aydin
  1991 Attitudes toward new organizational technology: Network proximity as a mechanism for social information processing. *Administrative Science Quarterly* 36(2):219–244.

Ridgeway, C.L., and L. Smith–Lovin
  1996 Gender and social interaction. *Social Psychology Quarterly* 59(3):173–175.

Roethlisberger, F.J., and W.J. Dickson
  1939 *Management and the Worker.* Cambridge, MA: Harvard University Press.

Rogers, E.M.
  1995 *Diffusion of Innovations.* New York: Free Press.

Ross, L., T.M. Amabile, and J.L. Steinmetz
  1977 Social roles, social controls, and biases in the social perception process. *Journal of Personality and Social Psychology* 35:485–494.

Salancik, G.R., and J. Pfeffer
  1978 Social information processing approach to job attitudes and task design. *Administrative Science Quarterly* 23:224–253.

Salas, E., R.J. Stout, and J.A. Cannon-Bowers
    1994   The role of shared mental models in developing shared situational awareness.
            Pp. 297–304 in *Situational Awareness in Complex Systems*, R.D. Gilson, D.J. Garland,
            and J.M. Koonce, eds. Daytona Beach, FL: Embry-Riddle Aeronautical University
            Press.
Sampson, S.
    1969   Crisis in a cloister. Unpublished Ph.D. dissertation. Cornell University, Ithaca,
            NY.
Sanil, A., D. Banks, and K. Carley
    1995   Models for evolving fixed node networks: Model fitting and model testing. *Social
            Networks* 17(1):65–81.
Simon, H.A.
    1976   *Administrative Behavior*. 3d ed. New York: Free Press.
    1979   Rational decision making in business organizations. *American Economic Review*
            69(4):493–513.
Smith, M.
    1973   Political Attitudes. In *Handbook of Political Psychology*, Jeanne Knutson, ed. San
            Francisco: Jossey-Bass.
Smith, M., J. Bruner, and R. White
    1956   *Opinions and Personality*. New York: Wiley.
Smith-Lovin, L.
    1987a   Affect control theory: An assessment. *Journal of Mathematical Sociology* 13:171–192.
    1987b   The affective control of events within settings. *Journal of Mathematical Sociology*
            13:71–101.
Sproull, L., and S. Kiesler
    1991   *Connections: New Ways of Working in the Networked Organization*. Cambridge, MA:
            MIT Press.
Stokman, F.N., and E.P.H. Zeggelink
    1996   "Self-organizing" friendship networks. Pp. 385–418 in *Frontiers in Social Dilemmas
            Research*, W.B.G. Liebrand and D.M. Messick, eds. Berlin: Springer Verlag.
Strang, D., and J.W. Meyer
    1993   Institutional conditions for diffusion. *Theory and Society* 22:487–512.
Strang, D., and N. Tuma
    1993   Spatial and temporal heterogeneity in diffusion. *American Journal of Sociology*
            99:614–639.
Thoits, P.A.
    1991   Patterns in coping with controllable and uncontrollable events. Pp. 235–258 in
            Life-span Developmental Psychology: Perspectives on Stress and Coping, E.M. Cum-
            mings, A.L. Greene, and K.H. Karraker, eds. Hillsdale, NJ: Lawrence Erlbaum
            Associates.
Tversky, A., and D. Kahneman
    1974   Judgment under uncertainty: Heuristics and biases. *Science* 185:1124–1131.
    1981   The framing of decisions and the psychology of choice. *Science* 211:453–458.
Valente, T.W.
    1995   *Network Models of the Diffusion of Innovations*. Cresskill, NJ: Hampton Press.
    1996   Social network thresholds in the diffusion of innovations. *Social Networks* 18:69–
            89.
Valente, T.W., Y.M. Kim, C. Lettenmaier, W. Glass, and Y. Dibba
    1994   Radio and the promotion of family planning in The Gambia. *International Family
            Perspectives Planning* 20(3):96–100.

Valente, T.W., S. Watkins, M.N. Jato, A. Van der Straten, and L.M. Tsitsol
  1997   Social network associations with contraceptive use among Cameroonian women in voluntary associations. *Social Science and Medicine* 45:677–687.
Walsh, J.P., and L. Fahey
  1986   The role of negotiated belief structures in strategy making. *Journal of Management* 12:325–338.
Wasserman, D., R.O. Lempert, and R. Hastie
  1991   Hindsight and causality. *Personality and Social Psychology Bulletin* 17(1):30–35.
Weenig, M.W., and C.J. Midden
  1991   Communication network influences on information diffusion and persuasion. *Journal of Personality and Social Psychology* 61(5):734–742.
Weesie, J., and H. Flap, eds.
  1990   *Social Networks Through Time.* Belgium: ISOR/University of Utrecht.
Wegner, D.M.
  1987   Transactive memory: A contemporary analysis of the group mind. Pp. 185–208 in *Theories of Group Behavior*, B. Mullen and G.R. Goethals, eds. New York: Springer-Verlag.
  1995   A computer network model of human transactive memory. *Social Cognition* 13(3): 319–339.
Wegner, D.M., R. Erber, and P. Raymond
  1991   Transactive memory in close relationships. *Journal of Personality and Social Psychology* 61:923–929.
Wellman, B.
  1992   Which ties provide what kinds of support? *Advances in Group Processes* 9:207–235.
  1997   An electronic group is virtually a social network. Pp. 179–203 in *Culture of the Internet*, Sara Kiesler, ed. Mahwah, NJ: Lawrence Erlbaum Associates.
Wellman, B., and S.D. Berkowitz
  1988   *Social Structures: A Network Approach.* Cambridge, Eng.: Cambridge University Press.
Wellman, B., and S. Wortley
  1990   Different strokes from different folks: Community ties and social support. *American Journal of Sociology* 96(November):558–588.
White, H.C., S.A. Boorman, and R.L. Breiger
  1976   Social structure from multiple networks. I. Blockmodels of roles and positions. *American Journal of Sociology* 81:730–780.
Whittaker, J.
  1967   Resolution and the communication discrepancy issue in attitude change. In *Attitude Ego–Involvement and Change*, C. Sherif and M. Sherif, eds. New York: Wiley.
Zeggelink, E.P.H.
  1993   *Strangers Into Friends: The Evolution of Friendship Networks Using an Individual Oriented Modeling Approach.* Amsterdam: Thesis Publishers.
  1995   Evolving friendship networks: An individual oriented approach implementing similarity. *Social Networks* 17:83–110.
  1996   "Self–organizing" networks of affective relations. Pp. 899–903 in *Third European Congress on Systems Science*, E. Pessa and M.P. Penna, eds. Rome: Edizione Kappa.
Zeggelink, E.P.H., F.N. Stokman, and G.G. van de Bunt
  1996   The emergence of groups in the evolution of friendship networks. *Journal of Mathematical Sociology* 21:29–55. Also in *Evolution of Social Networks*, P. Doreian and F.N. Stokman, eds. Amsterdam: Gordon and Breach.

7

Mass Media and Fertility Change

ROBERT HORNIK AND EMILE MCANANY

Does the spread of access to mass media in a society affect the rate of decline in fertility? This essay organizes the thicket of issues bundled in that simple question and then reviews the relevant evidence, which will provide some tentative answers. We close with some comments about what we believe to be the most promising ways to think about this issue.

There is evidence of a very substantial association between access to mass media and the level of fertility in a country. That is true at the most aggregated level, when national levels of per capita television access are used to predict fertility rates. There is a strong association of the natural log of fertility with televisions per 1,000 population for 144 countries for which data are available (Figure 7-1). Excluding four oil-rich outlier countries, a regression equation fitting a linear and quadratic term shows that televisions per capita accounted for 74 percent of the variance in fertility in 1997. This is a substantially better prediction of fertility than one gets from measures of gross national product per capita (indicated by an index of purchasing power parity) or indices of female education.[1]

Robert Hornik is Wilbur Schramm professor of communication and health policy in the Annenberg School for Communication at the University of Pennsylvania. Emile McAnany is the Walter E. Schmidt, S.J. professor of communication and chair of the communication department at Santa Clara University. The authors extend a special note of gratitude to R. Kirkland Ahern, Jennifer Horner, and Jo Stryker for research assistance, as well as Joseph Cappella for insightful suggestions in the preparation of this paper.

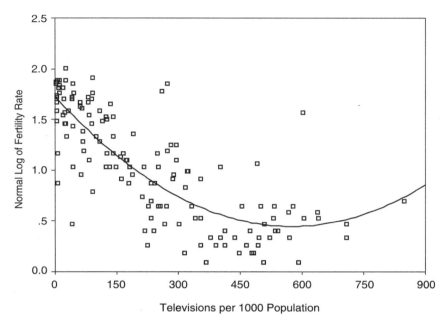

FIGURE 7-1 Fertility by television (N = 144), normal log of fertility rate, televisions per 1000 population.

The association of media access and fertility is also found at the subnational level; for example, Potter and his colleagues (1997) show the significant association between television ownership and fertility at the municipality level in Brazil. It is true also at the individual level; for example, Westoff and Bankole (1997) show the association between various types of media access and contraceptive behaviors and childbearing intentions in seven African countries. In that study, married women who are exposed to television are two to six times more likely to be current users of contraception than the nonexposed comparison group.

However, although these associations are consistent with a claim of media effects on fertility, they are far from definitive. They are not definitive, of course, because causal inferences from cross-sectional bivariate correlations are always tentative. Even though these associations generally are reduced but still significant when likely alternative explanations for them (such as education, urban residence, or occupation) are statistically controlled, inferences remain unsure. But they are also not definitive because, even if we were willing to make causal inferences from them, they do not tell us how the observed associations came about.

There is quite a broad set of explanations that might suggest mechanisms through which access to mass media in a society might affect fertility, even if we were willing to make a causal inference about that relation. We develop five major alternative (but not mutually exclusive) hypotheses. The first is about effects of the medium itself, the way it is used, separately from its content. The next three focus on the effects of ideas, each highlighting a different possible effect of the ordinary content of radio or television. The last considers effects of deliberate programs aimed at fertility control. It will turn out that tests of this last area of effect, evaluations of family planning communication programs, are the most common on the ground, but we suspect that the middle three hypotheses may deserve the most attention.

FIVE HYPOTHESES ABOUT MEDIA EFFECTS ON FERTILITY

Economic and Time Competition Effects

First, most hypotheses about media effects focus on their content, the effects of exposure to ideas in the media. However, the central fact of exposure to media is the act of exposure—the time spent with the medium. Given the fixed boundaries of the 24-hour day, time spent with mass media may mean time lost from other activities.

This effect may be particularly important when there are sharp increases in television ownership in individual homes. Individual ownership and the resulting heavy use of television may preclude or make some other activities more difficult, such as socializing with others at a central meeting place. If enough people are engaged with television in their homes, then the availability of such places for socializing in the community may be lost. This is an argument made strongly by Putnam (1995) in his oft-quoted paper "Bowling Alone," which attributes the decimation of Americans' social involvement to the spread of television.

How might this relate to fertility? We can only speculate. In some societies courting behavior precedes marriage. If the amount of socializing young people do is reduced by watching television at home and age at marriage is responsive to the amount of socializing potential mates do with marriage waiting until a certain amount of socializing has occurred, then television might produce delays in age at marriage with resultant reductions in fertility. Or, if nonmarital sex and resulting pregnancy are a function of the amount of time people spend socializing, and television means people spend more time at home and have less opportunity for nonmarital sex, there may be less nonmarital fertility.

Television may also compete with marital sex. If sex is, in part, a response to the lack of other things to do, and television watching takes up time that would otherwise be spent in sexual activity, fertility reductions might result. Or, contrarily, if television keeps spouses at home, and they spend more time in each other's company, the opportunities for sex may be increased. Anecdotal reports of increased births about nine months after power blackouts in the United States are consistent with this suggestion. Availability of power and access to television may suppress fertility. Clearly the credibility of these noncontent-based mechanisms depends on the statement of plausible paths of effect and evidence to corroborate them.

A second noncontent-related path of effect relates to the cost of purchasing a television. In poorer countries such a purchase is a significant expense relative to annual income. In Brazil, for example, there is evidence that television sets are often the first major consumer purchase, even in households with quite low incomes. If fertility reflects a deliberate allocation of scarce resources to children versus other forms of expense, then the decision to purchase and maintain a television may directly compete with childbearing, and reduce fertility. The more usual version of this competing use of resources hypothesis, which focuses on the materialist content of television and its influence on individual interests in consumption, is discussed below.

These time and cost models are less commonly proposed than ideational models, perhaps for good reason. We turn to them now.

Mass Media Effects on Elites

Public policy in a country may favor or constrain fertility control. There is good evidence that deliberate family planning efforts have accelerated the decline in fertility (Freedman, 1997). There is also a fair consensus that other forms of public investment, in areas such as health care, female education, and social security, have important effects on fertility decisions. The question to be raised here is what leads elites to allocate resources to such programs? Is it possible that the ideas of elites on these issues are in some part the reflection of the world they see pictured on their television screens?

Over a number of years beginning in the 1960s, American television programming dominated other countries' entertainment (Varis, 1984.) In recent years, however, a number of larger countries have managed to produce more of their own prime time fare, which generally is more popular. Even so, such national programming reflects cosmopolitan points of view from the national capital or other large urban centers, and may still reflect the production norms of foreign program sources. Elites may have more direct contact with foreign cultures, regardless of television use, than do nonelites and especially rural audiences, but television and other media may reinforce and add to these direct influences on elites within a country. Thus values such as female equality, small families, open discussion of sexuality and contraception, and the acceptance of medical and other technology as a solution to problems all may be typical of imported or cosmopolitan national content and affect how elites view the world and what policy decisions they make.

Mass Media Effects on Population Values Indirectly Relevant to Fertility Decisions

Like the elites described above, general populations, if they watch television, watch content that typically comes from outside national boundaries, or they watch programs produced by writers and directors who are influenced by an international standard or a national cosmopolitan view. Although there are exceptions, the values of audiences who are not yet committed to reduced fertility may differ from those implicit in television content. That content, full of advertising of bright goods, may glorify consumption: when viewers must choose between consumption and childbearing, they may move toward consumption. Also, that content may tell stories which legitimate values associated with reduced fertility: a soap opera tells the story of a woman who delays marriage so she can achieve in a career. The value supporting achievement over early marriage influences viewers, which turns into lessened fertility. Locally produced dramas show that well-educated women are respected or that their education has a high economic return—parents accept the value of girls' education; increases in girls' education result in reduced fertility. (See very similar arguments in Faria and Potter, 1999; Westoff and Bankole, 1997; Kottak, 1990.) Fadul and colleagues (1996) show in a thematic analysis of popular telenovelas how, over a twenty-five-year period in Brazil, women's roles have changed from housewives, teachers, and nurses to other professional roles outside the home and even to being portrayed as CEOs of major corporations. The authors also point to the consistently smaller family size on these soap operas than the current norms in Brazil, and how soap operas provided an early introduction to controversial ideas such as divorce, abortion, and premarital sex to a large Brazilian audience.

News broadcasts may highlight reductions in child mortality, so that couples may take those reductions confidently into account when they decide how many children to bear. Coale (cited in Mason, 1997) argued for the importance of acceptance of the idea that it is possible to limit family size as a precondition to the fertility transition. Small families on television may carry that message to viewers. Television programs may say what it means to be modern, and that to be modern is good. These value diffusion effects may occur regardless of whether there is any explicit mention of the value of reduced fertility.

Unintended Direct Mass Media Effects on Fertility Decisions

Media content may not only carry messages about values, which are indirectly related to fertility; they may also carry content that bears directly on the subject. These messages may be included in news programming, in dramatic or other content, for their news or dramatic value, without any conscious intention to influence behavior. Soap operas may have scenes with couples deciding to limit family size or delaying having children or scenes with unmarried couples using birth control to avoid pregnancy. News programs may provide information about available methods of fertility control, or about services available in local clinics, or about new governmental policies in support of reduced fertility.

Mass Media Effects on Fertility Through Deliberate Information, Education, and Communication Programs

Family planning programs in many countries have tried to use mass media-based programs to influence contraceptive decisions and behavior—sometimes trying to increase awareness of the need for fertility control, sometimes providing information to increase utilization of available services, sometimes marketing specific products. Those programs may use a variety of approaches: didactic programs, advertising approaches, entertainment education approaches. They may use a variety of educational strategies: providing straightforward information; modeling desirable behaviors (e.g., showing "typical" people going into clinics for services, using condoms, or discussing family planning with partners); or emphasizing social norms. These programs are not always different in purpose than ordinary population education efforts, with one exception: in each case, program developers use mass media as the primary channel, assuming that media will improve cost-effectiveness and fidelity. They may believe that mass media are potentially less effective per person reached than alternative strategies (through outreach workers or through clinic-based staff), knowing that a field agent has the great advantage of being able to respond to the needs of individuals. But they expect that the heightened control over the messages delivered, and particularly the "reach and frequency" achieved through wide exposure to mass media, should counterbalance that advantage.

MAJOR ISSUES TO CONSIDER WHEN THINKING ABOUT MEDIA EFFECTS

These are all paths of influence for media effects. Regardless of the path, however, it would be a mistake to think about media influence as a simple direct learning phenomenon: that people learn about an idea or a behavior from mass media and they immediately put it into practice. Little mass communication theory relies on such an assumption. Evaluation of the evidence about media effects has to take into account the process through which the effects might occur. Before turning to the presentation of evidence about each hypothesis, we review some central issues in mass communication effects theory, relevant to developing expectations for what the evidence might show.

The Issue of the Social Process Around Media Effects

Media may be influential because of their direct effects on what people know and do, but they are also likely to be effective because they affect the social process around individual decision making. Media content may serve as a stimulus for discussion in which multiple individuals exposed to the same message develop a shared response; exposure to media content may create permission for open discussion of taboo topics in social networks; people considering adopting a new behavior inconsistent with the way things are done locally may gain from media exposure a sense of belonging to a broader social network; one individual exposed to media content may pass on what he or she learns to others inside his or her social network.

Fadul et al. (1996) documented how controversial topics were introduced into Brazilian society over time through soap operas. Kothari (1997) explored the controversy surrounding Islamic practices regarding women that were introduced in popular soap operas in Pakistan by important women writers. A soap opera in Mexico (*San Jose Mercury*, 3 January 1998, 4A) stirred controversy by directly attacking in its story line the macho double standard about marital fidelity. In all cases the public nature and popularity of national television drama opens up opportunities to discuss sensitive social issues, including those regarding sexuality, divorce, abortion, and vasectomy.

This social view of the effects process has an important implication for the search for evidence. It says that the effects of mass media diffuse beyond those who are directly exposed to the content. Then comparisons between those individuals who are or are not exposed to media may tend to underestimate effects. Thus if person A is exposed to televised messages and person B isn't, but person A shares the content of the messages with person B, then a measure of exposure will show a difference between them but such exposure will not be associated with effect, even if there are effects. This idea of a diffused effect, likely to be lost if one focuses on individual differences, also can operate at a higher level of aggregation. If a certain proportion (about 30 percent) of a village is exposed to television, then the entire village may be substantially exposed because the messages are shared throughout the social network. A comparison of villages with 30 percent versus 60 percent access may not show the true effects of exposure, because the effects of exposure may be diffused in both places. We are often appropriately concerned about the ecological fallacy when we risk making erroneous inferences about individuals from aggregated data. But also we need to be careful on the other side. We can miss an effect if the evidence is based on individual comparisons of exposed and not exposed individuals, but the appropriate unit of effect is not the individual but the social network with whom the individuals affiliate.

Media May Be Effective Because They Change the Frame People Use to Think About an Issue

Media may be influential because people learn specific messages, but they are also influential because they influence the frame through which people process information (compare Iyengar and Kinder, 1987). This phenomenon is sometimes called agenda setting (compare McCombs et al., 1997). Here is an example regarding a woman's decision to obtain a modern method of contraception. Assume that two beliefs influence her decision: her (lack of) belief that her living children will survive to adulthood, and her belief that repeated pregnancies will make her less attractive to her husband. Media content may provide information about one or another of these beliefs, but it also may provide messages that influence which of the beliefs should matter more in her calculus of the contraceptive decision. If television tells her she ought to weigh her potential attractiveness to her husband more highly, then she might adopt contraception, without changing the level of either belief. These possible framing effects of exposure to media content may complement effects on the levels of beliefs or attitudes. Research that focuses only on level changes but ignores complementary framing effects may underestimate effects.

The Issue of Active Audiences Versus Universal Effects (Strong Audiences Versus Strong Media)

Since the beginnings of mass media research, a consistent controversy has been the extent to which effects are universal, widely shared among audience members, or contrarily, highly conditional on characteristics of individual audience members and their social networks. One view focuses on the common effects, stressing the widely shared experience of media viewing, and while recognizing that individuals will vary in response, they are mostly interested in the main effects (compare Gerbner et al., 1994; Schiller, 1976). These theorists are interested in how society at large is affected by media, and assume that those effects will be large. Others insist that audiences make use of media largely to solve their own problems and are highly active in the process, reading the content, making sense of it, from within their particular belief system and social context (compare Katz and Liebes, 1990). These scholars tend to expect more limited effects of media as media influence is constrained by the characteristics of audiences. This theoretical dispute has important implications when we begin the search for evidence for effects of mass media on fertility.

If the universal effects hypothesis is substantially true, then main effects are the appropriate place to focus our analyses, whether those were effects on knowledge or attitudes or behavior. We would look for noticeable average effects across the entire population. If, in contrast, effects are highly conditional on the beliefs and contexts of individuals, then main effects may be small, and only interaction terms will show effects. In that case a focus on the average correlation in a population, or the average effects of a media-based purposive program, may be misleading; if they are small they may be obscuring larger effects for particular subgroups for which the message was most relevant. An example: a media program that provides information about clinic services may be quite effective for the subset of people who are currently seeking contraception and are unaware of available services. An evaluation that asks for the average change in the population may fail to include enough of those people to show worthwhile effects. Early AIDS education evaluations foundered when they looked for increased condom use among all sexually active adults. But when they focused on people who reported "casual" sexual encounters, they found sharp increases in condom use (compare Dubois-Arber et al., 1997).

The Issue of Effects on Awareness Versus Effects on Behavior

An additional controversy bears on the issue of where to look for effects. The established diffusion literature stresses a claim that media effects are largely on awareness, on getting people to think about a new behavior. In contrast, that literature is skeptical about whether media have much influence on decisions to adopt behaviors (Rogers, 1995), expecting interpersonal sources to be more influential at decision-making stages. The diffusionist view is analogous to a more recently popular version of the same argument, called stages of change theory. That theory expects people at different stages of a change process (labeled precontemplation, contemplation, ready for action, action, and maintenance— which are similar to the awareness, behavior, and other categories used by diffusion theorists) to be affected by different types of messages (Prochaska and DiClemente, 1983) rather than different channels.

A contrary position is more inclined to credit media with direct influence on behavior change, pointing to the examples of advertising effects and some other evidence (compare Hornik, 1989). That hypothesis expects direct learning effects, but also credits media with effects because they initiate person-to-person discussion and diffusion, which produce change, and because they crystallize latent demand—telling people how to act to realize what it is they have chosen to do.

The Issues of the Nature of the Relationships Between Media Exposure and Fertility Outcomes

This issue of what media can affect also relates to two final issues—the time lag for effects and the shape of the relationship. Some effects will occur rapidly with a limited exposure to a message. For example, women ready to adopt a modern contraceptive may respond quickly to information about eased access to a clinic. On the other hand, some behaviors are more deeply ingrained in the belief system and social context of individuals. Individuals might be affected by media content but require a broad change in the public communication environment, with mass media and other channels of communication providing new messages supportive of changed behavior, but then one would not expect instant response. Rather, the time lag of effects can be in years or even decades. For example, there has been an extraordinary decline in cigarette smoking in the United States, so the current level is half or less what it was at the height of smoking prevalence. But that change occurred at a slow pace, one or two percent per year, often not detectable in the short term with typical samples we can study. Programs that operate for a year or two, and evaluations that are only able to detect substantial and rapid change, may not be informative for change depending on communication effects on world views.

Gradual change over longer periods also suggests that consistent reinforcement of the change messages is necessary. Even though advertising campaigns, for example, can create important short-term changes in buyers' behavior, the longer term strategies of companies such as Coca-Cola or Nike is to reinforce short-term gains with follow-up ads. If the mass media are generally promodern, as many have argued since Lerner (1958) first introduced the idea of modernization and media's role in the process, then their reinforcing value may be considerable in promoting not only consumerist desires but also modern and even Western views about fertility ideals and practices.

A related concern is about the shape of the curve associating media exposure to effects, both for individuals and for larger aggregates. At the individual level, will the effects of media exposure be the same when an individual moves from no exposure to one hour of daily exposure as they are when he or she moves from three hours to four hours of exposure? Or, will the effects on a village be the same when the tenth percentile of households gets televisions as when the fiftieth percentile gets television? Some effects might be larger at the high levels of exposure (e.g., the effects on decline in social interaction); others may show little additional effect after a low level of exposure is achieved (effect on knowledge about the existence of contraceptive methods).

This issue explores three overlapping concerns: the absolute quantity of exposure, the distribution over time of the exposure, and the time lag before the exposure produces effects. Any assessment of the effects of mass media needs to ask whether the evidence used as the basis for inference is consistent with hypothesized expectations for how each of these operate.

Thus far we have laid out the various paths through which mass media might influence fertility, and pointed to a series of conceptual controversies in mass media research that bear on the search for evidence. These discussions followed a brief presentation of the global evidence for an association between media spread and fertility. We now turn to a more extended treatment of the evidence. It contains two major sections: evidence for overall effects of media spread on fertility, and evidence for effects of specific programs that have used mass media to influence fertility. The first of these is relevant to all of the first four hypotheses. Each would predict an overall association between media access and fertility. The second section tests the final path of direct effects of purposive programs.

EVIDENCE ABOUT OVERALL EFFECTS

Studies Showing Associations at the Aggregate Level

We have noted the very substantial correlation (.86) between television access and fertility rates across 140 countries for which data were available (excluding 4 oil-rich outliers). The relation is still strong (.76) when the analysis is restricted to lower income countries (the countries classified as below the median on the purchasing power parity index used by the World Bank).

There are two typical threats to a causal inference from this type of association. One is a concern with causal order. Is it possible that the association reflects not the effects of television on fertility but the effects of fertility on television ownership? After all, we did previously argue that television and children compete for scarce family resources. Isn't it possible that in countries where there are families with fewer children, there are more people who can afford televisions? There is no useful way to distinguish these hypotheses from the cross-sectional associations, but some evidence from studies of individuals over time, presented below, may ease this concern.

A more conventional threat to causal inference would be that the association is the product of the influence of other confounding variables. However, the television relationships with fertility are as strong or stronger than those between purchasing power parity and fertility and are still significant when purchasing power parity is statistically controlled.

Nonetheless, there are rival hypotheses to the idea that these associations establish that media indeed have the hypothesized effects: one is that television ownership is a very good measure of average economic position of people in a country, and correlates with fertility because it is a measure of income. It may correlate better than do measures of wealth, such as purchasing power parity per capita, because it is a better measure of average income than that measure which is distorted as a measure of average income by income inequities. Or it may be that television ownership is a very good indicator of a broad range of social and institutional development variables, and one or more of them is the true causes(s) of fertility level. Nonetheless these results are consistent with an aggregate effect of media access on fertility, and the sheer size of the correlation is worth attention.

The second type of aggregated evidence comes from the Potter et al. study cited in this volume and from an earlier paper. Potter et al. (1997) do a quite elegant analysis of fertility rates in two Brazilian regions, showing that unmet demand for televisions in municipalities in one year predicts fertility rates ten or eleven years later, controlling for prior fertility and other likely determinants. They attribute these effects to Brazil-specific television content (the extraordinary telenovelas that dominate the airwaves), but we see no reason to assume that the effects are unique. They estimate that each 1-percent drop in television access is associated with a .10 increase in the total fertility rate in one region and a .16 increase in the other.

In both of these cases, even if one considers the evidence relevant to a claim of causal influence, one must be careful to avoid claims about individual-level effects, that individual exposure produces individual reductions in fertility. Insofar as they are credible, they are consistent with a claim of aggregate-level effects; nations or municipalities in which televisions are more widely owned are nations or municipalities in which there is lower fertility. Because some of the hypotheses about media effects on fertility operate at levels of aggregation higher than the individual, this is suitable and relevant evidence. The evidence may also be consistent with individual-level effects, but those effects are addressed directly by individual-level analyses.

Studies Showing Associations at the Individual Level

There is a long history of studies that have shown relationships between individual media exposure and "modern" attitudes, including those that bear on fertility. Lerner (1958), among the earliest scholars interested in effects of mass media on development, found in his six-country study of the Middle East that people who were more exposed to radio and film were more likely to express prodevelopment attitudes of various sorts. Inkeles and Smith (1974), in what was probably the biggest project involving survey-based investigation of determinants of modernity, found that television, radio, and newspaper use were good predictors of "modern" attitudes, even when other likely predictors of both media use and attitudes were controlled. Inkeles and Smith's measures of modernity included attitudes toward limiting family size.

Westoff and Bankole (1997) have updated those studies using cross-sectional African Demographic and Health Surveys (DHS); previously we noted that they found quite substantial associations of media use with a wide range of reproductive attitudes and behaviors. They examined associations of television, radio, and newspaper exposure with (a) knowledge of any modern method, (b) intention to use a method, (c) current use of any method, and (d) desire to stop childbearing, among other outcomes, while controlling likely covariates. Their data came from samples of 2,200–5,300 women in six Sub-Saharan countries (Burkina Faso, Ghana, Kenya, Madagascar, Namibia, and Zambia) as well as from Morocco. Although the magnitude of the associations varies with the country and with the outcome, they are virtually all consistent with a positive effect of media exposure on outcome. Odds ratios for one representative measure of media access, exposure to two of the three media, are reproduced in Table 7-1.[2]

The authors are extremely careful in interpreting these cross-sectional data, recognizing that the associations simply cannot eliminate the possibility that some other characteristic of the women, not controlled here, made them both more likely to expose themselves to mass media and more likely to use a contraceptive method. Nonetheless these data are also consistent with a media effects hypothesis.

An additional analysis enhances their argument. The authors have data from a three-year cohort study in Morocco in which the same women were reinterviewed. They show that both among women who were not using contraception in 1992 and separately among those who were, media

TABLE 7-1 Adjusted Odds Ratios of Media Use with Reproductive
Attitudes/Practices, Controlled for Other Characteristics

Country	Has Knowledge of Modern Method	Currently Using a Method	Intention to Use a Method	Expresses a Desire to Stop Childbearing
Burkina Faso	6.23	1.98	2.50	.96
Ghana	4.30	1.50	1.33	1.02
Kenya	NR	1.71	1.82	1.29
Madagascar	2.18	2.40	1.64	1.35
Namibia	1.63	1.25	2.73	1.15
Zambia	2.40	1.30	1.51	1.46

NOTES: Odds ratios comparing those with exposure to exactly two versus no mass media,
controlling for age, education, urban residence, number of living children, number of
husband's other wives, husband's occupation, electricity at home, refrigerator at home, car,
motorcycle or bicycle, religion, and exposure to family planning on radio. NR = 97 percent
of Kenyan women knew a modern method, so data not reported.
SOURCE: Adapted from Westoff and Bankole (1997).

use in 1992 predicted current use in 1995, while controlling for all of the
covariates listed in Table 7-1. In both cases, women who were heavy
users of media in 1992 were more than 2.5 times as likely to be using a
method in 1995 than were women who did not use any media. They also
show that media use in 1992 predicted a desire to stop childbearing in
1995, when only those women who wanted more children in 1992 were
included; heavy media users were about twice as likely as nonusers to
express a desire to stop childbearing. These longitudinal analyses add to
the claims of effects, but the authors do not claim definitive support. It
remains possible that women who were heavy media users in 1992 were
already on a different reproductive trajectory (what Cook and Campbell,
1979, call a "selection by maturation" threat to inference) that was independent of but correlated with their media use.

It is customary and legitimate to express wariness about making
causal inferences from correlational data of this sort, even with the extra
longitudinal information from the Moroccan data. But it is good to recognize that these data also might well underestimate the effects. If the
effects occur at a level of aggregation higher than the individual, the
individual associations will be too small. If the effects occur for some
people but not others (e.g., for those who lack interpersonal sources of
antinatalist information), the associations will be too small. If the effects
occur only in some contexts (e.g., where there is easy access to contraceptive supplies), the associations will be too small. Causal inferences from
these data are unsure, both because they are at risk of overestimating
effects and because they are at risk of underestimating effects.

EVIDENCE ABOUT INTERVENTION PROGRAM EFFECTS

There are two types of evidence available here: the first are evaluations of discrete projects, and the second are associations between self-reported exposure to family planning messages and reproductive behavior. We begin with the evaluation studies.

Most efforts at IEC (information, education, communication) in population programs are deeply integrated into multipronged programs, involving changes in government policies, increased access to contraceptive methods, and improvements in other aspects of service delivery (Ross and Mauldin, 1996). In most of those programs, it is impossible to isolate the effects of all of the IEC aspects of such programs, never mind the specific contributions of a mass media subcomponent of a broader IEC strategy. Although this complicates our search for relevant evidence, it is sensible policy. Although some might argue that a change in ideas about family limitation produced by mass media content would be enough and that couples would find some way of limiting family size even absent access to contraceptives, that is a long-term view. When the focus is on achieving short-term effects, for example, it is unlikely that one would find effects of IEC on contraceptive behavior absent sufficient access to contraceptive supplies.

A particularly important group of programs that often makes heavy use of media, but that does not allow isolation of media effects, is the variety of programs that fall under the term "social marketing." Several major operations, including the Social Marketing of Contraceptives (SOMARC) program sponsored by the United States Agency for International Development (USAID) and Population Services International (PSI) as well as particular national programs, have created sophisticated contraceptive social marketing programs. They couple new contraceptive brand development with appropriate pricing and packaging, private distribution networks, and major promotion campaigns, including mass media-based advertising. These programs have published regular reports (e.g., Ferreros, 1990; Harvey, 1991) that describe major successes in numbers of contraceptives sold in some countries. Although the nature of their evidence precludes any specific claims of success due to the mass media component in isolation, the results are relevant to our review; they represent a class of projects that make serious use of mass media and are successful, in some cases, but about which we cannot make specific media effects claims.

There is some 1970s-era evidence referenced by Rogers et al. (1978) that points to the aggregate association between the level of IEC in a country program and its national level of contraceptive use. Nonetheless, for the great majority of programs that incorporate media into their population programs, we have not seen published reports that permit us to isolate media effects. Also, small programs and programs without international funding are much less likely to make it into the literature. The lack of evidence from those programs is not evidence that such components do not work; indeed, the fact that IEC components are so often incorporated is evidence that policy makers on the ground value them. It just means that the media-specific evidence we do have has to be treated as a highly biased sample of the population of IEC and mass media-based programs. It is biased because it underrepresents programs for which there are no reports or for which the media component is not studied in isolation.

There are some evaluations of programs that do attempt to isolate media-specific effects. With one exception, they claim that media campaigns were associated with contraceptive adoption. This is no surprise; programs that find no effects are much less likely to make it into the literature. In a 1976 Rogers and Agarwala-Rogers study (summarized in Rogers et al., 1978), the authors describe evaluations of media campaigns in Colombia and Isfahan in Iran. Both evaluations involve interrupted time series and estimate changes in the number of adopters visiting family planning clinics. The Colombia results describe the reversal of a two-year decline in clinic adopters during the first nine months of a radio campaign, with effects fading during the final months. Isfahan shows a particularly strong increase in clinic demand in that region relative to the rest of Iran (30 percent greater), reflecting a three month "all-out media campaign" in that region, although there was some possibility that "other changes in the family planning program . . . may have contributed to increases" (Rogers et al., 1978:37). In any case the Isfahan advantage faded after the media campaign was over.

Hornik et al. (1987) evaluated a national media campaign in Peru designed to increase demand at government clinics for contraceptive services. It was the first such campaign in the country in which television spots were used to encourage modern contraceptive use. The campaign was associated with a substantial increase in such demand, but the increases could be accounted for by the preexisting secular trend in demand for family planning services, and an overall tendency for people to increase their use of government clinics for all purposes. The evaluators concluded that they could not claim effects.

An evaluation of a controlled four-community study meant to increase demand for vasectomy in Guatemala (Bertrand et al., 1987) provides mixed results. Compared to the control community, the community that was subject to a one-year radio intervention showed some increases in awareness and knowledge but not in behavior in a sample survey. However, clinic demand did increase quite rapidly in the radio community, with nearly three times the number of vasectomies occurring in the radio community than would have been expected on the basis of precampaign behavior. Consistent with the results of the Colombia and Isfahan projects, the monthly demand for vasectomies appeared to have returned to close to baseline after the radio campaign ended.

Strikingly, these results are consistent with some of the additional evaluations reported below: they show no behavioral effects when studied on a population level, but have evidence consistent with effects when clinic demand is examined. This is not surprising. If, at baseline, clinics are serving a small proportion of the population, and all effects are realized in increased clinic demand, then a very small population increase will appear as a very large increase in clinic demand. For example, the radio town in Guatemala had 38,000 people and was producing demand for two vasectomies a month before the campaign. The campaign appears to have tripled that demand, to around six vasectomies a month. But as a proportion of all adult males in the community, which is what would be reflected in a good sample survey, that increase would not be detectable.

Kincaid et al. (1996) describe the results of a series of media campaigns in Brazil designed to encourage vasectomy demand. They present a time series of number of vasectomies performed over a twelve-year period at one large Sao Paulo clinic, and from that note two important tendencies. Each media campaign was associated with a sharp rise (around 80 percent for a 1989 campaign) in demand for vasectomies during a six-month period, and the end of each media campaign was associated with a subsequent return to prior tendencies, including a sharp downward trend in demand through 1992.

The 1989 Brazilian campaign was one of a large number of programs that USAID has sponsored through its work with the Johns Hopkins University Population Communication Services Program. The Johns Hopkins program has been the major channel through which the USAID has provided support to countries that wish to include IEC in their population programs. Johns Hopkins has been a major advocate for an approach often called Entertainment-Education, which is a broad title for a number of distinct programs that incorporate population messages in entertainment formats, including the use of music videos, serial dramas, feature films, and advertising spots.

Although most of Johns Hopkins' work is provision of technical advice to government and private agencies, they have published evaluations of some of their programs. Piotrow and colleagues (1990) report the results of an evaluation of an entertainment education program in three states in Nigeria. They show that their interventions, which involved the incorporation of narrative vignettes in ongoing televised variety programs, all were associated with a substantial rise in demand for services at family planning clinics, and frequent reports among clinic visitors that the television programs had stimulated the visits.

Piotrow et al. (1992) also report the results of their "Male Motivation Project" in Zimbabwe. This program involved the production and broadcast of a 52-episode serial drama meant to affect men's willingness to make new reproductive choices with their partners. In contrast to the evidence from Nigeria, they focus their evaluation on before and after national survey data rather than only clinic records. They provide some evidence for improvements in beliefs and attitudes associated with the period of their campaign; however, the evidence for behavior change is much less secure. A very small change in self-reported behavior is not shown to be statistically significant and, in any case, relies on two imperfectly matched samples whose noncomparability could easily account for small observed differences in behavior.

Valente et al. (1994) provide an additional evaluation of a Johns Hopkins-advised radio drama, in The Gambia. The report relies on before and after surveys of 400 men and women in three villages in one region of the country. The surveys were taken about nine months apart and report a large gain in contraceptive practice, from 19 percent to 30 percent "using a modern method," including a jump from 9 percent to 22 percent among people with no education. And it appears that the reported increase in use rates is underestimated, since the authors report that nearly all of the increase in use was for pill use among women, who make up only half the sample. They also show some evidence that individuals who report listening to the programs held better knowledge, attitudes, and practices than did nonlisteners.

However, these results seem almost too good to be true: this would have to be an extraordinary program, indeed, to produce a doubling of use rates in a nine-month period. A suspicion that there was some problem in administration of the instrument is enhanced when one looks at scores on a 12-item "attitude towards family planning" scale. Precampaign attitudes had a mean of 4.9, while postprogram attitudes were a near perfect 11.2, including a score of 10.6 for those who were classified as not having radios and not hearing the program. It appears that these apparently strong results may be unreliable.

Another published evaluation of a serial drama campaign was undertaken in Zambia, but was not, in fact, a family planning campaign. Rather it was an AIDS campaign, but with an ultimate objective of affecting rates of condom use. The evaluation (Yoder et al., 1996) concludes that although there were substantial changes in condom use, and in other process variables (in beliefs and attitudes and talking about AIDS with family members) during the period of the campaign, they were not associated with exposure to the campaign. There was lots of public information and discussion about HIV/AIDS in Zambia during the period of the campaign, and presumably the observed changes were associated with those inputs, but they could not be attributed to specific listening to this serial drama.

A three-month family planning multimedia campaign in Mali used television plays and spots and radio songs (Kane et al., 1998) to encourage adoption of family planning. A pre-and postevaluation design showed a high level of recall of exposure to the campaign, some striking changes in attitudes including intention to use "a modern method" in the future, but only statistically nonsignificant trends toward increased use of any modern method.

Rogers et al. (1999) report about a radio serial drama in Tanzania that targeted both family planning and HIV/AIDS prevention objectives. The evaluators were plagued by large differences in precampaign practices between their treatment and comparison areas, making difficult the interpretation of advantages in rates of change to the treatment area. To deal with this unfortunate problem, the authors undertook correlational analysis at the ward (a small geographical unit) level, examining the associations between the average level of program exposure in a ward and rates of change on process and outcome variables. Many analyses are reported, and some of those related to beliefs and attitudes show positive slopes (e.g., changes in rates approving of the use of family planning, and proportion mentioning a higher ideal age for marriage for women). If we focus on behavioral outcomes relevant to family planning, there is a significant association between ward-level exposure and change in women's "always or sometimes use of family planning." The authors also report evidence from time series data of new adopters at 34 family planning clinics divided between the treatment and comparison areas. They show a long period, precampaign, of similar levels and trends in demand, and a quite sharp differentiation between the treatment and comparison area clinics six months into the broadcast of the serial drama, with the treatment area clinics serving 45 adopters per month and the comparison area clinics serving around 30 per month.

Storey et al. (1999) evaluated a radio communication project in Nepal involving both entertainment education through a soap opera, and additional radio and print programs aimed at consumers and health service personnel. They followed a cohort of currently married women for roughly 2-1/2 years, and found that exposure to the radio programs was associated with new adoption and with continuation of use. They also showed that much of the effects of exposure on behavior was mediated by changes in attitudes and perceived normative support, the explicit targets of the campaign. In a separate analysis of clinic service data from some sentinel clinics, they established sharp increases in demand for services accompanying the initiation of broadcasts, a decline during a nonbroadcast period, and a renewed demand associated with the reintroduction of broadcasts.

These studies represent the major published studies of discrete programs that used mass media in a way that permitted some exploration of their effects. The central results are summarized in Table 7-2. The most optimistic results from the credible studies say that there are effects of mass media programs, but they seem constrained in two ways: first, they are effective at increasing demand on clinics, but only in one or two cases seem to show much detectable effect on population-level behavior. Second, when data are available over a longer period, it seems as though program effects last as long as the programs are operating at a high level, but the effects seem not to stick; behavior returns to prior trends soon after the broadcasts stop. The lack of evidence of long-term effects may reflect the too short lives of these programs and the resulting premature collection of behavior data; funding agencies want evidence of effects on a schedule that may be inconsistent with the time it takes to realize behavioral change that can be detected on the population level.

At the beginning of this presentation of results of discrete programs, we noted that they represent a highly biased sample of all of the IEC, media-using, purposive programs. There are some additional results that do have relevance to the more ordinary programs. In their useful analyses of African DHS, Westoff and his colleagues establish a substantial association between self-reports of exposure to family planning messages on the mass media and reproductive beliefs, attitudes, and behaviors.

TABLE 7-2 Summary of Mass Media Intervention Projects

Country/Project	Effect on Clinic Demand	Effect on Population Behavior	Comments
Colombia	Yes	—	Fading after project end
Iran/Isfahan	Yes	—	Fading after project end
Peru	No	—	
Guatemala	Yes	No	
Brazil	Yes	—	Return to preproject level
Nigeria	Yes	—	
Zimbabwe	—	No?	Data quality issues
The Gambia	—	Yes?	Data quality issues
Zambia	—	No	
Tanzania	Yes	Yes?	Research design makes inference hard
Mali	—	No?	Nonsignificant trend
Nepal	Yes	Yes	

NOTES: — means effect not examined in published study.

The results reported previously referred to general media exposure; the results reported here refer specifically to recall of exposure to family planning messages on the mass media.

Westoff and Rodriguez (1995) show, using the 1989 Kenyan DHS data, that exposure to family planning messages on radio, print, and television were associated with current use of a method and use of a modern method, intentions to use in the future, and mean number of ideal children among other outcomes, while controlling for a wide range of covariates.

Bankole et al. (1996) show that reports of exposure to media messages in 1990 in Nigeria predicted current use of a modern method in 1993, among a small sample of women for whom data were available at both time periods. Among women who had never used a method by 1990, 28 percent of those who heard messages by 1990 claimed current use of a modern method in 1993, while only 9 percent who did not claim exposure to media messages by 1990 were modern method users in 1993.

Westoff and Bankole (1997) also use the DHS data already described above to show that self-reports of exposure to family planning messages on radio were positively associated with several outcomes in the five countries for which data were available about such exposure. These include significant associations with knowledge of modern methods and intention to use a method in all five countries studied and with current use of any fertility control method in three out of five countries studied. They control for general exposure to television, radio, and newspapers and to the other covariates listed in Table 7-1. In the same report of results, they also provide supplemental longitudinal analysis for Morocco. In Morocco, 1992 exposure to radio messages was also associated with 1995 use of a method, and with 1995 desire to stop childbearing.

In all of these studies there is a substantial association; as before, the question is whether these data permit a causal inference. Concerns about causal direction are partly dealt with through the longitudinal results from Nigeria and Morocco. Concerns about other variables causing both reported exposure to messages and the outcomes are partly dealt with by the analyses controlling for covariates. But as the authors cautiously indicate, they are unable to rule out a counterexplanation that suggests that people who are interested in family planning (or in the case of the longitudinal studies, about to become interested) are more likely to recall exposure to relevant messages.

Evidence from Qualitative Studies

There is another area of study of mass media that focuses on the microprocesses of reception and incorporation of messages into the daily lives of audiences. Most of the studies in this tradition have been concerned with defining how the reception process takes place and how audiences make sense of the ideas that come to them in the media (Katz and Liebes, 1990; Moores, 1993). There has been little attempt until now to link this body of evidence with evidence of change in receivers' attitudes or behaviors, partly because the focus was exclusively on reception processes and partly because changes were viewed as longer term and sometimes indirectly related to the ideas contained in the programs.

The link between reception and outcome is critical and one that Freedman (1997) has recently highlighted for understanding changes in fertility preferences due to family planning programs. He suggests that qualitative studies can add to the evidence about how ideational processes take place. He points out that the little evidence that we do have suggests the importance of discussion of demographic issues in social networks. He concludes:

> Interaction in social networks is likely to be an important basis for diffusion and legitimization of ideas about smaller families and birth control. But where do these ideas come from? Establishing their origins and pathways in the growing national and international networks, in the direct and indirect influence of local programs, and in the changing life situations of the population is a primary challenge. (p. 9)

The argument of models three and four above is partly based on the assumption that large numbers of people are exposed daily to information about issues relating to norms and values of family relations, women's roles, and sexuality coming from metropolitan or international mass media sources that generate reactions and discussions among audiences over long periods of time. Serial dramas like the Latin American telenovelas or equivalent genres in Asia, Africa, and the Arab countries often raise demographically relevant issues (Fadul et al., 1996; McAnany and La Pastina, 1994). Moreover, there is consistent evidence that audiences strongly identify with these stories and discuss issues of norms and values in family, neighborhood, and social groups (Brown, 1994, for English-speaking countries; McAnany and La Pastina, 1994, for Latin America; Mankekar, 1993, for India; Diase, 1996, for Egypt; and Kothari, 1997, for Pakistan).

In an ongoing study of Brazilian television and demography (Potter et al., 1997; Faria and Potter, 1999; Rios-Neto et al., 1998; McAnany, 1997), a series of qualitative studies of audience reception and incorporation have been carried out to delineate how demographically relevant ideas enter social networks and circulate beyond the family. The preliminary evidence (Hamburger, 1998; La Pastina, 1997) suggests several pathways and processes: (1) new ideas about nontraditional roles for women and taboo ideas, such as divorce, abortion, and vasectomy, reach the public sphere over time through television narratives that reach all levels of a national audience; (2) audiences engage with these narratives, discuss the issues raised in them, and compare and apply them to their own lives; (3) other media such as newspapers, magazines, and radio, not only reinforce and popularize the stories but discuss issues and debates raised by government, religious, and social groups; (4) mothers and fathers sometimes intervene in television viewing by their children to discuss issues about sexuality, authority, and social roles; most parents express the conviction that their children are influenced by the models, norms, and values presented in the stories. All of the evidence suggests a pathway for entry of new ideas concerning modern value issues confronting national audiences. Some behavioral outcomes are immediate, such as the buying of recorded music appearing in the series or adopting new fashions and styles of characters, but most are longer term and less direct, such as attitudes about women's work roles, the value of virginity before marriage, or the legitimization of divorce for women in loveless marriages. Historical records of the first treatment of such sensitive issues as divorce or abortion in a public medium such as national television (Fadul et al. 1996) provide some basis for tracking the debate surrounding such issues. The long-term nature of such changes, however, makes it difficult but not impossible to establish the link between changes in fertility practice and the spread of television (thus the integration of various sources of evidence within a single project like the one in Brazil is a critical step).

There is one more conclusion to the audience reception literature: there are a wide variety of reactions to messages received. The macro studies reviewed earlier suggest that media exposure is somehow related to a series of similar practices resulting in lowered fertility. One is left with the impression that it is a single, simple process of influence. What ethnographic audience studies reveal is that audiences represent a wide variety of positions on value and normative issues. The commonality of audiences is that they receive on a daily basis the stories and situations that they will discuss and debate with family and neighbors. Moreover, this process is repeated again and again over months and years, with varying degrees of intensity, depending on the issue that a particular story may raise.

The process outlined here is not, for the most part, an ideational campaign from government or other social agency. It is often random and even chaotic. The media, especially radio and increasingly television for developing countries, carry many messages in their programs, but in many countries the serial narratives making up the prime listening and viewing hours deal consistently with family matters that legitimate or at least open for debate problems facing their societies regarding women and their roles, families, premarital sex, and other modernizing pressures. Scriptwriters with an intent of raising debate (compare Kothari,

1997, on women's issues in Pakistani soaps) often consciously introduce these issues, but there may not be any immediately observable change. Looked at in the long term, however, and linked with studies of media exposure and changes in fertility beliefs and practices, the process of ideational change takes on a clearer path.

DISCUSSION

Thus far we have painted a complex picture of evidence around the hypothesis that the spread of mass media is associated with reductions in fertility. The correlational evidence, both cross-sectional and longitudinal, but not associated with discrete programs, is consistent with such an effect. The evidence from discrete programs is much less convincing about broad effects, although it provides some evidence for (short-lived) increases in demand for clinic services. The evidence that falls between the two types, reporting on the association of exposure to family planning messages but not tied to a specific program, is more optimistic.

However, we recognize there are problems with these data. The correlational studies do not permit us to reject the rival hypothesis that selection, the effects of unmeasured exogenous variables, accounts for the observed association. The discrete program evaluations have suffered from mischance in data collection, or too short a time frame for the intervention programs and for the estimation of effects, or too complex an environment to attribute effects cleanly. In some sense, the very attempt to make them open to study as discrete interventions may have worked against producing or measuring their success. The problem of openness to study relates directly to the issue of a proposed model of effect. How is it that mass media are to have their effects?

The review of specific evidence just completed corresponds to two particular models of media effects. The first model often underpins the evaluations of discrete programs. They assume that a focused input can produce specific effects in the short term. This may be a reasonable model when the effects involve shifting people from intending to engage in a behavior to actually engaging in the behavior. A good example from the evidence presented here would be a program designed to stimulate those people who are already intending to use modern methods to actually visit the clinic to obtain a contraceptive. The evidence from several programs of increases in clinic demand, without corresponding evidence of a population change in contraceptive use, is consistent with this model. It would suggest that the success of short-term programs might rely on a substantial population of people who are ready to act and just need a final push. Although in these family planning examples this group was apparently small, limiting the size of population effects, that does not have to be the case. In another area, encouraging immunization of young children, there is evidence that the ready-to-act population is much larger and media campaigns can stimulate rapid changes in immunization rates. In the Philippines, the proportion of urban children fully immunized by their first birthday increased from 32 percent to 52 percent as a result of a one-year media campaign. It apparently worked mostly by teaching parents who were having their children vaccinated, but on a delayed schedule, that they needed to bring their children in before their first birthdays (Zimicki et al., 1994).

However, there is also a second model of media effect, particularly relevant when behavior is not so close to realization. People may be aware of the new behavior but do not yet intend to do it, and then the model of effect may be different. Media may still have profound effects but the process may be slower and have a different character. Then the process of influence may take substantial time, and require reinforcement through repetition and transmission through multiple channels. This complex process of effects is described in studies of how people respond to prime time soap operas (compare McAnany and La Pastina, 1994; Brown, 1994). A program exposes television owners to messages directly; it generates conversation among those who watch it and with others not exposed; newspapers may regularly report about ongoing story lines, especially those stories that cause controversy. Soap operas, and other programs, address similar issues. This constant lapping against the shore, rather than a single large wave, may produce slow, long-term changes in values underlying fertility intentions.

There is some recent work analyzing health communication programs in the more developed world that has bearing here. There have been a series of discrete intervention programs directed toward smoking and other heart disease-related behaviors. These have included the Stanford Heart Disease Prevention Program, the Minnesota Heart Health Program, and the Community Intervention Trial for Smoking Cessation (COMMIT) trial (Farquhar et al., 1990; COMMIT, 1995; Luepker et al., 1994). Each has compared treatment and control groups to measure the effects of media (and other IEC efforts) on behavioral outcomes. Each has had to conclude that the evidence is inconsistent with an effect, or at best that the evidence is ambiguous. These discrete programs may contrast with a series of uncontrolled efforts at public education that are associated with massive changes in behavior. To point to just two: the Swiss AIDS program was associated with an increase from 8 percent to 56 percent of young people always using condoms for casual sex (Dubois-Arber et al., 1997); the National High Blood Pressure Education Program (NHBPEP) was associated with a 57-percent drop in stroke rate in a 12-year period (Roccella and Lenfant, 1992). (See Hornik, 1997, for a fuller discussion of these cases and others.)

One explanation for the difference between the small success of the discrete programs and major successes of the uncontrolled programs may be that the evaluations were of radically different quality. But a more important distinction may come from an understanding about how communication programs have big effects.

First, there is relatively little evidence for big differences in exposure to messages over time between the treatment and control areas in the discrete studies, while for the messy programs (like Swiss AIDS and NHBPEP), the levels of exposure achieved are much higher. This may be less of a problem in many developing country contexts in which the media environment is less competitive. Indeed, in many of the evaluations summarized here, authors are able to point to quite substantial levels of basic exposure to messages.

People may also change behavior when many aspects of their environments communicate new messages in a repeated and reinforcing way over time. They may change when there is substantial diffusion of those messages through social networks in the ways previously described. That is the way that programs that are considered strong family planning programs operate. Elsewhere one of us has speculated about the way that someone might initiate new practices related to high blood pressure:

> How might the NHBPEP have worked? One can imagine how the process of change occurs: a person sees some public service announcements and a local TV health reporter's feature telling her about the symptomless disease of hypertension; she checks her blood pressure in a newly accessible shopping mall machine, those results suggest a problem; she tells her spouse who has also seen the ads and encourages her to have it checked; she goes to a physician who confirms the presence of hypertension, encourages her to change her diet and then return for monitoring. Meanwhile the physician has become more sensitive to the issue because of a recent *Journal of American Medical Association* article, and some recommendations from a specialist society, and a conversation with drug detailer, as well as informal conversations with colleagues and exposure to television discussion of the issue. The patient talks with friends at work or family members about her experience; they also increase their concern and go to have their own pressure checked. She returns for another checkup and her pressure is still elevated although she has reduced her use of cooking salt; the physician decides to treat her with medication. The patient is ready to comply because all the sources around her, personal, professional and mediated, are telling her that she should (Hornik, 1997:49-50).

We would suspect that the story, while different in the details for a developing country, would not be radically different in essence for adoption of family planning behavior.

This may be why many of the discrete evaluations are unable to find population-level effects that stick. They are evidence about media effects on fertility within the first model. If the question at issue here is how media affect fertility in the broadest sense, although these projects get the lion's share of research, they may represent only quite a small share of the influence. They examine a small proportion of all the media content developed to affect fertility because for most programs media effects cannot be isolated from other program effects. Of greater moment, they are an even smaller proportion of all the media materials that may affect fertility, if we speculate that most fertility effects are due to hypotheses two, three, and four stated at the start—the ideational effects of ordinary media content. In that case, if what we are interested in is the long-term large effects of multifaceted programs, and of natural exposure to media content, the discrete evaluations are much less interesting than are the correlational studies. The correlational studies, both cross-sectional and longitudinal, address the model of effect that is most likely to have produced big fertility effects. And the correlational studies, for all their methodological tentativeness, support the claim that the spread of mass media affects fertility.

The evidence base is certainly open to challenge, but here are conclusions and speculations based on what is available:

- There is good evidence that short-term campaigns can affect clinic demand, which may relate to shortening the time lag between intention and behavior for those who are ready to act. The evaluations of those campaigns have been less successful in establishing that they produce detectable population-level changes in behavior.
- Access to mass media is substantially related to fertility (or fertility-related behavior), at three levels of aggregation—individual, municipal, and national—even when other likely causes of the relation are controlled. There is some evidence that mass media access predicts subsequent changes in fertility-related behavior.
- This second type of evidence is the strongest support for the argument that the spread of media affects fertility on a scale that is important. However, even if that claim was accepted, the mechanism of effect is undetermined. We have suggested at least four paths for such influence: medium noncontent effects, influence on elites, influence on basic values of general audiences, and influence on fertility-specific knowledge of general audiences.
- Nonetheless, we would speculate that if the spread of mass media has effects on fertility, it reflects a complex social process rather than a medium effect or a discrete learning process: multiple channels, providing reinforcing messages, over time, producing inter-

personal discussion and a slow change in values, and working at a level of social aggregation higher than the individual.

- Most of our discussion has focused on two types of effects: those related to discrete mass media interventions, and those related to general media access and exposure to ordinary media content. But there is a third type of possible effect: the effects of continuing messages delivered through the IEC efforts of general profamily planning programs. The explicit evidence relevant to these programs is that self-reported attention to media family planning messages, not in the context of a discrete intervention, is related to fertility-related behavior in the African sites studied by Westoff and Bankole. Most programs incorporate such efforts, but they are of unknown heft and quality, and of unknown effect. These programs cannot separate IEC or mass media messages from the rest of their activities, but they operate over the long term and with constant reinforcement of messages. In some ways they may behave more like the general media content, long-term effects model than they do the discrete, short-term effects model. More attention to these operational programs may produce evidence of long-term effects not seen with the short-term evaluations of discrete programs, just as the messy NHBPEP showed effects that the better evaluated but less comprehensive Stanford and COMMIT programs did not.

NOTES

1. Analysis based on 1997 data from World Development Indicators (World Bank, 1999); the predicted variance including the omitted countries is still a very substantial 66.1 percent.
2. The self-reported exposure to family planning messages on radio is also controlled in these analyses. Because that measure is likely to be highly correlated with radio exposure, it probably artifactually reduces the observed associations with overall media use.

REFERENCES

Bankole, A., G. Rodriguez, and C.F. Westoff
1996   Mass media messages and reproductive behavior in Nigeria. *Journal of Biosocial Science* 28(2):227–239.
Bertrand, J.T., R. Santiso, S.H. Linder, and M.A. Pineda
1987   Evaluation of a communications program to increase the adoption of vasectomy in Guatemala. *Studies in Family Planning* 18(6):361–370.
Brown, M.E.
1994   *Soap Opera and Women's Talk: The Pleasure of Resistance.* Thousand Oaks, CA: Sage Publications.

Community Intervention Trial for Smoking Cessation (COMMIT)
1995 I. Cohort results from a four year intervention. *American Journal of Public Health* 85:183–192.

Cook, T.D., and D. Campbell
1979 *Quasi-Experimentation*. Boston, MA: Houghton-Mifflin.

Diase, M.
1996 Egyptian Television Serials, Audiences and "The Family House": A Public Health Enter-Educate Serial. Unpublished Ph.D. dissertation, University of Texas at Austin.

Dubois-Arber, F., A. Jeannin, E. Konings, and F. Paccaud
1997 Increased condom use without other major changes in sexual behavior among the general population in Switzerland. *American Journal of Public Health* 87(4):558–559.

Fadul, A., E. McAnany, and O. Torres Morales
1996 Telenovela and Demography in Brazil: A Working Paper. Unpublished paper presented at the International Association for Mass Communication Research, August 18–22, Sydney.

Faria, V.E., and J.E. Potter
1999 Television, telenovelas and fertility change in northeast Brazil. Pp. 252–272 in *Dynamics of Values in Fertility Change*, Richard Leete, ed. Oxford, Eng.: Clarendon Press.

Farquhar, J.W., S.P. Fortmann, J.A. Flora, C.B. Taylor, W.L. Haskell, P.T. Williams, N. Maccoby, and P.D. Wood
1990 Effects of communitywide education on cardiovascular disease risk factors. The Stanford five-city project. *Journal of the American Medical Association* 264(3):359–365.

Ferreros, C.
1990 *Social Marketing of Condoms For AIDS Prevention in Developing Countries: The Zaire Experience*. Washington, DC: Population Services International.

Freedman, R.
1997 Do family planning programs affect fertility preferences? A literature review. *Studies in Family Planning* 28(1):1–13.

Gerbner, G., L. Gross, M. Morgan, and N. Signorielli
1994 Growing up with television: The cultivation perspective. In *Media Effects: Advances in Theory and Research*, J. Bryant and D. Zillman, eds. Hillsdale, NJ: Lawrence Erlbaum Associates.

Hamburger, E.
1998 Producing Culture in Contemporary Brazil: Theories and Practices Involved in Production and Reception of Telenovelas. Working paper. Population Research Center, University of Texas at Austin.

Harvey, P.D.
1991 *The Correlation Between Consumer Prices and Per Capita Sales of Condoms in Seventeen Social Marketing Programs*. Washington, DC: Population Services International.

Hornik, R.C.
1989 Channel effectiveness in development communication programs. In *Public Communication Campaigns*, 2d ed., R. Rice and C. Atkins, eds. Beverly Hills: Sage.
1997 Public health education and communication as policy instruments for bringing about changes in behavior. Pp. 45–60 in *Social Marketing: Theoretical and Practical Perspectives*, M. Goldberg, M. Fishbein, and S. Middlestadt, eds. Hillsdale, NJ: Lawrence Erlbaum Associates.

Hornik, R.C., ed.
  2001   Public Health Communication: Evidence for Behavior Change. Mahnah, NJ: Lawrence
         Erlbaum Associates.
Hornik, R.C., J. McDowell, J. Romero, and R. Pareja
  1987   Communication and Health Literacy: Evaluation of the Peru Program 1984–1985. Phila-
         delphia: Annenberg School, University of Pennsylvania and Washington, DC:
         Academy for Educational Development.
Inkeles, A., and D.H. Smith
  1974   Becoming Modern. Cambridge, MA: Harvard University Press.
Iyengar, S., and D.R. Kinder
  1987   News That Matters: Television and American Opinion. Chicago: University of Chi-
         cago Press.
Kane, T.T., M. Gueye, I. Speizer, S. Pacque-Margolis, and D. Baron
  1998   The impact of a family planning multimedia campaign in Bamako, Mali. Studies
         in Family Planning 29(3):309–323.
Katz, E., and T. Liebes
  1990   Interacting with Dallas: Cross cultural readings of American TV. Canadian Journal
         Of Communication 15:45–65.
Kincaid, D.L., A.P. Merritt, L. Nickerson, S. Buffington de Castro, M.P. de Castro, and B.M.
         deCastro
  1996   Impact of a mass media vasectomy promotion campaign in Brazil. International
         Family Planning Perspectives 22:169–175.
Kothari, S.
  1997   From Genre to Zanaana: Women and Urdu Drama Serials in Pakistan. Unpub-
         lished Ph.D. dissertation, University of Texas at Austin.
Kottak, C.K.
  1990   Prime Time Society: Anthropological Analysis of Television and Culture. Belmont, CA:
         Wadsworth.
La Pastina, A.
  1997   Watching "O rei do gado" in Timbabuba: A Short Account of an Ethnographic
         Research. Working paper. Population Research Center, University of Texas at
         Austin.
Lerner, D.
  1958   The Passing of Traditional Society. New York: Free Press.
Luepker, R.V., D.M. Murray, D.R. Jacobs Jr., M.B. Mittelmark, N. Bracht, R. Carlaw, R.
         Crow, P. Elmer, J Finnegan, and A.R. Folsom
  1994   Community education for cardiovascular disease prevention: Risk factor changes
         in the Minnesota Heart Health Program. American Journal of Public Health 84(9):
         1383–1393.
Mankekar, P.
  1993   National texts and gendered lives: An ethnography of television viewers in a
         north Indian city. American Ethnologist 20(3):543–563.
Mason, K.O.
  1997   Explaining fertility transitions. Demography 34(4):443–454.
McAnany, E.
  1997   Television and Demographic Transition in Brazil: A Model for Studying Long Term
         Change. Unpublished paper prepared for Long Term Consequences Through Mass
         Media, University of Saarlandes, February, Saarbrucken, Germany.
McAnany, E., and A. La Pastina
  1994   Telenovela audiences: A review and methodological critique of Latin American
         research. Communication Research 21(6):828–849.

McCombs, M., D.L. Shaw, and D. Weaver, eds.
    1997   *Communication And Democracy: Exploring The Intellectual Frontiers In Agenda-Setting Theory.* Mahwah, NJ: Lawrence Erlbaum Associates.
Moores, S.
    1993   *Interpreting Audiences: The Ethnography of Media Consumption.* Thousand Oaks, CA: Sage Press.
Piotrow, P.T., D.L. Kincaid, M.J. Hindin, C.L. Lettenmaier, I. Kuseka, T. Silberman, A. Zinanga, F. Chikara, D.J. Adamchak, M.T. Mbizvo, W. Lynn, O.M. Kumah, and Y.-M. Kim.
    1992   Changing men's attitudes and behavior: The Zimbabwe male motivation project. *Studies in Family Planning* 23(6 p 1):365–375.
Piotrow, P.T., J.G. Rimon 2d, K. Winnard, D.L. Kincaid, D. Huntington, and J. Convisser
    1990   Mass media family planning promotion in three Nigerian cities. *Studies in Family Planning* 21(5):265–274.
Potter, J.E., R.M. Assuncao, S.M. Cavenaghi, and A.J. Caetano
    1997   The Spread of Television and Fertility Decline in Brazil: A Spatial Temporal Analysis. Unpublished paper presented at the XXIIIrd IUSSP General Conference, October 11–17, Beijing, China.
Prochaska, J.O., and C.C. DiClemente
    1983   Stages and processes of self-change of smoking: Toward an integrative model of change. *Journal of Consulting & Clinical Psychology* 51(3):390–395.
Putnam, R.D.
    1995   Bowling alone: America's declining social capital. *Journal of Democracy* 6(1):65–79.
Rios-Neto, E., P. Miranda-Rebeiro, and J. Potter
    1998   I Saw It on TV: Television and Demographic Change in Brazil. Paper presented at the Workshop on the Social Dynamics of Fertility Change in Developing Countries, National Research Council, January 28–30, Washington, DC.
Roccella, E.J., and C. Lenfant
    1992   Family physicians and the battle against hypertension. (Editorial) *American Family Physician* 46(5):1390.
Rogers, E.M.
    1995   *Diffusion of Innovations,* 4th ed. New York: Free Press.
Rogers, E.M., D. Solomon, and R. Adhikarya
    1978   *Further Directions for USAID's Communication Policies in Population.* Stanford: Institute for Communication Research.
Rogers, E.M., P.W. Vaughan, R.M.A. Swalehe, N. Rao, P. Svenkerud, and S. Sood
    1999   Effects of an entertainment-education radio soap opera on family planning behavior in Tanzania. *Studies In Family Planning* 30(3):193–211.
Ross, J.A., and W.P. Mauldin
    1996   Family planning programs: Efforts and results, 1972–1994. *Studies in Family Planning* 27(3):137–147.
Schiller, H.I.
    1976   *Communication And Cultural Domination.* White Plains, NY: Pantheon Books.
Storey, D., M. Boulay, Y. Karki, K. Keckert, and D.M. Karmacharya
    1999   Impact of the integrated radio communication project in Nepal, 1994–1997. *Journal of Health Communication* 4(4):271–294.
Valente, T.W., Y.M. Kim, C. Lettenmaier, W. Glass, and Y. Dibba
    1994   Radio promotion of family planning in the Gambia. *International Family Planning Perspectives* 20:96–100.
Varis, T.
    1984   The international flow of television programs. *Journal of Communication* 34(1):143–152.

Westoff, C.F., and A. Bankole
  1997   *Mass Media and Reproductive Behavior in Africa.* Demographic and Health Surveys Analytical Reports No. 2, April. Calverton, MD: Macro International.
Westoff, C.F., and G. Rodriguez
  1995   The mass media and family planning in Kenya. *International Family Planning Perspectives* 21:1, 26–31, 36.
World Bank
  1999   *World Development Indicators.* Washington, DC: World Bank.
Yoder, P.S., R.C. Hornik, and B. Chirwa
  1996   Evaluating the program effects of a radio drama about AIDS in Zambia. *Studies in Family Planning* 27(4):188–203.
Zimicki, S., R.C. Hornik, C.C. Verzosa, J.R. Hernandez, E. de Guzman, M. Dayrit, A. Fausto, M.B. Lee, and M. Abad
  1994   Improving vaccination coverage in urban areas through a health communication campaign: The 1990 Philippine experience. *Bulletin of the World Health Organization* 72(3):409–422.

8

Ready, Willing, and Able: A Conceptualization of Transitions to New Behavioral Forms

RON LESTHAEGHE AND CAMILLE VANDERHOEFT

INTRODUCTION

In this paper we shall try to present a simple mathematical model for describing the adaptation to new forms of behavior and for studying the subsequent generalization of these forms among populations. Such transitions obviously involve processes of innovation and diffusion. In this conceptualization we shall use basic concepts that correspond to three preconditions for the adaptation to a new mode of behavior. These three preconditions are *readiness*, *willingness* and *ability*. This formulation is taken directly from Coale (1973), who grouped the preconditions for a fertility transition under these headings. To the best of our knowledge, this simple conceptualization has not received any further attention in the 25 years following its introduction.

The notion of readiness refers to the fact that the new forms of behavior must be advantageous to the actor; that is, their utility must be evident and outweigh their disutility. As such, the condition of readiness refers to the microeconomic cost-benefit calculus that actors utilize in decision processes.

The notion of willingness refers to considerations of legitimacy and normative (e.g., ethical, religious) acceptability of the new pattern of ac-

Ron Lesthaeghe and Camille Vanderhoeft are professors in the department of social research at Vrije University, Brussels. The authors extend a special note of gratitude to Jan Mariën at Vrije University for further mathematical research on the location of the minimum of three beta-distributions, and Martin Vaessen at Macro International for making available several tabulations from the raw data.

tion. Such an evaluation occurs against the backdrop of internalized normative structures existing in societies at any point in time. The basic question addressed by willingness is to what extent new forms of behavior run counter to established traditional beliefs and codes of conduct, and to what extent there is a willingness to overcome moral objections and fears.

The adoption of new forms of behavior may also depend on the availability of new techniques. The notion of ability then refers to the accessibility of these innovations. Also, this access may have a cost that reduces ability, even if it is merely psychological. Obviously this third precondition disappears when the issue of accessibility to new facilitating factors does not arise.

The conceptual model built around "ready, willing and able" (R,W,A for short) may have many applications in a variety of fields. In general, the R and W conditions arise in all matters that have both an economic and a moral dimension.

The use of the R,W,A preconditions also has the advantage of creating links between the various social science disciplines, and particularly between economics concentrating on the R condition, and the other social sciences that pay more attention to normative and cultural aspects, that is, to the W condition. The present conceptualization is therefore also meant as an overarching framework for the integration of hitherto segregated "narratives" existing in the various social science disciplines (compare van de Kaa, 1996; Burch, 1996; Lesthaeghe, 1997).

Finally, the model will also attempt to build bridges to the literature dealing with processes of diffusion or contagion and with social learning (self-initiated) and social influence (other initiated) (compare Montgomery and Casterline, 1996).

The structure of the paper is as follows. First we shall revisit the R,W,A preconditions and their use in various narratives of the fertility transition. After all, this was the empirical field where this general formulation was initiated. Then we shall present transitions as a function of changing distributions of R, W, and A. Here we shall adopt three beta-distributions and define the outcome variable S as the minimum of the R, W, and A scores. If success (S) with respect to the adoption of a new form of behavior is dependent on meeting the three preconditions *jointly*, that is,

$$S = R \cap W \cap A$$

and if R, W, and A are distributions on a zero to unity scale, then for an individual i:

$$S_i = \text{Min } (R_i,\ W_i,\ A_i)$$

which means that the weakest link (the smallest of the three scores) will determine the outcome.

In the next section, we shall link the shape of the beta-distributions to the Montgomery-Casterline formulation of social learning and social influence, thereby introducing outside influences in the decision process and degrees of heterogeneity within a population with respect to all three preconditions.

In the last section, we return to a demographic application by relating the R,W,A concepts to actual data taken from the Demographic and Health Service (DHS) surveys in African countries. The purpose here is to establish where the bottleneck conditions are located.

R,W,A AND FERTILITY TRANSITION NARRATIVES

As indicated in the introduction, the RWA preconditions were introduced in 1973 by Coale in an article that attempted to summarize the findings of the Princeton European Fertility Transition Project (EFT). Coale clearly meant that the onset and the speed of European fertility transitions was contingent on the *joint* meeting of the three preconditions, that is, $S = R \cap W \cap A$. But just like in the "nature-nurture" debate in psychology, the findings of the EFT project were quickly converted by others into a "culture *versus* economics" debate despite the fact that $R \cap W$ specifies a "culture *and* economics" model. This misinterpretation continues today. In this paper we consider the "economics versus culture" formulation as a dead-end street (see Lesthaeghe, 1997), and we shall not devote any more time to it. Rather, we shall give a short overview of the "sub-narratives" attached to R, W, and A.

First, the R precondition has been extensively discussed and conceptually modeled in the economic literature dealing with demographic outcome variables. All schools of thought in the microeconomics of the family give a great weight to the classic cost-benefit calculus. The starting point is simple: the essence of the model is the presumption that families would balance utilities against disutilities ascribed to the nth child to determine whether a family wanted this child (Liebenstein, 1957). The neoclassic formulation that followed introduced the assumptions of fixed preferences, maximizing behavior and equilibrium solutions. In 1960, Becker introduced the concept of a household production function. The demand for children depends on the utility (economic, social, and psychological) of offspring to the parents and on the costs of children (i.e., costs of parental time, labor, and external inputs). Caldwell's "wealth flow reversal" (1982) equally states that a fertility decline starts when the "wealth flow" over a lifetime from children to parents changes into a "wealth flow" in the opposite direction.

So far, and this holds for Easterlin's, Caldwell's, and the early neoclassical versions, the parental decisions are based solely on the parental interests. The much older theory of "social capillarity," formulated by Dumont in 1880, introduced the welfare of the children themselves and altruistic behavior of parents in favor of the children's future well-being. In Dumont's conceptualization all individuals aspire to upward social mobility, but when the parents cannot achieve this for themselves, they project this ambition onto their children and invest in children's health and especially education. This is an early formulation of Becker's "dynastic multi-generational model" that introduces a preference shift in favor of "higher quality" children. From this a "quantity-quality swap" is derived. In Dumont's version, industrialization, urbanization, and economic growth opened up new opportunities for the incoming generations and higher real wages allowed parents to invest more in the education of a smaller set of children, thereby maximizing the social mobility chances of their offspring. It is clear that in this version bequests and investments are added to parental time, labor, and external inputs.

In Easterlin's version extra attention is being paid to several other crucial factors. First, a corrective response can also be generated by an increase in the supply of children. Such an increase can stem from a variety of factors, such as declining infant and childhood mortality (increasing the supply of surviving children), reduced birth spacing (decreasing length of breastfeeding and postpartum abstinence), and increased fecundity. Even with a constant demand for children, an increase in the supply would produce excess fertility and generate a corrective response in the other direction. Furthermore, Easterlin and Crimmins (1985) pay considerable attention to factors associated with the costs of fertility regulation, which, in our framework, fall under the ability precondition. He also emphasizes that the key variables are reflecting the subjective perceptions and not the objective costs and benefits.

The advantage of economic theories dealing with the R condition has been their conceptual richness and the predilection for formal specifications. The disadvantages are related to the facts that (i) many concepts (e.g., child utility, child quality) are multidimensional and therefore difficult to measure, (ii) the nature of motivations is very difficult to extract from respondents, and (iii) the calculation of a balance between costs and benefits is not easy for actors, let alone observers (compare Burch, 1997; Robinson, 1997). The outcome is that we have a set of theories that explain conceptually why fertility control may be advantageous, but that we are still far removed from reliable and valid measurements of the key ingredients. Incidentally, the studies that tried to measure the key concepts pertaining to child utility in a direct way, rather than through rough proxies, were fielded by social psychologists rather than by economists. The "Value of Children Project" by Fawcett, Arnold, and Bulatao (Fawcett, 1972; Fawcett and Arnold, 1995; Bulatao, 1979) is a prominent example of such attempts.

The W condition, by contrast, has received far less attention than the R condition. The main reason for this is that willingness is taken to follow immediately in the wake of readiness. In other words, there is no moral dilemma or "cultural lag." This may be true in problems of firms adopting a new technology, but not in the field of fertility transitions. Much of the discussion of the W condition in narratives of fertility transition stems from the Princeton EFT project and is therefore linked to the concept of secularization, meaning the reduced credibility given to religious prescriptions. Also, the measurement of secularization in European historical settings was facilitated by the fact that secularism was often an overt element of the political-ideological dimension of social organization. This permitted operationalizations through voting behavior or through adherence to religious practices (e.g., Lesthaeghe and Wilson, 1986; Livi-Bacci, 1977; Le Bras and Todd, 1981). But the fact that the degree of secularization was readily measurable only in Western Europe does not mean that the W condition is irrelevant elsewhere. Clearly, the W condition refers to a much broader set of issues than Western-style secularization in relation to Christianity.

Secular political mobilization (e.g., Nag, 1989) and growing female empowerment in developing countries (e.g., Mason, 1985), all in relation to fertility control and health, show the relevance of the W condition. First, the W condition deals with the *legitimacy* of interfering with nature or with a "natural order" as a cultural construction. Second, it deals with the belief in the *power* that individuals have to alter this natural order, and hence W depends, inter alia, on dimensions such as fatalism. Third, the W condition depends on the degree of *internalization* of traditional beliefs and codes of conduct. And fourth, W depends on the *severity of sanctions* (even imaginary ones such as those stemming from avenging spirits) attached to transgressions of normative prescriptions. Much of this is not only dependent on individual psychological dispositions, but equally on institutional agency and on what Delumeau describes as the "politics of culpabilization" (1983). Occasionally sociological studies conducted in other than Western countries have attempted to operationalize such dimensions of "control over nature" or of "fatalism versus self-directed destiny" (e.g., Inkeless and Smith, 1974, is a classic in this field), but these batteries of questions have never found their way into the large-scale demographic surveys (e.g., World Fertility Survey, DHS). Generally speaking, the broader context of the W condition has remained inadequately documented in the areas of fertility or health transitions.

The A condition has again received ample attention, predominantly in the family planning literature. In fact, the precursor of the World Fertility Survey (WFS) has been the series of knowledge, attitude, and practice (KAP) surveys dealing with the assessment of knowledge, attitudes, and practice of contraception in developing countries. These studies were predominantly designed to show that there was a knowledge gap, that is, it was essentially the lack of knowledge about contraception and the lack of accessibility to reliable contraception that formed the bottleneck. Others argued vividly that a lack of motivation constituted the weakest link. Stronger still, if there was no "reversal of the wealth flow," family planning efforts would run against the interests of large segments of populations of developing nations. In short, we had a clear debate about the relative locations of the W and A distributions. Also, national politics in many countries got involved in both local and world-wide debates on the feasibility of promoting ability, and the United Nations (World Population Conferences, United Nations Fund for Population Activities) assumed a leading role in promoting the legitimacy (W) and the accessibility (A) of family planning. More recently, academic interest in the issue of ability has taken the forms of studies in diffusion mechanisms and models (e.g., Rosero-Bixby and Casterline, 1993; Montgomery and Casterline, 1996). Several of these ideas will be used in this paper as well.

To sum up, the R and A conditions for fertility transitions are covered extensively by the literature, but the W precondition in Coale's formulation has been given much less attention. The various dimensions involved in cultural change in developing countries need to be given greater priority.

R,W,A DISTRIBUTIONS AND THE WEAKEST LINK MODEL

In the following section, we assume that the degree of fertility control (S) is an outcome variable with a continuous intensity ranging from 0 to 1. This outcome variable is, as in Coale's original verbal formulation, dependent on three preconditions, R, W, and A, as shown in the Boolean expression:

$$S = R \cap W \cap A$$

that is, all three conditions must be met jointly. However, for S to be a continuous variable, we must also assume that R, W, and A are continuous and comprised between 0 and 1. In this new formulation, a score of 0 for R would mean that limiting fertility would have 0 advantages and only entail disadvantages. A score of 0.5 would typify the situation where advantages and disadvantages are in perfect balance, and obviously a score of unity would mean there are only advantages in adopting the new strategy. Similarly, a score of 0 on W means that fertility control is ethically or religiously totally unacceptable, a score of 0.5 identifies the point of indecision, and a score of unity implies that there are no moral or cultural obstructions to adopting the new form of behavior. Finally, a score of 0 on A means that the individual has no means whatsoever to control fertility, a score of 0.5 implies that there would only be ineffective traditional methods, and a score of unity corresponds to complete ability to regulate fertility. An index of contraceptive use efficiency would be equally appropriate. In this model one could convert these scores into a dichotomy (controller/no controller) if the score on the outcome variable is larger than a given cutting point, say 0.5. For each individual in a population, a score is available on all three preconditions (R_i, W_i, and A_i). In the weakest link model, the outcome score for that individual, i.e., S_i, is the smallest value of the three, R_i, W_i, or A_i. Hence:

$$S_i = \text{Min } (R_i, W_i, A_i).$$

This means, for instance, that precondition A would be the bottleneck if A_i is the lowest score: the individual could be highly ready and willing, but has few means of controlling fertility (e.g., only abstinence).

This principle is readily generalizable to entire populations. In this instance we deal with three distributions for R, W, and A, respectively, and the weakest link rule gives the distributions of the outcome variable S as

$$S = \text{Min } (R, W, A).$$

These distributions need a particular shape. Here we have opted for a beta-distribution, because this distribution is contained between 0 and 1 and because it has the feature of bell-shaped distributions if its mean is 0.5 and if the variance is small. If the mean is lower than 0.5, the distribution is positively skewed, and if it is larger than 0.5, the distribution is negatively skewed. In Figure 8-1, we have produced three such beta-distributions, respectively with means = .1667 (var = .0106), .5 (var = .0357), and .7778 (var = .0173). The distribution to the left in Figure 8-1 would show the population distribution at the onset of an R, W, or A transition. The vast majority would see little economic advantage in controlling fertility, or would largely be unwilling or unable to do so. However, there would already be an upper tail of "innovators" for whom R, W, or A would come closer to the 0.5 mark or even surpass it. Halfway during the transition of the three preconditions, the distribution would assume a classic bell shape and half the population would be located beyond the 0.5 cutting point. Finally, near the end of the transition, only the lower tail of the skewed distribution would drag behind the majority of the population. Such a general movement of the distribution from left to right in Figure 8-1 seems an attractive representation of a general transition because it does accommodate the features of "early initiators" and "late joiners."

As indicated, our problem consists of finding the distribution of the minimum of R_i, W_i, and A_i. Assuming *stochastic independence* between the

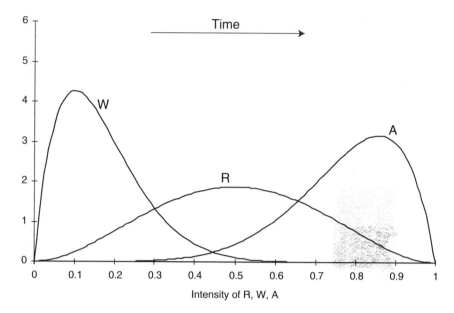

FIGURE 8-1 Shift over time of the beta distribution of the intensity of either R, W, or A from low (less than 0.5) to high (greater than 0.5).

random variables R, W, and A (subscripts are dropped to simplify the notations), the distribution of S = Min(R,W,A) can easily be obtained from the following probabilistic statement (which holds for any s between 0 and 1):

$$Pr(S > s) = Pr((R > s) \cap (W > s) \cap (A > s))$$
$$= Pr((S > s)Pr(S > s)Pr(S > s)$$

which, in terms of the cumulative distribution functions of R, W, and A, also can be written as:

$$1 - F_S(s) = (1 - F_R(s))(1 - F_W(s))(1 - F_A(s)).$$

Differentiating with respect to s gives the following expression for the probability density function (pdf) of S:

$$fs(s) = f_R(s)(1 - F_W(s))(1 - F_A(s))$$
$$+ f_W(s)(1 - F_R(s))(1 - F_A(s))$$
$$+ f_A(s)(1 - F_R(s))(1 - F_W(s))$$

Using the interpretation of a random variable's density in s as the probability that the random variable takes the value s, this formula becomes intuitively appealing and clear: the probability that the minimum S assumes the value s is the probability that one of the three underlying variables assumes that value s, while the other two have at least that value s. Moreover, if, for fixed s, both $1 - F_W(s)$ and $1 - F_A(s)$, for example, are large (i.e., close to 1), then $f_S(s)$ is close to $f_R(s)$. Thus, if two of the underlying random variables (e.g., W and A) are heavily right skewed, then the distribution of S is close to that of the third random variable (e.g., R). We used the above formula to calculate and draw the pdf of S in Figures 8-2 to 8-4, which will be discussed hereafter. Notice that although R, W, and A are assumed to be beta-distributed, S generally will not be beta-distributed. An explicit formula for the pdf of S, however, is not our concern here, and would not even be useful for our purposes, as it involves incomplete beta functions (which are to be evaluated by numerical integration).

This can also be understood intuitively. In Figure 8-2 we have reproduced the same three beta-distributions as those of Figure 8-1. Assume that the left-hand distribution now represents the individuals' scores for one of the preconditions, say W, and that the other two are representing R and A. From the "weakest link" rule S = Min (R, W, A), it follows that the

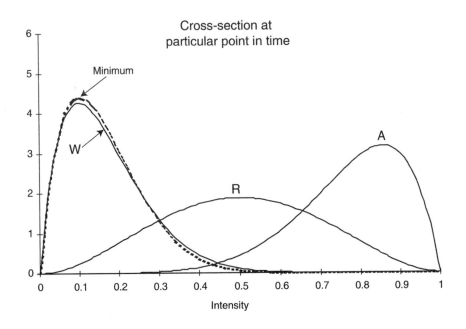

FIGURE 8-2 Location of W (left), R (middle), and A (right) at one point in time (example) and location of the distribution of the minimum (R_i, W_i, A_i) (= dotted line).

outcome for S would closely resemble the distribution of the weakest link, that is, of W. In fact, an overwhelming majority of individuals have scores W_i that would be the lowest of the three, and only for a few persons, mostly located at the upper tail of W, one would find scores of R_i and A_i that could be smaller than their W_i. Hence, the distribution of S must always be slightly to the left of the distribution of the weakest link condition (here W). Hence, the upper tail of W will be pulled in, S would have a slightly higher peak than W, and consequently the mean of S must be smaller than the mean of W. Similarly, the variance of S also will be reduced compared to the variance of W. As expected, the calculation of the S-distribution (see dotted line on Figure 8-2) shows exactly these features.

Two other examples will bring this out in a more striking way. In Figure 8-3 we have plotted (full lines) three beta-distributions with the same mean (= 0.25) but a different variance (respectively .0208, .0144, and .0110). The distribution of their minimum (dotted line) has a mean of 0.14 only, and also a variance that is much smaller, that is, .0052. This example further illustrates that each of the three beta-distributions for R, W, and A

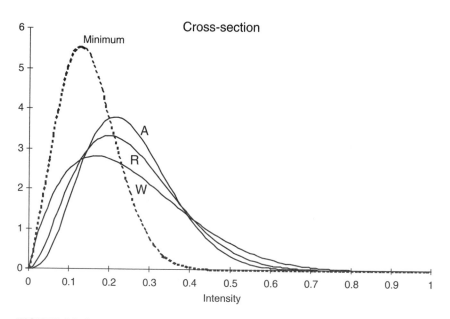

FIGURE 8-3 Location of W (left), R (middle), and A (right) at one point in time (second example) and location of the distribution of the minimum (R_i, W_i, A_i) (= dotted line).

may have an upper tail (innovators) larger than the "indecision"-cutting point of 0.5, but that such an upper tail for the distribution of the minima would be virtually nonexistant.

In the third example (Figure 8-4) we present a situation in which the distributions again have different means (0.4, 0.5, and 0.7) and different variances (.04, .0278, and .0191). Suppose we are dealing with a situation in which the vast majority of the population is already quite ready to control fertility (right-hand distribution), that willingness is following in the wake of readiness (middle distribution), but that availability and accessibility to efficient contraception would be lagging (left-hand distribution). In this instance, the distribution of the minima of scores (dotted line) would typically be situated further to the left than the distribution of the weakest link and a much smaller proportion would have S_i scores greater than 0.5 than in any of the other three distributions. In this example the mean of the S distribution is only 0.33 and the variance is again smaller than that of the weakest link distribution (.022 compared to .04). (In the next section we shall see that Figure 8-4 very closely resembles the situation found in Niger.)

This section has illustrated the rules of the game. We shall now take up the issue of diffusion and shifting distributions.

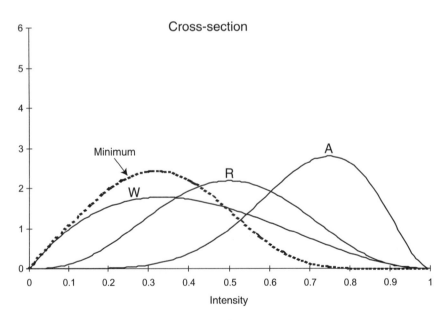

FIGURE 8-4 Location of W (left), R (middle), and A (right) at one point in time (third example) and location of the distribution of the minimum (R_i, W_i, A_i) (=dotted line).

THE MEANING OF THE R,W,A MODEL FOR
SOCIAL LEARNING AND SOCIAL INFLUENCE

Montgomery and Casterline have recently presented (1996) a simple formulation of the impact of social environment factors. They assume that an outcome variable Y at time t would be a function of two components: first, a set of individual characteristics $X_{i,t}$, and second, a weighted set of social influences Z_{t-1}. This equation is as follows:

$$Y_{i,t} = \beta X_{i,t} + \delta_i \sum_{j \in N} \omega_{i,j} Z_{j,t-1} + E_{i,t}.$$

The greek letters identify coefficients and roman capitals are variables. The social influence component is made up as follows: $Z_{j,t-1}$ is the opinion or behavior of another individual j observed by the actor i at an earlier point in time, given that individual j belongs to the network N of individual i. The latter will give a weight $\omega_{i,j}$ to the influence of j, and will furthermore do so for all other members of his network. The coefficients $\omega_{i,j}$ illustrate which network co-members will be more or less influential. To this package of outside influences, individual i will also give a general influence or credibility weight in the form of coefficient δ_i. This coefficient will be high for an impressionable learner or quick follower and low for someone with a conservative mindscape. Finally, E is a vector of residuals.

Obviously one can include a variety of actors into the relevant network. The subscript j can stand for husbands, kin, friends, or others, but also for institutional influences operating via media, religious groups, political parties, or others. This distinction is a crucial one because the underlying models of diffusion are distinct. If information, and more crucially, messages about intentions (compare Kohler, 1997) stem from individuals in the actor's own primary group environment (kin, close friends), the growth curve of adoption of new behavior is likely to follow a logistic S curve. In other words, it may take some time before adoptive behavior reaches momentum. This feature obviously is caused by the fact that the adoption has to start from a restricted group of early innovators who can only reach their immediate environment. By contrast, messages initiated by the mass media through mobilization immediately reach a broad audience, so that the rate of increase of adoptive behavior is likely to reach a maximum right from the onset (compare Lave and March, 1975:chapter 7). However, diffusion via individual contact may be less ephemeral and more convincing than that via media, so that the ultimate proportions in a population who alter behavior can be higher.

One can also make a distinction, as Montgomery and Casterline have done, between social learning that is actor initiated and social influence that is initiated by others. In the case of institutional actors, one would then refer to processes of "mobilization" or "propagation." In the European historical experience, we know that such institutional actors played a significant role in the process of fostering or obstructing secularism in the various regions, and that this had a nonredundant extra effect on the pace of the marital fertility decline. The same can be said for contemporaneous countries with a strong propagation, if not a coercive form of family limitation. Furthermore, we know that people are willing to listen to those in their immediate, trusted environment, but that such interaction density circles are not completely impermeable. Permeability across social classes, for instance, often results in a "trickle down" effect, with the behavior or attitudes of the lower classes following those of the higher ones (cultural mobility, reference group behavior, bandwagon effects).

In the model of three preconditions, we need to specify the Montgomery-Casterline expression not just for social learning and social influence with respect to family planning (i.e., ability) alone, but for *all three* preconditions:

$$R_{i,t} = \beta X^R_{i,t} + \delta_i \sum \omega_{i,j} Z^R_{j,t-1} + E_R$$

$$W_{i,t} = \beta X^W_{i,t} + \delta'_i \sum \omega_{i,j} Z^W_{j,t-1} + E_W$$

$$A_{i,t} = \beta^* X^A_{i,t} + \delta^*_i \sum \omega_{i,j} Z^A_{j,t-1} + E_A$$

With this specification, a number of new features emerge.

(i) R, W, and A are likely to be correlated. This is so because the sets of individual attributes relevant for R, W, and A, respectively (i.e., X^R, X^W, and X^A) are overlapping. Education, urban residence, income, and other factors are indeed likely to have an impact, be it each time with a different coefficient, on R, W, and A. Furthermore, the same holds for the impact of the social environment, because people largely maintain a fairly well-circumscribed social network.

(ii) In this social network, the messages tend to have some consistency. This may be particularly true for institutional agents who propagate a coherent "total attitude." If they favor family planning, they will also propagate the economic advantages of a smaller family and send out ethical messages about responsibility, foresight, and other subjects. This means that action on A, for example, will also have an impact on R and on W. The mere fact of showing that family planning is safe also alters one's views on nature, self-directedness, secular values, and related areas.

(iii) The correlations between R, W, and A can vary substantially across contexts (e.g., countries, neighborhoods, social groups), and the assumption of complete endogeneity of W is not likely to hold. For instance, counterpropagation or gossip about the physical effects or comfort of contraception can reduce willingness considerably, even if R and A would be high. Hence, the chain model R→W→A need not be general either. In a good family planning message the chain is reversed: A→W→R.

(iv) The empirical task therefore consists of locating members of a population along an RWA classification, from all three conditions being met (R,W,A) to none being met (rwa). This yields information about the bottleneck conditions (see next section) and about the factors that are responsible for it (see equations above).

(v) The three equations simultaneously determine the outcome $S_{t,i}$ via the weakest link rule, and hence all too-exclusive stress on A could result in one of the other two distributions lagging behind. Examples of negative effects of A on R and W are the cases of coercive or poor-quality family planning programs. Actually, W and R can be adversely affected at a considerable speed through the network part in the Montgomery-Casterline equations.

(vi) The Montgomery-Casterline equation may also inform us about the variance of the R, W, and A distributions as related to the rapidity of shifts in their means. In the beta-distributions that we have proposed, a small group of "innovators" is capable of pulling the rest of the population with them. This assumes permeability between social networks in an area. The greater the degree of permeability, the smaller the variance can be expected to be as the mean moves to the right. However, impermeable and distinct networks are likely to be formed on the principle that the like minded also assemble. In such instances the overall variance is likely to remain substantial. If this holds for the weakest condition, this lower tail will pull the distribution of S toward the left and the transition of S will be slowed down. If one has reasons to believe that a society has important social cleavages that cause impermeability, messages about R, W, and A need to be tailor made to suit each of these segregated networks.

The bottom line from this discussion is that the sole application of social learning and social influence models to the factors affecting the ability condition may lead to lopsided policy inputs. If the two other conditions, and predominantly the W condition, are overlooked, the final S distribution may show a surprising lag as a result of the weakest link rule.

R,W,A AS SEEN THROUGH THE AFRICAN DHS SURVEYS

A conceptual model should also derive some credibility from an application. In this section we shall try to locate the proportions of women of reproductive age in African countries in eight categories, ranging from obviously ready, willing and able (RWA) to none of these three (rwa). In this application the conditions are seen as discrete, that is, satisfied or not, and this will be denoted by upper case or lower case letters. The following eight categories can obviously be established:

1. RWA
2. RWa
3. RwA
4. Rwa
5. rWA
6. rWa
7. rwA
8. rwa

We shall apply this classification to all women who are currently married, fecund, and exposed to risk of becoming pregnant (i.e., excluding those who are amenorrheic, or already pregnant). Among such women, those who are current users of contraception plainly fall in category 1, RWA. The others are nonusers and must be distributed over the remaining seven slots. Those among them who are nonusers in order to conceive ("want another child soon") are obviously members of categories 5 through 8, and have the attribute r, meaning not ready to delay the next pregnancy. Those nonusers who want to delay the next birth or to avoid it altogether are ready to control, but do not do so, either because they are not willing and/or not able. They must therefore belong to categories 2, 3, or 4.

The three-way classification can now be abbreviated as follows:

*RWA: current users
* r..: nonusers who want their next pregnancy soon
*R-RWA: all other nonusers who want to delay the next pregnancy (2+ years) or avoid it altogether (i.e., RWa + RwA + Rwa).

Such a three-way classification can be obtained from the African DHS surveys for all currently married, fecund, and exposed women; the results are presented in Table 8-1. Before going into the details of this table, we shall first establish a link with the theoretical distributions presented in Figure 8-4.

Suppose that the beta-distributions of Figure 8-4 would represent, from left to right, the distributions of willingness (mean = 0.4), readiness

TABLE 8-1 Distribution of Currently Married, Fecund, and Exposed Women According to Their Planning Status of the Next Birth; African DHS surveys

DHS Country and Date	N of Women	Nonusers (Proportion)		Users (proportion) RWA
		Pregnancy Wanted r..	Next Pregnancy to be Delayed (2+ years) or No More Wanted R-RWA	
CAR 1994–1995	2,306	.62	.22	.16
Niger 1992	1,840	.52	.34	.14
Mali 1995–1996	4,160	.46	.42	.12
Uganda 1995	2,382	.46	.28	.26
Benin 1996	2,041	.44	.29	.27
Nigeria 1990	2,478	.39	.45	.16
Senegal 1992–1993	1,722	.39	.42	.19
N. Sudan 1989–90	2,187	.39	.40	.21
Tanzania 1991–1992	2,543	.35	.40	.25
Cameroon 1991	1,337	.35	.31	.34
Zambia 1992	2,006	.34	.32	.34
Burkina F. 1993	2,338	.33	.49	.18
Zimbabwe 1994	2,331	.28	.13	.59
Madagascar 1992	1,727	.25	.39	.36
Malawi 1992	1,471	.24	.45	.31
Namibia 1992	1,308	.24	.26	.50
Rwanda 1992	1,627	.21	.30	.49
Ghana 1993	1,502	.16	.41	.43
Morocco 1992	3,129	.14	.20	.66
Kenya 1993	2,657	.12	.31	.57
Egypt 1992	6,370	.11	.21	.68

NOTE: Exposed = not amenorrheic or pregnant; also women reporting not having sex, infrequent sex, menopausal/hysterectomy, subfecund and infecund or in postpartum abstinence are eliminated from N.
SOURCES: Adapted from (before 1994): computed from Westoff & Bankole (1995) table 4.1 p. 5; (from 1994–1996) computed from special output prepared by Macro International, personal communication, Dr. M. Vaessen.

(mean = 0.5), and ability (mean = 0.7). Assume, furthermore, that we use a cutting point value of 0.5 for dichotomizing these distributions. The proportions in each of the eight discrete categories are then:

RWA:	0.142	rWA:	0.142
RWa:	0.014	rWa:	0.014
RwA:	0.313	rwA:	0.313
Rwa:	0.031	rwa:	0.031
R..:	0.500	r..:	0.500

Given that the mean for readiness in this example has been set at 0.5, the population would obviously be split equally over the R.. and r.. slots. Furthermore, since willingness is defined as the weakest link, each of these halves must contain much smaller proportions satisfying W than A. Using the three-way classification adopted in Table 8-1 for real population, the above example corresponding to Figure 8-4 would yield the following outcomes:

    RWA: 0.142
    r..:   0.500
    R-RWA: 0.358

This can be compared to the values observed for Niger in 1992 (see Table 8-1):

    RWA: 0.140
    r..:   0.520
    R-RWA: 0.340

Hence, Figure 8-4 can be taken as a fairly close representation of the Niger situation. Roughly half the population of married, fecund, and exposed women would not be ready to postpone or avoid the next pregnancy (r = 0.520) at any rate, and of the other half, more than two-thirds (R-RWA = 0.340) would either be unwilling, unable, or both. The bottleneck condition is, furthermore, especially a lack of willingness (left-hand distribution on Figure 8-4), and hence we would expect that ethical or religious objections, health fears and beliefs, or social pressure from others would be the key factors in pulling the S curve for Niger to the left, thereby preventing a contraceptive breakthrough.

In their study of "unmet need," Westoff and Bankole (1995, nr. 4.1:5) present a table that allows us to establish this first three-way division for many other African countries. Those classified as RwA, Rwa, or Rwa in this paper differ from the Westoff-Bankole women with unmet need in a number of ways. First, our denominator only contains exposed women, whereas theirs also includes currently pregnant or amenorrheic women. Second, our numerator only contains the nonusers with a desire to postpone or avoid the next pregnancy, whereas theirs also uses the non-exposed women who report a mistimed or unwanted previous birth. The classification we adopt has the advantage of concentrating exclusively on the next birth (which we need conceptually to assess R or r), but it has the disadvantage of excluding substantial numbers of women who are pregnant or amenorrheic. Information on their future intentions rather than past experience would have helped. The proportions that we derive for Rwa + RWa + RwA are often larger than the figures derived by Westoff and Bankole for unmet need, not only because of the smaller denominators used in our computation, but also because we suspect that the number of mistimed or unwanted last or current pregnancies is likely to be underreported in African populations. In other words, we suspect that Westoff-Bankole unmet need is underestimated (which, in fact, makes their argument for countries with large unmet need even more powerful). The other distinction is that Westoff and Bankole imply, by virtue of the label "unmet need" (we assume: need for family planning), that the bottleneck condition is nonability (a). In our conceptualization, the bottleneck can equally be nonwillingness (w) or nonwillingness and nonability jointly (wa).

Finally, a short note on the calculations is required. The results in Table 8-1 stem from the Westoff-Bankole table for all DHS surveys prior to 1994. The percentages were recalculated by eliminating the infecund women and the pregnant or amenorrheic women from the Ns used in the Westoff and Bankole table. For DHS surveys with dates 1994 or later, the results were obtained from special tabulations provided by Macro International starting from the raw data tapes. In these tables, although produced for fecund, married, and exposed women, a number of respondents still give reasons for not using contraception pertaining to not being married, having no or infrequent sex, being infecund or subfecund, or having reached menopause. These women were also eliminated from the analysis.

We can now turn to Table 8-1. The outcomes for Morocco and Egypt were added to Table 8-1 for comparison. In our logic we start with a first dichotomy pertaining to readiness, that is, to r.. or R.. Two countries have more than half the population of married, fecund, and exposed women who are not ready to postpone or avoid the next pregnancy (r..): Niger and the CAR (Central African Republic). Another three have proportions for r.. in excess of 40 percent: Mali, Uganda, and Benin (see column 2). However, Uganda and Benin must have distributions of W and A that have shifted further to the right than in the other three countries, because their values of R,W,A are already larger than 0.25.

The next group of countries has values for r.. of between 30 and 39 percent, indicating that a larger part of the R distribution has moved to the right. This group contains Senegal, Nigeria, Burkina Faso, Northern Sudan, Cameroon, Tanzania, and Zambia. But, in addition, Cameroon and Zambia have significantly higher proportions in R,W,A, meaning that they must have more favorable locations of the W and A distributions as well.

In the third group of countries, the subpopulation with r.. is already smaller than 30 percent; some, such as Ghana and Kenya, have proportions lower than 20 percent, which is already typical for Northern Africa. Yet, in this group, the A or W distributions seem to act as a stronger brake in Malawi or Madagascar, since proportions in R,W,A are still below 40 percent. To a lesser extent, this also holds for Ghana, especially when compared to Kenya, Rwanda, Namibia, and Zimbabwe with proportions in R,W,A close to or in excess of 50 percent.

The analysis conducted so far illustrates that the planning status of the next birth already sheds some light on the approximate locations of the R, W, and A distributions. The three-way classification can, however, be refined a bit further for women falling in the R-RWA category (column 3 in Table 8-1) because more information is available that helps to clarify the respective roles of W and A.

The DHS surveys of the late 1980s probed reasons for not using contraception among married, fecund, and exposed women who also stated that they would "be unhappy to have the next pregnancy soon" or for whom "such a pregnancy would cause problems." The results are also published in the DHS country reports for these years (chapter 4). Among the answers, some categories are indicative of infecundity or subfecundity or nonexposure, and we have eliminated such respondents from our analysis. The recalculated percentages are reproduced in Table 8-2.

The DHS country reports for the 1990s either do not have such tables or do not publish them for married, fecund, and exposed women. However, Macro International could produce tabulations at our request for five surveys between 1994 and 1996 that satisfy our needs. Again, women who want to postpone the next pregnancy (2+ years) but were not using contraception for reasons of infecundity or nonexposure were eliminated. These results for the later five surveys should be comparable to those published for the late 1980s, and they are reproduced in Table 8-3.

In both tables we have regrouped the response categories in two large classes. First, the reasons for not using contraception, despite a manifest need for postponing or altogether avoiding a next pregnancy pertaining to a lack of knowledge about methods of contraception, a lack of knowledge about Family Planning (FP) services, difficulty of access to FP, or costs, are grouped in the category "nonability" (i.e., condition a). Reasons related to personal opposition to FP, to opposition from others, to religious objections, to fatalistic attitudes, or to fears for health are regrouped in the category "nonwillingness" (i.e., condition w). Only one response item could be specified, so that no information is available for the proportion satisfying both conditions, that is, aw. Finally, in some countries the frequencies for "other reasons" without further specification and/or the nonresponse are fairly high—sometimes in excess of 30 percent—so that extra caution is needed in interpreting the outcomes.

The first question that can be addressed with this additional information is whether, for those in R-RWA, the dominant bottleneck is either a or w. A ratio a/w is therefore calculated in Tables 8-2 and 8-3. For the late 1980s, the a/w ratio is larger than unity in all but three countries. The

TABLE 8-2 Breakdown of Reasons for Not Using Contraception Among Fecund and Exposed Women Who Want to Delay or Avoid the Next Pregnancy (Condition R), but Who Are Also Nonusers (Conditions a, w, or aw); Various DHS Sub-Saharan Countries in the Late 1980s

	Mali 1987	Senegal 1986	Togo 1988	Liberia 1986	Ghana 1988	Burundi 1987	Uganda 1988-89	Kenya 1989	Zimbabwe 1988	Botswana 1988
A. Bottleneck = nonability (a)	N=835	264	610	331	786	486	1388	1818	400	697
- Lack of information	48.3	30.3	38.9	11.8	32.1	39.7	37.6	25.8	8.0	6.5
- Access difficult	2.3	1.1	2.6	12.7	2.5	3.3	9.9	13.9	23.2	0.1
- Too expensive	Na	Na	4.4	15.1	2.8	2.3	1.8	2.2	4.5	12.9
Total	50.6	31.4	45.9	39.6	37.4	45.3	49.3	41.9	35.7	19.5
B. Bottleneck = nonwillingness (w)										
- Religion opposed	10.1	20.4	5.4	2.7	4.4	1.0	22.0	5.7	5.8	1.4
- Others opposed, social control	2.0	Na	Na	Na	0.9	0.2	0.6	0.9	1.2	3.9
- Husband opposed	12.7	8.0	Na	9.4	5.1	4.3	4.3	11.2	11.3	8.0
- Opposition to family planning	Na	Na	14.3	6.3	4.8	4.8	5.5	4.2	6.2	18.2
- Fatalistic	Na	Na	Na	Na	0.6	3.3	0.9	1.4	1.8	0.9
- Inconvenient, bad for health	4.6	8.0	15.7	20.8	15.0	4.3	10.5	11.4	20.3	20.2
Total	29.4	36.4	35.4	39.2	30.8	17.9	43.8	34.8	46.6	52.6
Ratio a/w	1.72	.86	1.30	1.01	1.21	2.53	1.13	1.20	.77	.37
C. Bottleneck-not specified										
- Other reason	15.0	21.6	17.9	21.1	17.6	28.3	5.8	16.0	13.8	3.7
- Don't know	4.8	10.6	Na	Na	13.4	8.2	Na	6.2	3.5	23.0
- No answer	0.2	Na	0.8	Na	0.8	0.2	0.9	1.0	0.5	1.1
Total	20.0	32.2	18.7	21.1	31.8	36.7	6.7	23.2	17.8	27.8

NOTE: Excluded from the calculations are: breastfeeding or amenorrheic women, women with "infrequent sex," and, for Togo, Senegal, and Mali, also women who want a birth soon (in the other countries, such women were already eliminated from the published analysis). Na = response category not used in published table.
SOURCE: Adapted from DHS individual country report.

TABLE 8-3 Breakdown of Reasons for Not Currently Using Contraception Among Fecund and Exposed Married Women Who Have Indicated That They Want to Postpone (2+ years) or Avoid the Next Pregnancy (R-RWA); Selected DHS Countries in the 1990s

	Mali 1995–96	Benin 1996	Centr. Afr. Rep. 1994–95	Uganda 1995	Zimbabwe 1994
A. Nonability (a)					
- Lack of information	42.5	47.4	36.1	41.2	3.7
- Access difficult	0.6	0.4	0.3	2.2	3.9
- Too expensive	1.0	3.0	0.4	4.0	1.3
Total a	44.0	50.8	36.8	47.4	8.9
B. Nonwillingness (w)					
- Religion opposed	2.6	3.3	5.4	2.9	10.6
- Husband opposed	4.8	4.8	6.4	13.9	12.4
- Others opposed	0.2	0.2	0.2	0.2	0.7
- Opposition to FP	10.8	18.1	10.6	4.2	14.3
- Health fears	19.2	14.5	8.1	19.9	45.5
- Inconvenient to use	2.6	0.8	Na	1.4	1.6
Total w	40.2	41.7	30.7	42.5	85.1
C. Not specified					
- Other reasons	2.2	4.5	6.0	8.2	3.3
- Don't know	13.5	3.0	1.4	1.8	2.6
- No answer	Na	Na	25.2	Na	Na
Total unspecified	15.7	7.5	32.6	10.0	5.9
a/w ratio	1.10	1.22	1.20	1.12	0.10

NOTE : Na = response category not used in published table.
SOURCE: Adapted from DHS data files ; personal communication, Dr. M. Vaessen, Macro International.

first of these is Senegal, but unfortunately this is a case with more than 30 percent of unspecified or missing answers. The other two are Zimbabwe (a/w = .77) and Botswana (.37), which are countries with high proportions in RWA and low proportions in R-RWA. By 1994 the a/w ratio for Zimbabwe (see Table 8-2) further declines to only 0.10, and in Mali, the ratio diminishes from 1.72 in 1987 to 1.10 in 1995–1996. This suggests that a/w ratios decline when proportions of users (RWA) increase. In such circumstances, the bottleneck condition at the onset would be primarily the A distribution, which is logical for most of Sub-Saharan Africa given the lower knowledge levels and the much weaker FP organization during the 1980s. But when overall need for contraception increases over time, that is, when the R distribution shifts to the right, the W distribution rather than the A distribution increasingly becomes the weakest link. Hence, one can expect for the future that the reasons for not using contraception among those with a spacing or stopping need will increasingly be associated with nonwillingness rather than nonability, as was already the case in Botswana and Zimbabwe in the 1980s. This does not imply that the W distribution remains static—in fact, it too shifts to the right—but that in the course of the transition the distributions for R and A are moving faster. At this later stage, despite greater willingness than before, willingness becomes the bottleneck condition.

Finally, Tables 8-2 and 8-3 also lend more support to the hypothesis that reasons for nonwillingness may be increasingly associated with health fears (bad for health, side effects, inconvenient to use) rather than with social opposition to fertility control in general. The items concerning health fears already had the highest frequencies in the 1980s in Togo, Ghana, Liberia, Kenya, Zimbabwe, and Botswana (Table 8-2) and in the 1990s in Mali, Uganda, and Zimbabwe (Table 8-3). Moreover, these items were more frequently cited in the 1990s than in the late 1980s in the three countries for which we have two observations: an increase in Mali from 4.6 to 21.8 percent, in Uganda from 10.5 to 21.3 percent, and in Zimbabwe from 20.2 to 47.1 percent.

Admittedly, the evidence from Tables 8-2 and 8-3 is not yet conclusive and needs to be checked out for more countries with at least two observations tabulated for the R-RWA subpopulations. But it does at least advance two new hypotheses:

(i) The take-over hypothesis: As the three distributions for R, W, and A shift to the right, the A distribution is likely to move faster than the W distribution, leading to a situation in which increasing willingness still becomes the bottleneck condition.

(ii) The shifting objections hypothesis: As the W distribution moves to the right, nonwillingness becomes increasingly associated with beliefs about the health impact of contraception and less with general ethical, religious, or social opposition.

Nevertheless, country-specific features associated with differences in culture, social organization, and FP program implementation are likely to exert their influence as well.

CONCLUSIONS

The reintroduction of the triple concepts of readiness R, willingness W, and ability A in social demography has a set of advantages:

(i) It allows us to integrate economic and noneconomic paradigms of transitions to new forms of behavior, a crucial requirement for the study of fertility transitions in particular.

(ii) It avoids dead-end streets such as the "economics versus culture" debate.

(iii) It sharpens awareness of the fact that transitions can take many forms depending on the shapes of the R, W, and A distributions and the speed at which they move.

The model presented here hinges on the weakest link principle, that is, it is the minimum of either R, W, or A that determines the final speed of the adoption of fertility regulation (either for spacing or stopping). Such a bottleneck model elucidates the role of leads and lags and recognizes that, during the course of a transition, different factors may be responsible for slower change or for barrier effects in diffusion. With respect to the latter effects, models should not only be constructed with respect to diffusion of contraceptive knowledge and availability (i.e., ability), but equally pay attention to the diffusion of readiness or perceptions of economic advantage and of willingness or perceptions of cultural, social, and psychological obstacles.

The R, W, A model further allows for the detection of bottleneck conditions. The application to the data from African DHS surveys illustrates that a simple three-way classification of the fecund and exposed population according to the planning status of the next pregnancy can already shed light on the approximate locations of the R, W, and A distributions in each of the countries concerned. As such, the application is a variant of the "unmet need" concept, but it fully recognizes that such unmet needs also can be associated with a lack of willingness, and not solely with a lack of ability. The heterogeneity of the sub-Saharan populations with respect to the planning status of the next birth (i.e., the distribution over the categories r.., R-RWA, and RWA) testifies to this effect. This heterogeneity indicates that factors associated with low readiness and ability tend to be responsible for the bottleneck at the onset, but that the willingness condition is likely to become the weakest link at a later stage. In other words, as the distributions of R, W, and A move to the right, the shift in the W distribution may be slower than that of the other two. In such circumstances policies become necessary that confront cultural, social, and psychological barriers to the use of contraception, in addition to policies that further facilitate access to FP. Finally, a closer inspection of the reasons given for not using contraception among fecund and exposed women who manifestly want to delay or avoid their next pregnancy (i.e., those in the R-RWA category) reveals that a shift may be occurring in the nature of nonwillingness. More specifically, as the distribution of W also shifts to the right, the remaining obstacles seem to be increasingly associated with health-related fears rather than with more general ethical, religious, or social objections. This equally implies that public messages related to FP should be increasingly attentive to such fears, particularly in countries that have to pull in the tail of "late joiners."

Further research starting from Coale's three preconditions can easily be imagined. First, locations and shapes of beta-distributions for the R, W, and A conditions can easily be constructed, and the location of S determined. As was done for the case of Niger, the actual proportions in the categories RWA, r.., and R-RWA can be obtained from the DHS data, and these can be compared to a set of model situations to infer the approximate locations of R, W, and A distributions. Second, the DHS data on reasons for not using contraception among the R-RWA subpopulation of fecund and exposed women should be produced systematically and in a comparable fashion. To estimate Rwa, the questionnaire should also allow for the specification of multiple reasons rather than just one. The breakdown of the fecund and exposed female population in the categories r.., RWA, RwA, RWa, and Rwa would further facilitate the estimation of the location of the R, W, and A distribution in each country and their subgroups, thereby shedding more light on the prevailing weakest link at various points in time.

REFERENCES

Bulatao, R.
  1979 On the Nature of the Transition in the Value of Children. EWPI Paper 60-A. Honolulu: East-West Center.
Burch, T.K.
  1996 Icons, straw men and precision: Reflections on demographic theories and fertility decline. The Sociological Quarterly 37(1):59–81.
  1997 Fertility Decline: Toward a Synthetic Model. Unpublished paper for the International Conference on Computer Simulation and the Social Sciences, September, Cortona, Italy.
Caldwell, J.C.
  1982 Theory of Fertility Decline. New York: Academic Press.
Coale, A.J.
  1973 The demographic transition reconsidered. In IUSSP—Proceedings of the International Population Conference. Liège, Belgium: Eds. Ordina.
Delumeau, J.
  1983 Le Péché et la Peur—La Culpabilisation en Occident. Paris: Fayard.
Dumont, A.
  1880 Dépopulation et Civilisation—Etude Démographique. Paris: Eds. Lecrosnier et Babé.
Easterlin, R., and E. Crimmins
  1985 The Fertility Revolution: A Supply-Demand Analysis. Chicago: University of Chicago Press.
Fawcett, J., ed.
  1972 The Satisfactions and Costs of Children: Theories, Concepts and Methods. Honolulu: East-West Population Institute.

Fawcett, J., and F. Arnold
    1975   The value of children: Theory and method. Representative Research in Psychology 4(1):23–26.
Inkeless, A., and D.H. Smith
    1974   Becoming Modern: Individual Change in Six Developing Countries. Cambridge, MA: Harvard University Press.
Kohler, H.-P.
    1997   Fertility and Social Interaction—An Economic Approach. Unpublished Ph.D. thesis, University of California, Berkeley.
Lave, C., and J.G. March
    1975   An Introduction to Models in the Social Sciences. New York: Harper & Row.
Le Bras, H., and E. Todd
    1981   L'Invention de la France. Paris: Hachette.
Lesthaeghe, R.
    1997   Imre Lakatos' views on theory development: Applications to the field of fertility theories. In IPD-Working Papers 97-1. Brussels: Vrije Universiteit.
Lesthaeghe, R., and C. Wilson
    1986   Modes of production, secularization and the pace of the fertility decline in Western Europe, 1879–1930. Pp. 261–292 in The Decline of Fertility in Europe, A.J. Coale and S.C. Watkins, eds. Princeton: Princeton University Press.
Liebenstein, H.
    1957   *Economic Backwardness and Economic Growth.* New York: Wiley & Sons.
Livi-Bacci, M.
    1977   A History of Italian Fertility During the Last Two Centuries. Princeton: Princeton University Press.
Mason, K.O.
    1985   The Status of Women. New York: Rockefeller Foundation.
Montgomery, M., and J. Casterline
    1996   Social learning, social influence, and new models of fertility. Population and Development Review 22(supplement):151–175.
Nag, M.
    1989   Political awareness as a factor in accessibility of health services. Economic and Political Weekly (Bombay) 24(8):417–426.
Robinson, W.C.
    1997   The economic theory of fertility over three decades. Population Studies 51:63–74.
Rosero-Bixby, L., and J. Casterline
    1993   Modeling diffusion effects in fertility transition. Population Studies 47:147–167.
van de Kaa, D.J.
    1996   Anchored narratives: The story and findings of half a century of research into the determinants of fertility. Population Studies 50:389–432.
Westoff, C., and A. Bankole
    1995   Unmet need: 1990–1994. In Demographic & Health Surveys, Comparative Studies no. 16. Calverton, MD: Macro International Inc.

Index